Human Nature: Darwin's View

HUMAN NATURE: DARWIN'S VIEW

Alexander Alland, Jr.

COLUMBIA UNIVERSITY PRESS
New York 1985

Library of Congress Cataloging in Publication Data

Darwin, Charles, 1809–1882.
  Human nature, Darwin's view.

  "All selections in this book are taken from the second,
revised, John Murray editions—1845 for the Journal of
researches, 1874 for the Descent of man, and 1890 for
the Expression of the emotions"—Pref.
  Bibliography: p.
  Includes index.
  1. Social evolution.   2. Race.   3. Social Darwinism.
4. Ethnology.   I. Alland, Alexander, 1931–
II. Title.
GN360.D382   1985   305'.01   85-4108
ISBN 0-231-05898-5 (alk. paper)
ISBN 0-231-05899-3 (pbk.)

Columbia University Press
New York   Guildford, Surrey
Copyright © 1985 Columbia University Press
All rights reserved

Printed in the United States of America

This book is dedicated to
the great modern evolutionist and naturalist
Stephen Jay Gould

CONTENTS

PREFACE

OF THE SEVERAL COLLECTIONS of Darwin's writings published to date, none extract his major writings on humans; yet such writings, taken together, tell us much about his attitudes toward race and what has come to be known in the twentieth century as "social darwinism." It is only by reading the scattered material on our species found in the *Journal of Researches, The Expression of the Emotions in Man and Animals,* and *The Descent of Man* that we can fairly judge what Darwin's complex and sometimes contradictory ideas on racial intelligence and social darwinism really were. This book, then, consists of almost all Darwin's writings on the human species found in these three works. Except for the selections from *The Expression of the Emotions,* which include major extracts from the theory chapter and chapter summaries dealing with humans, but exclude extended discussions of the same topics from several chapters, I have left out only a few paragraphs that provide short passing comments of little value to the issues under consideration. In addition to the three works presented in the body of this book, the introduction includes quotes from a few of Darwin's letters. In all cases footnotes have been excluded.

Ms. Deborah Blincoe assisted me by reading and abstracting articles on Darwin concerning his views on race and social darwinism. I do not discuss all these in my introduction, and therefore all of them are not cited in its bibliography, but they were all helpful in deciding how to frame this essay and in seeing where the debates really lie. Although I am responsible for the views expressed in the introduction, including any errors of fact or judgment, I wish to thank Ms. Blincoe for her valuable help, without which I might have missed several valuable sources.

I also wish to thank Joel Wallman with whom conversations about Darwin have always been thought-provoking and Anne McCoy, my patient manuscript editor at Columbia University Press, who helped me well beyond the call of duty.

The major point I wish to make in this book, and I hope it is made both in the introduction and in Darwin's own words, is that his attitudes toward the subjects of race and social darwinism were shaped by three sometimes contradictory sources. These included his own observations, particularly during the voyage of the Beagle; his readings on race and intelligence; and the exigencies of the theory of natural selection. The fact that Darwin was often inconsistent can be traced to inconsistencies in the three sources of his ideas. As one might expect from the kind of outstanding natural historian Darwin was, his own observations and his comments on them are often far superior to what his contemporaries were writing on the same subjects. But Darwin overvalued the scientific authority of his contemporaries and was often led astray by their claims. In the case of theory, the situation is more complicated. The theory of natural selection led Darwin correctly to accept the monogenic origin of human races, but it also led him to propose contemporary primitive societies as examples of intermediate forms between modern humans and the lower primates. Here Darwin was profoundly wrong.

All selections in this book are taken from the second, revised, John Murray editions—1845 for the *Journal of Researches,* 1874 for *The Descent of Man,* and 1890 for *The Expression of the Emotions.* In the last case Darwin's son incorporated his father's revisions into the posthumous edition. Darwin's own spelling and punctuation are used throughout, even where inconsistent. For example, in one case he spells "Negro" with both lower and uppercase letters in the same paragraph, and we find "civilisation" in one volume and "civilization" in another. Typographical errors are silently corrected, and editorial clarifications or interpolations are indicated by square brackets. Numbers at the beginning of paragraphs are the page numbers on which these paragraphs begin. In the selections from the *Journal,* I have indicated the date of the entry before each section.

Human Nature: Darwin's View

INTRODUCTION

CHARLES DARWIN is justly acclaimed for his theory of evolution through natural selection and, at least among biologists and geologists, for the many contributions he made to biology and earth science. Darwin was one of those great nineteenth-century voyager-naturalists who, during the now famous voyage of the Beagle, kept his weather eye alert to every aspect of the world around him, including even political events. Humans are not mentioned, except briefly, in *The Origin of Species*. Darwin was aware that his theory would shock the clerics and their sympathizers even without the explicit inclusion of our species in the evolutionary process. It was for this reason that he reserved his ideas about human evolution for a later publication, *The Descent of Man*. In spite of this reticence, he maintained an active interest in human biology and in what we would now call anthropology throughout his life.

Darwin's major published writings on humans can be found in *The Descent of Man, The Expression of the Emotions in Man and Animals,* and in the *Journal of Researches*. The last documents floral, faunal, and geological observations from the South American continent and Oceania, including Australia and New Zealand, It also contains relatively short but nonetheless interesting accounts of Gauchos, Guasos (the Chilean equivalent of Gauchos), the Argentine army and one of its generals, the Indians of Tierra del Fuego, Araucanian Indians, copper and gold miners in Chile, Tahitians, the Maoris of New Zealand, Australian aborigines, Tasmanians, missionaries among these various groups, and Australian convicts. Darwin was no anthropologist, nor in his time had this discipline yet risen from its armchair to study native cultures in depth. Darwin spoke Spanish but could not communicate in the native languages of any of the peoples he observed during the course of his journey. Still, he was as interested in the human life around him as he was in natural history. His observations, imperfect as they were, and in spite of occasional stereotyping, allowed him to make shrewd judgments about race and intelligence that were, for the most part, ahead of their time. Although he would, undoubtedly, have been against slavery even if he had not voyaged (such feelings were consistent with his nineteenth-century liberalism), Darwin's first-hand observations of the cruelties of this institution shocked him deeply and influenced his attitudes toward native peoples. Generally, Darwin was sympathetic to the plight of the underdog even when he allowed his sympathy to be tempered by personal distaste for certain customs. Darwin was no relativist. He was an English gentleman who knew exactly what was right and what was wrong. He approved of order, cleanliness, and total honesty in human relations. Although not a pacifist, he disapproved of violence and trickery. He looked down upon exploitation but did not favor total equality. He was distrustful of republicanism and respected capitalist enterprise under the laws of the English monarchy. He attempted, however, to keep most overt political judgments out of his writings; when they do occur they are, in most cases, less obviously political than the work of his fellow evolutionist and contemporary, Herbert Spencer. Darwin was self-protective and, more important, protective of his theory of evolution through natural selection. He apparently realized that he would have enough trouble convincing the scientific and intelligent lay public of the truth of evolution without discussing its social and political implications.

Writing approvingly of Darwin's strong abolitionist sentiments, Stephen Jay Gould reminds us that, as a creature of his age, Darwin had strong prejudices:

> Yet I do not wish to portray Darwin as a man of cardboard, for then he would be dull in his one dimensionality, however admirable. Darwin had faults aplenty, even if most were the common attitudes of his age. Don't think that his many favorable words about blacks reflect a general egalitarian perspective. Virtually no white male of that era—neither Franklin, nor Jefferson, nor Lincoln— doubted the innate superiority of his race. Darwin spoke well of blacks because he had respect for this race as well, but read his

words about the people of Tierra del Fuego if you wish to encounter the conventional intolerance of his age (1982:xix).

In a letter to C. Whitley on July 23, 1834, Darwin illustrates Goulds' point:

> But I have seen nothing which more completely astonishes me than the first sight of a savage. It was a naked Fuegian, his long hair blowing about, his face besmeared with paint. There is in their countenances an expression which I believe, to those who have not seen it, must be inconceivably wild. Standing on a rock he uttered tones and made gesticulations, than which the cries of domestic animals are far more intelligible.

In the *Journal of Researches*, a long description of Tierra del Fuego is full of negative remarks about the low position of the natives. Darwin was clearly disturbed by the notion that any humans (and he recognized in the Fuegians the same humanity he saw in other peoples) could live in such abject misery, be so dirty, and lack, or so it seemed to him, the most basic elements of culture. Darwin was unable to penetrate Fuegian culture because he could not speak the language and because his contact with the Indians was short and superficial. Given the immense inequality of material goods between the English and the Indians and the way the English presented themselves as bearers of trade items, it was natural for the natives to define the English as people with whom one bartered or begged and, when neither worked, from whom one stole. Under these conditions, it was easy for Darwin to view the Indians as excessively demanding, at best, and dishonest, at worst. The latter notion was confirmed for Darwin when a missionary left behind with the Fuegians by the Beagle expedition for a few days was robbed of all his belongings by the Indians.

I believe, however, that Darwin's negative views of the Fuegians were most strongly influenced by the peculiar events surrounding his adventures with them. A few years before Darwin's trip, Captain Fitz Roy of the Beagle had brought a small group of natives from Tierra del Fuego to England in order to educate and convert them to Christianity. It was Captain Fitz Roy's hope that he could later return the Indians to their own country in the company of a missionary in order to plant the seeds of Christian civilization among this very primitive population. Three Fuegians who had learned some English and had somewhat acculturated to English ways were therefore Darwin's companions on the long voyage to the tip of South America. Darwin saw all of them as individuals with separate personalities and looked upon them as intelligent human beings. Of course, being a good Englishman he was also impressed with their adopted, if imperfect, English culture. That they could "revert" to the native way of life after only a few months back in Tierra del Fuego was a shock to Darwin who certainly did not approve of what he understood as the native culture. Thus he wrote to J. S. Henslow on April 11, 1834:

> I forgot to mention the fate of the Fuegians whom we took back to their country. They had become entirely European in their habits and wishes, so much so that the younger one [Jemmy Button] had forgotten his own language, and their country-men paid but very little attention to them. We built houses for them and planted gardens, but by the time we return again on our passage round the horn, I think it will be very doubtful how much of their property will be left unstolen.

Darwin's fears about the result of resettlement were confirmed when in 1834 his ship returned to the Beagle Channel. On April 6, he wrote to his sister:

> My Dear Catherine,
> . . . After visiting some of the southern islands, we beat up through the magnificent scenery of the Beagle Channel to Jemmy Button's country. We could hardly recognise poor Jemmy. Instead of the clean, well-dressed stout lad we left him, we found him a naked, thin, squalid savage. York and Fuegia [the other two Fuegians from the Beagle] had moved to their own country some months ago, the former having stolen all Jemmy's clothes. Now he had nothing except a bit of blanket round his waist. Poor Jemmy was very glad to see us, and, with his usual good feeling, brought several presents (otter-skins, which are most valuable to themselves) for his old friends.

This encounter is also mentioned in the *Journal*. There, Darwin informs us that after a bath and a change of clothes, Jemmy once more resembled the little Englishman he had become. He notes approvingly that Jemmy ate dinner with good manners, using knife and fork, and was his usual polite self. Also of interest is Darwin's final remark in the *Journal* concerning the mental capacities of the Fuegians: On the 5th of March, 1834, he said:

> The Australian, in the simplicity of the arts of life, comes nearest the Fuegian: he can, however, boast of his boomerang, his spear and throwing-stick, his method of climbing trees, of tracking animals, and of hunting. Although the Australian may be superior in acquirements, it by no means follows that he is likewise superior in mental capacity: indeed, from what I saw of the Fuegians when on board, and from what I have read of the Australians, I should think the case was exactly the reverse.

Here, Darwin compares his first-hand and relatively long-term personal acquaintance with Fuegians with what he has *read* of the Australians. It is clear in this passage that Darwin is able to make a distinction between innate mental capacities and learned culture even if he misjudges the intelligence of Australian aborigines. Later, after a short personal experience in Australia, Darwin also corrected his judgment of the mental capacities of the aborigines.

In an interesting discussion of "the native" as a projection of historically determined European values James Boon tries to show that assumed differences between Renaissance and Enlightenment views of non-Europeans have been exaggerated. Thus he states:

> What, though, of medieval and Renaissance recourse to superstitious monstrosities versus Enlightenment skepticism and caution? Did not the lumieres at last outgrow that 'tide of ethnological fantasy' bemoaned by Hodgen? Our case study will reveal as much evidence of exaggeration and nonobjectivity in Enlightenment formulaic generalizations as in those of the Renaissance. Furthermore the same instance of monstrosity serves to exemplify two different styles of expressing cross-cultural diversity, both of them limited,

but—and herein lies their anthropological interest—in different ways (1982:36).

Boon's point is a good one, but his use of Darwin's putative lack of observational judgment to strengthen his case for historical continuity does not fit the facts. Boon attempts to illustrate this historical continuity by citing reports of giants in Patagonia. In a section bearing the title "Patagonian Marvels: Pigafetta, Darwin, Sagan" Boon notes that the myth of Patagonian giants began with Magellan's chronicler Pigafetta who said of these natives:

> This giant was so big, that the head of one of our men, of a nice stature, came but to his Waste. He was of good corporature, . . . painted with divers colors, but for the most part yellow. (Pigafetta quoted in Boon 1982:37).

For Boon, the Patagonian "giants" represent a superficial conversion of diabolical monstrosity, conceived in the Renaissance, into physical monstrosity conceived during the Enlightenment. Boon notes the fact that physical gigantism among Patagonians "was explicitly discredited and empirically disproved in 1670 by John Narborough" (1982:38), yet, he claims, even Darwin made use of this image in his description of Fuegians. The citation in question is one of Darwin's least perspicacious remarks about natives, but as we shall see below, it was based on fact rather than on his purported recourse to Renaissance myth:

> While going one day on shore near Wollaston Island, we pulled alongside a canoe with six Fuegians. These were the most abject and miserable creatures I anywhere beheld. . . . [They] were quite naked, . . . stunted in their growth, their hideous faces bedaubed with white paint, their skins filthy and greasy, their hair entangled, their voices discordant, and their gestures violent. Viewing such men, one can hardly make one's self believe that they are fellow-creatures, and inhabitants of the same world. we often try to imagine what pleasure in life some of the lower animals can enjoy: how much more reasonably the same question may be asked concerning these barbarians!
> The Fuegians of Good Success Bay are a very different race from the stunted, miserable wretches farther westward; and they seem

closely related to the famous Patagonians of the Strait of Magellan.
. . . Their skin is of a dirty coppery-red color. Their chief spokesman, an old man, had a . . . face . . . crossed by two broad bars:
one, white like chalk, stretched above the first. . . . His two companions . . . were ornamented by streaks of black powder, made
of charcoal. The party altogether closely resembled the devils which
come on the stage in plays like Der Freischutz. (Darwin's *Journal*
entry for December 25, 1832, quoted in Boon 1982:42)

Here Darwin draws on a clearly marked fictional device to end
his description of naked, painted natives who were, to say the least,
exotic to a nineteenth-century Englishman and more so to his
readers. The contrast these natives presented to Darwin's own
world was surely dramatic. Is it, therefore, surprising that he used
an analogy drawn from theatre to end his description of them? But
who were the "giants" of Patagonia referred to by Darwin? Were
they really projections of Renaissance fantasy or were they real
people, reasonably described by Darwin? The following quote from
the *Journal* of May 1834 will show not only that Darwin was familiar with the giant myth, but that he was able to overcome it
through sensible, if mundane, observation:

During our previous visit (in January), we had an interview at Cape
Gregory with the famous so-called gigantic Patagonians, who gave
us a cordial reception. Their height appears greater than it really
is, from their large guanaco mantles, their long flowing hair, and
general figure: on an average their height is about six feet, with
some men taller and only a few shorter; and the women are also
tall; altogether they are certainly the tallest race which we anywhere saw.

While Darwin was a good observer (even of people from different cultures), he was not very critical of what he *read* about non-
western peoples. Thus, he tended to trust racist conclusions published by others on those occasions when he had no first-hand
experience on which to base his opinion. On the other hand, when
he did have such experiences, he was able, at least partially, to
cut through the prejudices of his day. When he could actually talk
to natives, he discerned in each of them a unique personality and

intelligence. Nonetheless, it is true that Darwin had a very low opinion of Fuegian *culture*, if not of Fuegian racial capacities. Here his political views partially influenced his judgment, and in his *Journal* for March 5, 1834, he comes out strongly against equality:

> The perfect equality among the individuals composing the Fuegian tribes, must for a long time retard their civilization. As we see those animals, whose instinct compels them to live in society and obey a chief, are most capable of improvement, so is it with the races of mankind.

Darwin was not a racist, but, as I have already pointed out, neither was he a relativist when it came to judgments about alien cultures. He was often too quick to condemn social practices he did not understand fully or which deviated too far from his firm belief that the best (but not all) of English culture was the proper model for world civilization. A good part of his intolerance of certain aspects of native cultures was based (rightly or wrongly) on his strong sense of fairness. He was a committed humanitarian, highly critical of injustice among human beings. The *Journal* has long sections in which he deplores the mistreatment of Indians and slaves. Elsewhere, he describes in detail the brutal conditions of Chilean gold and copper miners. In other sections he denounces the tyranny and corruption of Latin American dictators in a voice that has a strong contemporary ring.

Furthermore, the fact that Darwin shared his abolitionism with others who, while against slavery, could still hold strong racist views does not indicate that Darwin himself shared their racist convictions. Compare, for example, the following two quotes from Darwin with a published statement made by Thomas Henry Huxley (known in his role as a strong advocate of evolution as Darwin's "bulldog") on the emancipation question. The first quote is from a letter Darwin wrote to Thomas Wentworth Higginson, and the second is from the *Journal*, August 11, 1833:

February 27th, 1873

My Dear Sir,

My wife has just finished reading aloud your "Life with a Black regiment," and you must allow me to thank you heartily for the very great pleasure which it has in many ways given us. I always thought well of the negroes, from the little I have seen of them; and I have been delighted to have my vague impressions confirmed, and their character and mental powers so ably discussed. When you were here I did not know of the noble position which you had filled. I had formerly read about the black regiments, but failed to connect your name with your admirable undertaking.

The house was situated at the base of a ridge, between one and two hundred feet high—a most remarkable feature in this country. This posta was commanded by a negro lieutenant, born in Africa: to his credit be it said, there was not a rancho between the Colorado and Buenos Ayros in nearly such neat order as his. He had a little room for strangers, and a small corral for the horses, all made of sticks and reeds; he had also dug a ditch round his house, as a defence in case of being attacked. This would, however, have been of little avail, if the Indians had come; but his chief comfort seemed to rest in the thought of selling his life dearly. A short time before, a body of Indians had traveled past in the night; if they had been aware of the posta, our black friend and his four soldiers would assuredly have been slaughtered. I did not any where meet a more civil and obliging man than this negro; it was therefore the more painful to see that he would not sit down and eat with us.

Huxley wrote the following in his essay "Emancipation—Black and White":

Quashie's plaintive inquiry, "Am I not a man and a brother?" seems at last to have received its final reply—the recent decision of the fierce trial by battle on the other side of the Atlantic fully concurring with that long since delivered here in a more peaceful way.

The question is settled; but even those who are most thoroughly convinced that the doom is just, must see good grounds for repudiating half the arguments which have been employed by the winning side; and for doubting whether its ultimate results will embody the hopes of the victors, though they may more than realise the fears of the vanquished. It may be quite true that some negroes are better than some white men; but no rational man, cognisant of the facts, believes that the average negro is the equal, still less the superior, of the average white man. And, if this be true, it is simply incredible that, when all his disabilities are removed, and our prognathous relative has a fair field and no favor, as well as no oppressor, he will be able to compete successfully with his bigger-brained and smaller-jawed rival, in a contest to be carried on by thoughts and not by bites. The highest places in the hierarchy of civilization will assuredly not be within the reach of our dusky cousins, though it is by no means necessary that they should be restricted to the lowest.

But whatever the position of stable equilibrium into which the laws of social gravitation may bring the negro, all responsibility for the result will henceforward lie between nature and him. The white man may wash his hands of it, and the Caucasian conscience be void of reproach for evermore. And this, if we look to the bottom of the matter, is the real justification for the abolition policy. (1865:115)

Huxley was not alone in his cynical judgment of intelligence among the nonwhite races. The American social evolutionist Lewis Henry Morgan saw primitives (read also nonwhites) as children in the scale of humanity. This view was shared by such well-known social evolutionists as Herbert Spencer and Edward B. Tylor. Morgan, who was also an abolitionist, believed that once the slaves were freed in the United States they would slowly disappear. In Morgan's view, the abolition of slavery was necessary to free *nature* to perform its noble work. This is a pure expression of what has, unfortunately, come to be known as "social darwinism." For Morgan, blacks under slavery were protected by that institution from direct competition with whites. Emancipation would allow natural selection to take its course, and blacks would be eliminated from the American scene.

If up to this point I have emphasized Darwin's enlightened position on race, let me consider his position from another point of view. Darwin was least racist in his *Life and Letters* and *Journal of Researches,* that is to say, when he formed his opinions on the basis of real encounters. His attitude toward race in *The Descent of Man* is much more complicated and often expresses unenlightened ideas. In my opinion these ideas can be traced directly to Darwin's theorizing. His overall method provides us with one of the best examples of empiricism we have. He based the theory of evolution on a long series of careful observations and only published it when he had amassed a hugh amount of evidence in its favor. But data only make sense when they are organized according to some set of theoretical principles. For Darwin, the order underlying the diversity so obvious in nature was the result of evolution. All organisms were related biologically. Those most obviously related were close relatives which had diversified only recently. Those most distant had diverged at a very early period. Thus Darwin realized that the human species and its apparently closest relatives, the great apes, must have a common and recent ancestry in some intermediate form. This led him to believe that between that form and modern humans there must be a series of biologically primitive humans. At the time *The Origin of Species* was published, the fossil record was very slim and in dispute. The only human fossils available were those of Neanderthal. Although these bones were used as evidence for human evolution, the link to living subhuman primates could only be weakly argued from them. Another line of evidence available at the time was to point out similarities in structure between apes and humans. These data did not satisfy Darwin. He was therefore faced, in *The Descent of Man,* with the problem of mustering greater evidence for a premodern stage of human development so that he could connect our species to the lower primates. Throughout the *Descent of Man,* he uses contemporary primitive societies as examples of biologically intermediate forms of the human species. At one point he goes so far as to say that "The belief that there exists in man some close relation between the size of the brain and the development of the intellectual faculties is supported by comparison of the skulls of savage and civilized races" (p. 54). Elsewhere he says of the Fuegians: "Their skill in some respects may be compared to the instincts of animals; for it is not improved by experience" (*Journal* entry for December 25, 1832).

This sort of nonsense came from Darwin's reading. But since his own observations told him that there are few profound morphological differences between the people of these societies and ourselves and because, as we shall see below, Darwin needed a monogenic explanation for the living races, he shifted from the notion of *primitive morphology* or structure to prove the existence of intermediate types, to what he assumed in preliterate peoples were genetically determined *primitive behaviors.* Thus, the noncivilized "primitive" cultures that Darwin observed and read about became, for him, examples of fossilized, but living, social life. This was then taken to be indicative of some former stage of human evolution already passed through by Europeans. To accept this, Darwin was forced to accept the notion that a large proportion of human social behavior was based on genetic patterns rather than on learning. It was easy for Darwin to confuse learned behavior patterns with instinct. Cultural anthropology had not yet shown that peoples who originated from the same gene pool could have vastly different behavioral systems. Indeed, the concept of gene pool was unknown. In addition, scientists lacked the knowledge of genetics which provides the necessary mechanisms to account for dynamic change in evolution. Darwin's attempts to explain certain aspects of social life in humans as instinct were justified in his mind by the belief that habits long practiced became hereditary. This essentially Lamarkian position (that acquired traits were inherited) was common in Darwin's time.

Another confusion that Darwin shared with his contemporaries was the equation between ethnic group and race. This confusion was partially the result of the linguistic ambiguity inherent in the word "race." (Even today it is often used, particularly in Europe, to mark a group that can properly be defined only by culture. To call the French or the English "races" is such a common error.) The major reason for this confused thinking, however, was the already noted frequent attribution of genetic causes to behavioral differences among cultures or societies. Thus Darwin's writings often reflect this mode of thinking, but here again we must correct our view of him. As I have shown above, he does, now and then, draw a distinction between race and culture. To give another example, he notes that the culturally impoverished Indians of Tierra del Fuego are racially identical to other Indians in South and even North America whose cultures are on a much higher plain: "The men [Argentinian Indians] were a tall, fine race, yet it was afterwards easy to see in the Fuegian savages the same countenance rendered hideous by cold, want of food, and less civilization. Some authors in defining the primary races of mankind, have separated these Indians into two classes; but this is certainly incorrect." His discussion of Tahiti and his notions about the effects of missionaries on the development of civilization among native peoples also demonstrate that Darwin realized, with the same set of contradictions as did many of his contemporaries, that native cultures were not genetically fixed. Primitives could be educated to behave in a "civilized" manner. This notion, of course, formed the justification for the ideology of the "white man's burden." Even though he also accepted, in large measure, the white man's burden and praised the work of missionaries in both New Zealand and Tahiti, Darwin could, on occasion, throw a barb in the direction of western "civilization." This was the case, at least, when the civilization in question was slave-holding and Spanish, rather than abolitionist and English.

> It is a pleasant thing to see the aborigines advanced to the same degree of civilization, however low that may be, which the white conquerors have attained.

> The fire, bed, and situation showed the dexterity of an Indian; but he could scarcely have been an Indian, for the race is in this part extinct, owing to the Catholic desire of making at one blow Christians and Slaves.

Jacob Gruber uses Darwin's basically Lamarkian position to argue that he was fully in the camp of cultural determinism: "Darwin consistently took these differences to be the products of history, culture, education, and habitat, rather than the reflection of a fixed inheritance of psychological traits" (Gruber 1981:184). Gruber goes on to support his argument by quoting the *Journal* entry for December 22, 1835, in which Darwin discusses the Indians of Chiloe Island off the coast of Chile. In this quote Darwin notes how the Indians had advanced to the same degree of civilization as their white conquerors. This opinion, the result of Darwin's honesty and observational skill, could easily be combined with the idea, found consistently in Darwin's writing, that hereditary traits (including behavioral traits) *could* be modified through experience. Such a conclusion cannot, for this reason, be equated with cultural determinism because the latter theory makes no demands whatsoever upon genetic mechanisms. For Darwin, as Gruber himself points out, habits had a tendency to become *hereditary*. In this way Darwin could have his cake and eat it too. Such reasoning allowed him to reconcile the contradictory "facts" that "primitive" peoples were indeed biologically inferior (that they were the missing links between apes and modern humans) and that they could rapidly be brought up to the standards of the modern world. This would take place not through natural selection, but through a process of Lamarkian selection in which the white man's burden could be translated into real progress providing the lessons taught by civilized people were the right ones.

In Darwin's time, a controversy raged over whether or not the so-called "races" of man were separate species or merely varieties of the same species. Those who favored special creation also favored the separate species notion because it suggested that each race was created by God as an immutable entity. For these individuals, races had existed since creation and would continue to exist unchanged until the final judgment. If Darwin's theory led him to see primitive societies as lower stages in social evolution, to be used as one form of evidence for the descent of man from lower forms, the same theory guided Darwin toward the notion that races were divisions of a single species and that, in general, racial differences were basically superficial. From Darwin's theoretical point of view, the human species had emerged once from lower primate forms. Races were merely divergent biological groups of the same species.

In order to explain the evolution of such superficial yet differential traits, Darwin developed the concept of sexual selection as an *alternative* to natural selection. Sexual selection is hypothesized to occur in those species in which mate choice is an aspect of genetically controlled behavior, and variation occurs in such physical aspects of males or females as color, size, body build, plumage, antler size, etc. Mate choice selects out preferred traits from within the species and is therefore different from natural selection because in the latter, selection comes from environmental pressures. For Darwin, such variable human racial traits as skin color, the texture and color of hair, the shape of such features as nose and lips were all seen as the result of sexual selection. Thus, he was led to say of races (*The Descent*, p. 198):

> Although the existing races of man differ in many respects as in colour, hair, shape of skull, proportions of the body, etc., yet if their whole structure be taken into consideration they are found to resemble each other closely in a multitude of points. Many of these are of so unimportant or of so singular a nature, that it is extremely improbable that they should have been independently acquired by aboriginally distinct species or races. The same remark holds good with equal or greater force with respect to the numerous points of mental similarity between the more distinct races of man. The American aborigines, Negroes and Europeans are as different from each other in mind as any three races that can be named; yet I was incessantly struck, whilst living with the Fuegians on board the "Beagle" with the many little traits of character, shewing how similar their minds were to ours and so it was with a full-blooded negro with whom I happened once to be intimate. (*The Descent*, p. 198)

Although Harris (1968) claims, on the basis of the above quote, that Darwin excluded intelligence from his monogenic theory of races, the last sentence shows, once again, the conflict between what Darwin read and wanted to believe for the sake of his theory, on the one hand, and his own observations, on the other. Unlike many of his contemporaries, for whom natives were essentially invisible people Darwin paid attention to his real encounters with a wide range of individuals from different ethnic stocks. When his personal experiences contradicted the accepted dogma that certain races were mentally inferior, Darwin took note of this fact. The best example of this comes from his Fuegian experience. As unfond as he was of Fuegian culture, his social encounters with the three acculturated Fuegians on board the Beagle convinced him that each was similar in intelligence to the average European and that each was endowed with a unique and individual personality. It is very clear that the few natives Darwin came to know well and his all too occasional contacts with blacks influenced his judgment enough to question the pasteboard stereotypes held by scholars in his time. Must we demand, in retrospect, that he should have seen with fuller clarity that the received wisdom on race was wrong?

The notion that human racial differences are but superficial was strengthened for Darwin by research he pursued on emotional displays in animals and humans. This was published in 1872 as *The Expression of the Emotions in Man and Animals.* In that study, which is recognized as a milestone of research in this field and as one of the very first cross-cultural studies ever undertaken, Darwin investigated a wide variety of emotional expressions in animals, the insane, and, on the basis of a questionnaire sent to missionaries and government officials around the world, a large sample of ethnic groups. The major purpose of the study, beyond its purely empirical value, was to test the monogenic theory of human evolution. If, Darwin reasoned, the various races of the world experience the same emotions and display them in similar fashion, then they must all have had a common origin in the once-evolved and single human species. For Darwin, the results were unequivocal. Thus, he concludes this work as follows:

> I have endeavoured to show in considerable detail that all the chief expressions exhibited by man are the same throughout the world. This fact is interesting, as it affords a new argument in favor of the several races being descended from a single parent-stock, which must have been almost completely human in structure, and to a large extent in mind, before the period at which the races diverged from each other.

*   *   *   *   *   *   *

It has often been said, and correctly so, that evolution was in the air when Darwin published his theory in 1859. Darwin's own grandfather, Erasmus, the German poet Goethe, the sociologist-philosopher Herbert Spencer, and Lamarck, not to mention Alfred Russel Wallace, were all evolutionists. What distinguished Darwin and Wallace was that in their co-theory of evolution, natural selection, acting on hereditary biological variation in given populations, drove the system. Natural selection removed teleological necessity from the evolutionary process. All the other evolutionists before and during Darwin's and Wallace's time were either finalists or vitalists who saw evolution as the expression of a grand plan of progressive development. Herbert Spencer's theory was inclusive of all natural phenomena from stellar origins to the development of political society. Spencer's principles demanded a steady *overall* (devolution could also occur) development from the simple to the complex and from the unordered to the highly ordered. Darwin and Wallace limited their theory to biology and, although Darwin did speculate about human social systems, he never did so on the grand scale so characteristic of Spencer. The latter intended that his theory should guide political choices while Darwin was wary of stepping beyond the boundary of biology.

Spencer's theory of social evolution along with its built-in ideology of laissez-faire politics was published before *The Origin Of Species*, but Spencer was much taken by Darwin's evidence for evolution in the biological realm. Thus, in his published works after *The Origin*, Spencer borrowed freely from Darwin. (This is not to say that Darwin was not himself influenced by Spencer's ideas; some of these are evident in *The Descent of Man*.) In any case, Spencerism, basically the teleological social evolution of human groups toward civilized perfection, came to be known as "social darwinism." Because Spencer's theory was based on a strong notion of *natural* progress, it fostered noninterference with social inequalities at home and imperialism in the growing empire. The "survival of the fittest," a slogan coined by Spencer ten years before the publication of *The Origin*, became the political rallying point for right-wing, expansionist politics in Victorian England.

Many scholars have argued over how much, if at all, Darwin himself was a social darwinian. (For an excellent review of this controversy, see Freeman 1974 with discussion by such authors as Bajema, Blacking, Carneiro, Harris, Mayr, and G. G. Simpson.) Although he never published any political tracts and took a strong social stand only against slavery, Darwin leaves a rather confusing record concerning his attitudes toward the application of evolutionary theory to social, historical, and political events. In *The Descent of Man* and *Journal of Researches*, we find several strong statements that suggest pure biological determinism. For example, consider the following from the *Journal* written on January 12, 1836:

> Besides the several evident causes of destruction, there appears to be some more mysterious agency generally at work. Wherever the European has trod, death seems to pursue the aboriginal. We may look to the wide extent of the Americas, Polynesia, the Cape of Good Hope, and Australia, and we find the same result. Nor is it the white man alone that thus acts the destroyer; the Polynesian of Malay extraction has in parts of the East Indian archipelago, thus driven before him the dark coloured native. The varieties of man seem to act on each other in the same way as different species of animals—the stronger always extirpating the weaker.

The next sentence provides a clue to one difference between the hard-hearted, pure social darwinian and Darwin himself when he says: "It was melancholy at New Zealand to hear the fine energetic natives saying, that they knew the land was doomed to pass from their children." Again, whenever Darwin had personal experiences with people, he tended to see them as individuals and could not bring a cold and pretended scientific objectivity to his observations. Thus in the *Journal* we find many sympathetic pages that document with a critical eye the destruction of Indian culture and the miserable conditions of gold and copper miners in Chile. Furthermore, he was able to say in *The Descent* that the conditions of the poor in England were due to English social institutions and *not* to the laws of nature.

A careful reading of *The Descent* reveals a series of contradictions in Darwin's rather unsystematic thinking about social as opposed to biological evolution. As we have already seen, because he uses primitives to link modern humans to our primate relatives, he makes some rather crude assumptions about primitive mentality and social customs. On the latter point, because he could not communicate with natives in their own languages, his observations are distant and often wide of the mark. This tendency is mitigated only when Darwin is confronted with obvious cruelty. On the other hand, *The Descent* is full of statements that suggest the strong role culture must play in human adaptation. In chapter five he notes, agreeing with A. R. Wallace, that humans are enabled, through their mental facilities and in spite of an unchanged body, to keep in harmony with the changing universe. He tells us that it is superiority in the arts that allows one group to win over another. But, in contradiction to these ideas, he also states that the intellectual powers of contemporary peoples are improved through natural selection. This, of course, is a crude biological determinism. Rather than generalize from this to the conclusion that civilization has developed among the most biologically gifted populations, Darwin admits that he has no good explanation for the "first advances of savages towards civilization." "The problem," he tells us, "is at present much too difficult to be solved."

What becomes abundantly clear on reading *The Descent* is the fact that while Darwin believed (complete with contradictions) in a kind of modified social darwinism as an explanation for the behavioral systems of primitive societies, he did not believe that such principles could be of much use in explaining modern society. Furthermore, he did not appear anywhere in his writings as a strong advocate of laissez-faire politics. Rather, he tended toward a moral position and then *sometimes* tried to justify this position on the basis of evolutionary principles. It is likely that Darwin's liberal humanism protected him from the more extreme forms of social darwinism. But his equivocation over the role of natural selection in the social process contributes to the confusion over his stand on the overall question concerning biological determinism and its relation to socio-political evolution. It would be helpful to give careful consideration to the distinction Darwin drew between the effects of natural selection on primitive societies, on the one hand, and civilized societies, on the other. Only then will we be able to achieve some understanding of his position. Thus he says in *The Descent*:

> With savages, the weak in body or mind are soon eliminated; and those that survive commonly exhibit a vigorous state of health. We civilized men, on the other hand, do our utmost to check the process of elimination; we build asylums for the imbecile, the maimed,

and the sick; we institute poor-laws; and our medical men exert their utmost skill to save the life of every one to the last moment. There is reason to believe that vaccination has preserved thousands who from a weak constitution would have succumbed to smallpox. Thus the weak members of civilized societies propagate their kind. No one who has attended to the breeding of domestic animals will doubt that this must be highly injurious to the race of man. The aid which we feel impelled to give to the helpless is mainly an incidental result of the instinct of sympathy, which was originally acquired as part of the social instincts, but subsequently rendered, in the manner previously indicated, more tender and more widely diffused. Nor could we check our sympathy, even at the urging of hard reason, without deterioration in the noblest part of our nature. (pp. 133–134)

Although it would be easy to argue as a social darwinian in favor of war, Darwin's moral stance leads him to hypothesize a negative biological value for it:

In every country in which a large standing army is kept up, the finest young men are taken by the conscription or are enlisted. They are thus exposed to early death during war, are often tempted into vice, and are prevented from marrying during the prime of life. On the other hand the shorter and feebler men, with poor constitutions, are left at home, and consequently have a much better chance of marrying and propagating their kind. (*The Descent*, p. 134)

Darwin comes down squarely on the side of civilization, including its tendency to ameliorate suffering, by adding up its positive aspects:

Although civilization thus checks in many ways the action of natural selection, it apparently favors the better development of the body, by means of good food and the freedom from occasional hardships. . . . With civilized nations as far as an advanced standard of morality, and an increased number of fairly good men are concerned, natural selection apparently effects but little; though the fundamental social instincts were originally thus gained. . . . The western nations of Europe, who now so immeasurably surpass their former savage progenitors, and stand at the summit of civilization, owe little or none of their superiority to direct inheritance from the old

Greeks, though they owe much to the written works of that wonderful people. . . . Who can positively say why the Spanish nation, so dominant at one time, has been distanced in the race. The awakening of the nations of Europe from the dark ages is a still more perplexing problem. (*The Descent*, pp. 135–136)

Even on this issue, Darwin is not completely consistent. He ends the section I have been quoting by accepting the role of natural selection in the success of the United States. Perhaps this is due to the unstated assumption on his part that young countries in the New World were more like primitive societies than older, established European nations. In any case, he says approvingly of the United States:

There is apparently much truth in the belief that the wonderful progress of the United States, as well as the character of the people, are the results of natural selection; for the more energetic, restless, and courageous men from all parts of Europe have emigrated during the last ten or twelve generations to that great country, and have there succeeded best. (*The Descent*, p. 142)

To call Darwin a pure social darwinist would be to oversimplify Darwin's own positions on social issues. He was, unlike such advocates, a reformer who clearly believed in a certain degree of intervention to ameliorate the worst social conditions. In addition, he was skeptical of the role natural selection could play in advanced societies given their complexity and the constant interaction of contradictory forces that acted on them. On the other hand, it would be fair to say that Darwin was a social evolutionist, subscribing, in large measure, to the idea that primitive societies represent different stages in human development and that civilization as he knew it was the most advanced as well as the best condition for our species.

One of the major themes of this essay has been the proposition that Darwin was an excellent observer, capable of accurate description and analysis, but that he was often gullible when forced to rely for information on the publications of individuals accepted by the intelligent public as scientists or scholars. It is as if, confi-

dent of his own powers of objective observation, Darwin sometimes let his critical guard down because he expected the same
accuracy and objectivity in the work of his peers. I believe that
my case for this argument is strengthened by Darwin's negative
opinions concerning the intellectual capacities of women. I hold
this view, as aberrant as it might appear at first glance, because a
look at Darwin's life shows that his opinions on this subject come
primarily from the judgments of others.

Darwin at his worst is Darwin on women. Here he is a pure
and crude biological determinist. On having a wife he wrote,
"Constant companion, (friend in old age) who will feel interested
in one, object to be beloved and played with—better than a dog
anyhow—Home and someone to take care of house—Charms of
music and female chitchat. These things good for one's health"
(quoted in Gould 1982:xix). This was said in his private papers,
but he also devotes a section of *The Descent* to a comparison of
men's and women's minds. Although married and a family man,
Darwin apparently had more personal experiences with, and lasting impressions of, natives in far away places than he had with
women of high intellectual abilities. The Beagle was, after all, a
male domain, and in his wanderings over half the globe, Darwin
lived in the company of men. His views on marriage and the role
of women in providing comfort, but not intellectual companion-
ship, may be due to the known views of his wife on evolution. As
Darwin drifted further and further away from religious belief and
as the apparent threat his theory posed to religion became an issue of the day, Darwin and his wife must have become increas-
ingly estranged from each other in their attitudes and opinions. It
is well known that Mrs. Darwin, a profoundly religious person,
had little understanding or sympathy for the theory of natural selection and was appalled by its implications for theology. These
experiences with his wife and his lack of experience with women
in general must have led Darwin to produce the kind of negative
evaluation of women's intellectual capacities we find in *The Descent* (p. 557):

Man is more courageous, pugnacious and energetic than woman, and has a more inventive genius. His brain is absolutely larger, but whether or not proportionately to his larger body, has not, I believe, been fully ascertained.

And on pp. 563–564:

It is generally admitted that with woman the powers of intuition, of rapid perception, and perhaps of imitation, are more strongly marked than in man; but some, at least, of these faculties are characteristic of the lower races, and therefore of a past and lower state of civilization. The chief distinction in the intellectual powers of the two sexes is shewn by man's attaining to higher eminence, in whatever he takes up, than can woman—whether requiring deep thought, reason, or imagination, or merely the use of the senses and hands. If two lists were made of the most eminent men and women in poetry, painting, sculpture, music (inclusive both of composition and performance), history, science, and philosophy, with half-a-dozen names under each subject, the two lists would not bear comparison. We may also infer, from the law of the deviation of averages, so well illustrated by Mr. Galton, in his work on 'Hereditary Genius,' that if men are capable of a decided pre-eminence over women in many subjects, the average of mental power in man must be above that of woman.

Unfortunately, this statement has a modern ring. Contemporary racists often speak of women in the same way they speak of what they consider to be inferior races. This is really no accident. Those who see cultural variables as determined by biological constants are also likely to see any apparent biological differences as prima facie evidence for mental and behavioral differences. More often than not, these differences are then cast in terms of superiority and inferiority. It is unfortunate that Darwin was excluded from contact with intellectual women for, given what we can see of his changing attitudes toward the intelligence of native peoples, if he had had the proper opportunity to interact with educated and talented women, he might have revised his negative attitudes toward females as creative and scholarly individuals.

In summary, Darwin's ideas, both accurate and inaccurate, were shaped by three factors: his excellent observations and interpretations of natural phenomena; the demands made by the theory of natural selection in an era when no knowledge existed about the mechanisms of genetics or the power of chemical mutations to change hereditary material; and Darwin's reliance on, and trust of, the available literature concerning data unavailable to his own direct observation. The theory of evolution through natural selection guided Darwin's interpretations of his own work and the work of others. On the question of race it led Darwin to take a monogenic position close to the modern view of human variation, but it also led him to make inaccurate judgments concerning primitive mentality. The latter error was due to his self-perceived need to muster evidence for a link between lower primates and modern humans. But here Darwin's personal experiences and observations of a variety of different ethnic groups led him finally to question the notion that certain races were intellectually inferior. In his publications we find statements reflecting the then accepted racist wisdom along with obvious caveats based on real experience. These are all the more unusual because, even as a creature of his time, Darwin, unlike so many of his contemporaries, often saw real people rather than accepted stereotypes. Another set of factors that must have protected Darwin from the extremes of laissez-faire social darwinism was his desire to disassociate the theory of evolution through natural selection from politics and, even if this seems contradictory, his overriding humanism and sympathy for his fellow creatures, which obviously tempered his political views.

REFERENCES

Boon, J. 1982. *Other Tribes, Other Scribes.* Cambridge: Cambridge University Press.

Darwin, C. 1896. *Life and Letters.* New York: Appleton.

Freeman, D. 1974. "The Evolutionary Theories of Charles Darwin and Herbert Spencer," *Current Anthropology,* 15:211–237.

Gould, S. J. 1982. "In Praise of Charles Darwin," Preface to *What Darwin Really Said* by Benjamin Farrington, New York: Schocken Books.

Gruber, H. 1981. *Darwin on Man: A Psychological Study of Scientific Creativity.* Second edition. Chicago: University of Chicago Press.

Harris, M. 1968. *The Rise of Anthropological Theory.* New York: Crowell.

Huxley, T. H. 1865. "Emancipation—Black and White." In *Huxley's Lecture and Lay Sermons.* New York: Dutton.

JOURNAL OF RESEARCHES

APRIL 14TH, 1832.—Leaving Socego, we rode to another estate on the Rio Macae, which was the last patch of cultivated ground in that direction. The estate was two and a half miles long, and the owner had forgotten how many broad. Only a very small piece had been cleared, yet almost every acre was capable of yielding all the various rich productions of a tropical land. Considering the enormous area of Brazil, the proportion of cultivated ground can scarcely be considered as any thing, compared to that which is left in the state of nature: at some future age, how vast a population it will support! During the second day's journey we found the road so shut up, that it was necessary that a man should go ahead with a sword to cut away the creepers. The forest abounded with beautiful objects; among which the tree ferns, though not large, were, from their bright green foliage, and the elegant curvature of their fronds, most worthy of admiration. In the evening it rained very heavily, and although the thermometer stood at 65°, I felt very cold. As soon as the rain ceased, it was curious to observe the extraordinary evaporation which commenced over the whole exent of the forest. At the height of a hundred feet the hills were buried in a dense white vapour, which rose like columns of smoke from the most thickly-wooded parts, and especially from the valleys. I observed this phenomenon on several occasions: I suppose it is owing to the large surface of foliage, previously heated by the sun's rays.

While staying at this estate, I was very nearly being an eye-witness to one of those atrocious acts which can only take place in a slave country. Owing to a quarrel and a law-suit, the owner was on the point of taking all the women and children from the male slaves, and selling them separately at the public auction at Rio. Interest, and not any feeling of compassion, prevented this act. Indeed, I do not believe the inhumanity of separating thirty fam-

ilies, who had lived together for many years, even occurred to the
owner. Yet I will pledge myself, that in humanity and good feeling he was superior to the common run of men. It may be said
there exists no limit to the blindness of interest and selfish habit.
I may mention one very trifling anecdote, which at the time struck
me more forcibly than any story of cruelty. I was crossing a ferry
with a negro, who was uncommonly stupid. In endeavouring to
make him understand, I talked loud, and made signs, in doing
which I passed my hand near his face. He, I suppose, thought I
was in a passion, and was going to strike him; for instantly, with
a frightened look and half-shut eyes, he dropped his hands. I shall
never forget my feelings of surprise, disgust, and shame, at seeing
a great powerful man afraid even to ward off a blow, directed, as
he thought, at his face. This man had been trained to a degrada-
tion lower than the slavery of the most helpless animal.

JULY 24TH, 1833.—The Beagle sailed from Maldonado, and on
August the 3rd she arrived off the mouth of the Rio Negro. This
is the principal river on the whole line of coast between the Strait
of Magellan and the Plata. It enters the sea about three hundred
miles south of the estuary of the Plata. About fifty years ago, under the old Spanish government, a small colony was established
here; and it is still the most southern position (lat. 41°) on this
eastern coast of America, inhabited by civilized man. . . .

The settlement is situated eighteen miles up the river. The road
follows the foot of the sloping cliff, which forms the northern
boundary of the great valley, in which the Rio Negro flows. On
the way we passed the ruins of some fine "estancias," which a few
years since had been destroyed by the Indians. They withstood
several attacks. A man present at one gave me a very lively description of what took place. The inhabitants had sufficient notice
to drive all the cattle and horses into the "corral" which surrounded the house, and likewise to mount some small cannon. The
Indians were Araucanians from the south of Chile; several hundreds
in number, and highly disciplined. They first appeared in two
bodies on a neighbouring hill; having there dismounted, and taken

off their fur mantles, they advanced naked to the charge. The only weapon of an Indian is a very long bamboo or chuzo, ornamented with ostrich feathers, and pointed by a sharp spear-head. My informer seemed to remember with the greatest horror the quivering of these chuzos as they approached near. When close, the cacique Pincheira hailed the besieged to give up their arms, or he would cut all their throats. As this would probably have been the result of their entrance under any circumstances, the answer was given by a volley of musketry. The Indians, with great steadyness, came to the very fence of the corral: but to their surprise they found the posts fastened together by iron nails instead of leather thongs, and, of course, in vain attempted to cut them with their knives. This saved the lives of the Christians: many of the wounded Indians were carried away by their companions; and at last one of the under caciques being wounded, the bugle sounded a retreat. They retired to their horses, and seemed to hold a council of war. This was an awful pause for the Spaniards, as all their ammunition, with the exception of a few cartridges, was expended. In an instant the Indians mounted their horses, and galloped out of sight. Another attack was still more quickly repulsed. A cool Frenchman managed the gun; he stopped till the Indians approached close, and then raked the line with grape-shot: he thus laid thirty-nine of them on the ground; and, of course, such a blow immediately routed the whole party.

The town is indifferently called El Carmen or Patagones. It is built on the face of a cliff which fronts the river, and many of the houses are excavated even in the sandstone. The river is about two or three hundred yards wide, and is deep and rapid. The many islands, with their willow-trees, and the flat headlands, seen one behind the other on the northern boundary of the broad green valley, forms, by the aid of a bright sun, a view almost picturesque. The number of inhabitants does not exceed a few hundreds. These Spanish colonies do not, like our British ones, carry within themselves the elements of growth. Many Indians of pure blood reside here: the tribe of the Cacique Lucanee constantly have their Toldos on the outskirts of the town. The local government partly supplies them with provisions, by giving them all the old worn-out horses, and they earn a little by making horse-rugs and other articles of riding-gear. These Indians are considered civilized; but what their character may have gained by a lesser degree of ferocity, is almost counterbalanced by their entire immorality. Some of the younger men are, however, improving; they are willing to labour, and a short time since a party went on a sealing-voyage, and behaved very well. They were now enjoying the fruits of their labour, by being dressed in very gay, clean clothes, and by being very idle. The taste they showed in their dress was admirable; if you could have turned one of these young Indians into a statue of bronze, his drapery would have been perfectly graceful. . . .

To the northward of the Rio Negro, between it and the inhabited country near Buenos Ayres, the Spaniards have only one small settlement, recently established at Bahia Blanca. The distance in a straight line to Buenos Ayres is very nearly five hundred British miles. The wandering tribes of horse Indians, which have always occupied the greater part of this country, having of late much harassed the outlying estancias, the government at Buenos Ayres equipped some time since an army under the command of General Rosas for the purpose of exterminating them. The troops were now encamped on the banks of the Colorado; a river lying about eighty miles northward of the Rio Negro. When General Rosas left Buenos Ayres he struck in a direct line across the unexplored plains: and as the country was thus pretty well cleared of Indians, he left behind him, at wide intervals, a small party of soldiers with a troop of horses (a posta), so as to be enabled to keep up a communication with the capital. . . .

AUGUST 11TH,—Mr. Harris, an Englishman residing at Patagones, a guide, and five Gauchos, who were proceeding to the army on business, were my companions on the journey. The Colorado, as I have already said, is nearly eighty miles distant: and as we travelled slowly, we were two days and a half on the road. The whole line of country deserves scarcely a better name than that of a desert. Water is found only in two small wells; it is called fresh; but even at this time of the year, during the rainy season, it was quite brackish. In the summer this must be a distressing passage; for now it was sufficiently desolate. The valley of the Rio Negro, broad as it is, has merely been excavated out of the sand-stone plain; for immediately above the bank on which the town stands, a level country commences, which is interrupted only by a few trifling valleys and depressions. Everywhere the landscape wears the same sterile aspect; a dry gravelly soil supports tufts of brown withered grass, and low scattered brushes, armed with thorns.

Shortly after passing the first spring we came in sight of a famous tree, which the Indians reverence as the altar of Walleechu. It is situated on a high part of the plain, and hence is a landmark visible at a great distance. As soon as a tribe of Indians come in sight of it, they offer their adorations by loud shouts. The tree itself is low, much branched, and thorny: just above the root it has a diameter of about three feet. It stands by itself without any neighbour, and was indeed the first tree we saw; afterwards we met with a few others of the same kind, but they were far from common. Being winter the tree had no leaves, but in their place numberless threads, by which the various offerings, such as cigars, bread, meat, pieces of cloth, etc. had been suspended. Poor Indians, not having anything better, only pull a thread out of their ponchos, and fasten it to the tree. Richer Indians are accustomed to pour spririts and maté into a certain hole, and likewise to smoke upwards, thinking thus to afford all possible gratification to Walleechu. To complete the scene, the tree was surrounded by the bleached bones of horses which had been slaughtered as sacrifices. All Indians of every age and sex make their offerings; they then think that their horses will not tire, and that they themselves shall be prosperous. The Gaucho who told me this, said that in the time of peace he had witnessed this scene, and that he and others used to wait till the Indians had passed by, for the sake of stealing from Walleechu the offerings.

The Gauchos think that the Indians consider the tree as the god itself; but it seems far more probable, that they regard it as the altar. The only cause which I can imagine for this choice, is its being a landmark in a dangerous passage. The Sierra de la Ventana is visible at an immense distance; and a Gaucho told me that he was once riding with an Indian a few miles to the north of the Rio Colorado, when the Indian commenced making the same loud noise, which is usual at the first sight of the distant tree; putting his hand to his head, and then pointing in the direction of the Sierra. Upon being asked the reason of this, the Indian said in broken Spanish. "First see the Sierra." About two leagues beyond this curious tree we halted for the night: at this instant an unfortunate cow was spied by the lynx-eyed Gauchos, who set off in full chace, and in a few minutes dragged her in with their lazos, and slaughtered her. We here had the four necessaries of life "en el campo,"—pasture for the horses, water (only a muddy puddle), meat and firewood. The Gauchos were in high spirits at finding all these luxuries; and we soon set to work at the poor cow. This was the first night which I passed under the open sky, with the gear of the recado for my bed. There is high enjoyment in the independence of the Gaucho life—to be able at any moment to pull up your horse, and say, "Here we will pass the night." The death-like stillness of the plain, the dogs keeping watch, the gipsy-group of Gauchos making their beds round the fire, have left in my mind a strongly-marked picture of this first night, which will never be forgotton. . . .

The encampment of General Rosas was close to the river. It consisted of a square formed by waggons, artillery, straw huts, etc. The soldiers were nearly all cavalry; and I should think such a villanous, banditti-like army was never before collected together. The greater number of men were of a mixed breed, between Negro, Indian, and Spaniard. I know not the reason, but men of such origin seldom have a good expression of countenance. I called on the Secretary to show my passport. He began to cross-question me in the most dignified and mysterious manner. By good luck I had a letter of recommendation from the government of Buenos Ayres to the commandant of Patagones. This was taken to General Rosas, who sent me a very obliging message; and the Secretary returned all smiles and graciousness. We took up our residence in the *rancho*, or hovel, of a curious old Spaniard, who had served with Napoleon in the expedition against Russia.

We stayed two days at the Colorado; I had little to do, for the surrounding country was a swamp, which in summer (December), when the snow melts on the Cordillera, is overflowed by the river. My chief amusement was watching the Indian families as they came to buy little articles at the rancho where we stayed. It was supposed that General Rosas had about six hundred Indian allies. The men were a tall, fine race, yet it was afterwards easy to see in the Fuegian savage the same countenance rendered hideous by cold, want of food, and less civilization. Some authors, in defining the primary races of mankind, have separated these Indians into two classes; but this is certainly incorrect. Among the young women or chinas, some deserve to be called even beautiful. Their hair was coarse, but bright and black; and they wore it in two plaits hanging down to the waist. They had a high colour, and eyes that glistened with brilliancy; their legs, feet, and arms were small and elegantly formed; their ankles, and sometimes their waists, were ornamented by broad bracelets of blue beads. Nothing could be more interesting than some of the family groups. A mother with one or two daughters would often come to our rancho, mounted on the same horse. They ride like men, but with their knees tucked up much higher. This habit, perhaps, arises from their being accustomed, when travelling, to ride the loaded horses. The duty of the women is to load and unload the horses; to make the tents for the night; in short to be, like the wives of all savages, useful slaves. The men fight, hunt, take care of the horses, and make the riding gear. One of their chief indoor occupations is to knock two stones together till they become round, in order to make the bolas. With this important weapon the Indian catches his game, and also his horse, which roams free over the plain. In fighting, his first attempt is to throw down the horse of his adversary with the bolas, and when entangled by the fall to kill him with the chuzo. If the balls only catch the neck or body of an animal, they are often carried away and lost. As the making [of] the stones round is the labour of two days, the manufacture of the balls is a very common employment. Several of the men and women had their faces painted red, but I never saw the horizontal bands which are so common among the Fuegians. Their chief pride consists in having everything made of silver; I have seen a cacique with his spurs, stirrups, handle of his knife, and bridle made of this metal: the headstall and reins being of wire, were not thicker than whipcord; and to see a fiery steed wheeling about under the command of so light a chain, gave to the horsemanship a remarkable character of elegance.

General Rosas intimated a wish to see me; a circumstance which I was afterwards very glad of. He is a man of an extraordinary character, and has a most predominant influence in the country, which it seems probable he will use to its prosperity and advancement. [Here Darwin later added the footnote: "This prophecy has turned out entirely and miserably wrong." 1845.]He is said to be the owner of seventy-four square leagues of land, and to have about three hundred thousand head of cattle. His estates are admirably managed, and are far more productive of corn than those of others. He first gained his celebrity by his laws for his own estancias, and by disciplining several hundred men, so as to resist with success the attacks of the Indians. There are many stories current about the rigid manner in which his laws were enforced. One of these was, that no man, on penalty of being put in the stocks, should carry his knife on a Sunday: this being the principal day for gambling and drinking, many quarrels arose, which from the general manner of fighting with the knife often proved fatal. One Sunday the Governor came in great form to pay the estancia a visit, and General Rosas, in his hurry, walked out to receive him with his knife, as usual, stuck in his belt. The steward touched his arm, and reminded him of the law; upon which turning to the Governor, he said he was extremely sorry, but that he must go into the stocks, and that till let out, he possessed no power even in his own house. After a little time the steward was persuaded to open the stocks, and to let him out, but no sooner was this done, than he turned to the steward and said, "You now have broken the laws, so you must take my place in the stocks." Such actions as these delighted the Gauchos, who all possess high notions of their own equality and dignity.

General Rosas is also a perfect horseman—an accomplishment of no small consequences in a country where an assembled army elected its general by the following trial: A troop of unbroken horses being driven into a corral, were let out through a gateway, above which was a cross-bar: it was agreed whoever should drop from the bar on one of these wild animals, as it rushed out, and should be able, without saddle or bridle, not only to ride it, but also to bring it back to the door of the corral, should be their general. The person who succeeded was accordingly elected; and doubtless made a fit general for such an army. This extraordinary feat has also been performed by Rosas.

By these means, and by conforming to the dress and habits of the Gauchos, he has obtained an unbounded popularity in the country, and in consequence a despotic power. I was assured by an English merchant, that a man who had murdered another, when arrested and questioned concerning his motive, answered, "He spoke disrespectfully of General Rosas, so I killed him." At the end of a week the murderer was at liberty. This doubtless was the act of the general's party, and not of the general himself.

In conversation he is enthusiastic, sensible, and very grave. His gravity is carried to a high pitch: I heard one of his mad buffoons (for he keeps two, like the barons of old) relate the following anecdote: "I wanted very much to hear a certain piece of music, so I went to the general two or three times to ask him; he said to me, 'Go about your business, for I am engaged.' I went a second time; he said, 'If you come again I will punish you.' A third time I asked, and he laughed. I rushed out of the tent, but it was too late; he ordered two soldiers to catch and stake me. I begged by all the Saints in heaven he would let me off; but it would not do;—when the general laughs he spares neither mad man nor sound." The poor flighty gentleman looked quite dolorous, at the very recollection of the staking. This is a very severe punishment; four posts are driven into the ground, and the man is extended by his arms and legs horizontally, and there left to stretch for several hours. The idea is evidently taken from the usual method of drying hides. My interview passed away without a smile, and I obtained a passport and order for the government post-horses, and this he gave me in the most obliging and ready manner.

In the morning we started for Bahia Blanca, which we reached in two days. Leaving the regular encampment, we passed by the toldos of the Indians. These are round like ovens, and covered with hides; by the mouth of each, a tapering chuzo was stuck in the ground. The toldos were divided into separate groups, which belonged to the different caciques' tribes, and the groups were again divided into smaller ones, according to the relationship of the owners. For several miles we travelled along the valley of the Colorado. The alluvial plains on the side appeared fertile, and it is supposed that they are well adapted to the growth of corn. Turning northward from the river, we soon entered on a country, differing from the plains south of the river. The land still continued dry and sterile; but it supported many different kinds of plants, and the grass, though brown and withered, was more abundant, as the thorny bushes were less so. These latter in a short space entirely disappeared, and the plains were left without a thicket to cover their nakedness. This change in the vegetation marks the commencement of the grand calcareo argillaceous deposit, which forms the wide extent of the Pampas, and covers the granitic rocks of Banda Oriental. From the Strait of Magellan to the Colorado, a distance of about eight hundred miles, the face of the country is everywhere composed of shingle: the pebbles are chiefly of porphyry, and probably owe their origin to the rocks of the Cordillera. North of the Colorado this bed thins out, and the pebbles become exceedingly small, and here the characteristic vegetation of Patagonia ceases.

Having ridden about twenty-five miles, we came to a broad belt of sand-dunes, which stretches, as far as the eye can reach, to the east and west. The sand-hillocks resting on the clay, allow small pools of water to collect, and thus afford in this dry country an invaluable supply of fresh water. The great advantage arising from depressions and elevations of the soil, is not often brought home to the mind. The two miserable springs in the long passage between the Rio Negro and Colorado were caused by trifling inequalities in the plain; without them not a drop of water would have been found. The belt of sand-dunes is about eight miles wide; at some former period it probably formed the margin of a grand estuary, where the Colorado now flows. In this district, where absolute proofs of the recent elevation of the land occur, such speculations can hardly be neglected by any one, although merely considering the physical geography of the country. Having crossed the sandy tract, we arrived in the evening at one of the post-houses; and, as the fresh horses were grazing at a distance, we determined to pass the night there.

The house was situated at the base of a ridge, between one and two hundred feet high—a most remarkable feature in this country. This posta was commanded by a negro lieutenant, born in Africa: to his credit be it said, there was not a rancho between the Colorado and Buenos Ayros in nearly such neat order as his. He had a little room for strangers, and a small corral for the horses, all made of sticks and reeds; he had also dug a ditch round his house, as a defence in case of being attacked. This would, however, have been of little avail, if the Indians had come; but his chief comfort seemed to rest in the thought of selling his life dearly. A short time before, a body of Indians had travelled past in the night; if they had been aware of the posta, our black friend and his four soldiers would assuredly have been slaughtered. I did not any where meet a more civil and obliging man than this negro; it was therefore the more painful to see that he would not sit down and eat with us.

In the morning we sent for the horses very early, and started for another exhilarating gallop. We passed the Cabeza del Buey, an old name given to the head of a large marsh, which extends from Bahia Blanca. Here we changed horses, and passed through some leagues of swamps and saline marshes. Changing horses for the last time, we again began wading through the mud. My animal fell, and I was well soused in black mire—a very disagreeable accident, when one does not possess a change of clothes. Some miles from the fort we met a man, who told us that a great gun had been fired, which is a signal that Indians are near. We immediately left the road, and followed the edge of a marsh, which when chased offers the best mode of escape. We were glad to arrive within the walls, when we found all the alarm was about nothing, for the Indians turned out to be friendly ones, who wished to join General Rosas.

Bahia Blanca scarcely deserves the name of a village. A few houses and the barracks for the troops are enclosed by a deep ditch and fortified wall. The settlement is only of recent standing (since 1828); and its growth has been one of trouble. The government of Buenos Ayres unjustly occupied it by force, instead of following the wise example of the Spanish Viceroys, who purchased the land near the older settlement of the Rio Negro, from the Indians. Hence the need of the fortifications; hence the few houses and little cultivated land without the limits of the walls: even the cattle are not safe from the attacks of the Indians beyond the boundaries of the plain, on which the fortress stands.

The part of the harbour where the Beagle intended to anchor being distant twenty-five miles, I obtained from the Commandant a guide and horses, to take me to see whether she had arrived. Leaving the plain of green turf, which extended along the course of a little brook, we soon entered on a wide level waste consisting either of sand, saline marshes, or bare mud. Some parts were clothed by low thickets, and others with those succulent plants, which luxuriate only where salt abounds. Bad as the country was, ostriches, deers, agoutis, and armadilloes, were abundant. My guide told me, that two months before he had a most narrow escape of his life: he was out hunting with two other men, at no great distance from this part of the country, when they were suddenly met by a party of Indians, who giving chace, soon overtook and killed his two friends. His own horse's legs were also caught by the bolas; but he jumped off, and with his knife cut them free: while doing this he was obliged to dodge round his horse, and received two severe wounds from their chuzos. Springing on the saddle, he managed, by a most wonderful exertion, just to keep ahead of the long spears of his pursuers, who followed him to within sight of the fort. From that time there was an order that no one should stray far from the settlement. I did not know of this when I started, and was surprised to observe how earnestly my guide watched a deer, which appeared to have been frightened from a distant quarter. . . .

Two days afterwards I again rode to the harbour: when not far from our destination, my companion, the same man as before, spied three people hunting on horseback. He immediately dismounted, and watching them intently, said, "They don't ride like Christians, and nobody can leave the fort." The three hunters joined company, and likewise dismounted from their horses. At last one mounted again and rode over the hill out of sight. My companion said, "We must now get on our horses: load your pistol;" and he looked to his own sword. I asked, "Are they Indians?"—"Quien sabe? (who knows?) if there are no more than three, it does not signify." It then struck me, that the one man had gone over the hill to fetch the rest of his tribe. I suggested this; but all the answer I could extort was, "Quien sabe?" His head and eye never for a minute ceased scanning slowly the distant horizon. I thought his uncommon coolness too good a joke, and asked him why he did not return home. I was startled when he answered, "We are returning, but in a line so as to pass near a swamp, into which we can gallop the horses as far as they can go, and then trust to our own legs; so that there is no danger." I did not feel quite so confident of this, and wanted to increase our pace. He said, "No, not until they do." When any little inequality concealed us, we galloped; but when in sight, continued walking. At last we reached a valley, and turning to the left, galloped quickly to the foot of a hill; he gave me his horse to hold, made the dogs lie down, and then crawled on his hands and knees to reconnoitre. He remained in this position for some time, and at last, bursting out in laughter, exclaimed, "Mugeres!" (women!) He knew them to be the wife and sister-in-law of the major's son, hunting for ostrich's eggs. I have described this man's conduct, because he acted under the full impression that they were Indians. . . .

During my stay at Bahia Blanca, while waiting for the Beagle, the place was in a constant state of excitement, from rumours of wars and victories, between the troops of Rosas and the wild Indians. One day an account came that a small party forming one of the postas on the line to Buenos Ayres, had been found all murdered. The next day three hundred men arrived from the Colorado, under the command of Commandant Miranda. A large portion of these men were Indians (*mansos*, or tame), belonging to the tribe of the Cacique Bernantio. They passed the night here; and it was impossible to conceive any thing more wild and savage than the scene of their bivouac. Some drank till they were intoxicated; others swallowed the steaming blood of the cattle slaughtered for their suppers, and then, being sick from drunkenness, they cast it up again, and were besmeared with filth and gore. . . .

In the morning they started for the scene of the murder, with orders to follow the "rastro," or track, even if it led them to Chile. We subsequently heard that the wild Indians had escaped into the great Pampas, and from some cause the track had been missed. One glance at the rastro tells these people a whole history. Supposing they examine the track of a thousand horses, they will soon guess the number of mounted ones by seeing how many have cantered; by the depth of the other impressions, whether any horses were loaded with cargoes; by the irregularity of the footsteps, how far tired; by the manner in which food has been cooked, whether the pursued travelled in haste; by the general appearance, how long it has been since they passed. They consider a rastro of ten days or a fortnight, quite recent enough to be hunted out. We also heard that Miranda struck from the west end of the Sierra Ventana, in a direct line to the island of Cholechel, situated seventy leagues up the Rio Negro. This is a distance of between two and three hundred miles, through a country completely unknown. What other troops in the world are so independent? With the sun for their guide, mares' flesh for food, their saddle-cloths for beds,—as long as there is a little water, these men would penetrate to the end of the world.

A few days afterwards I saw another troop of these banditti-like soldiers start on an expedition against a tribe of Indians at the small Salinas, who had been betrayed by a prisoner cacique. The Spaniard who brought the orders for this expedition was a very intelligent man. He gave me an account of the last engagement at which he was present. Some Indians, who had been taken prisoners, gave information of a tribe living north of the Colorado. Two hundred soldiers were sent; and they first discovered the Indians by a cloud of dust from their horses' feet, as they chanced to be travelling. The country was mountainous and wild, and it must have been far in the interior, for the Cordillera were in sight. The Indians, men, women, and children, were about one hundred and ten in number, and they were nearly all taken or killed, for the soldiers sabre every man. The Indians are now so terrified that they offer no resistance in a body, but each flies, neglecting even his wife and children; but when overtaken, like wild animals, they fight against any number to the last moment. One dying Indian seized with his teeth the thumb of his adversary, and allowed his own eye to be forced out sooner than relinquish his hold. Another, who was wounded, feigned death, keeping a knife ready to strike one more fatal blow. My informer said, when he was pursuing an Indian, the man cried out for mercy, at the same time that he was covertly loosing the bolas from his waist, meaning to whirl it round his head and so strike his pursuer. "I however struck him with my sabre to the ground, and then got off my horse, and cut his throat with my knife." This is a dark picture; but how much more shocking is the unquestionable fact, that all the women who appear above twenty years old are massacred in cold blood! When I exclaimed that this appeared rather inhuman, he answered, "Why, what can be done? they breed so!"

Every one here is fully convinced that this is the most just war, because it is against barbarians. Who would believe in this age that such atrocities could be committed in a Christian civilized country? The children of the Indians are saved, to be sold or given away as servants, or rather slaves for as long a time as the owners can make them believe themselves slaves; but I believe in their treatment there is little to complain of.

In the battle four men ran away together. They were pursued, one was killed, and the other three were taken alive. They turned out to be messengers or ambassadors from a large body of Indians, united in the common cause of defence, near the Cordillera. The tribe to which they had been sent was on the point of holding a grand council; the feast of mare's flesh was ready, and the dance prepared: in the morning the ambassadors were to have returned to the Cordillera. They were remarkably fine men, very fair, above six feet high, and all under thirty years of age. The three survivors of course possessed very valuable information; and to extort this they were placed in a line. The two first being questioned, answered, "No sé" (I do not know), and were one after the other shot. The third also said "No sé;" adding, "Fire, I am a man, and can die!" Not one syllable would they breathe to injure the united cause of their country! The conduct of the above-mentioned cacique was very different: he saved his life by betraying the intended plan of warfare, and the point of union in the Andes. It was believed that there were already six or seven hundred Indians together, and that in summer their numbers would be doubled. Ambassadors were to have been sent to the Indians at the small Salinas, near Bahia Blanca, whom I have mentioned that this same cacique had betrayed. The communication, therefore, between the Indians, extends from the Cordillera to the coast of the Atlantic.

General Rosas's plan is to kill all stragglers, and having driven the remainder to a common point, to attack them in a body, in the summer, with the assistance of the Chilenos. This operation is to be repeated for three successive years. I imagine the summer is chosen as the time for the main attack, because the plains are then without water, and the Indians can only travel in particular directions. The escape of the Indians to the south of the Rio Negro, where in such a vast unknown country they would be safe, is prevented by a treaty with the Tehuelches to this effect;—that Rosas pays them so much to slaughter every Indian who passes to the south of the river, but if they fail in so doing, they themselves are to be exterminated. The war is waged chiefly against the Indians near the Cordillera; for many of the tribes on this eastern side are fighting with Rosas. The general, however, like Lord Chesterfield, thinking that his friends may in a future day become his enemies, always places them in the front ranks, so that their numbers may be thinned. Since leaving South America we have heard that this war of extermination completely failed.

Among the captive girls taken in the same engagement, there were two very pretty Spanish ones, who had been carried away by the Indians when young, and could now only speak the Indian tongue. From their account they must have come from Salta, a distance in a straight line of nearly one thousand miles. This gives one a grand idea of the immense territory over which the Indians roam: yet, great as it is, I think there will not, in another half-century, be a wild Indian northward of the Rio Negro. The warfare is too bloody to last; the Christians killing every Indian, and the Indians doing the same by the Christians. It is melancholy to trace how the Indians have given way before the Spanish invaders. Schirdel says that in 1535, when Buenos Ayres was founded, there were villages containing two and three thousand inhabitants. Even in Falconer's time (1750) the Indians made inroads as far as Luxan, Areco, and Arrecife, but now they are driven beyond the Salado. Not only have whole tribes been exterminated, but the remaining Indians have become more barbarous: instead of living in large villages, and being employed in the arts of fishing, as well as of the chace, they now wander about the open plains, without home or fixed occupation.

I heard also some account of an engagement which took place, a few weeks previously to the one mentioned, at Cholechel. This is a very important station on account of being a pass for horses; and it was, in consequence, for some time the head-quarters of a division of the army. When the troops first arrived there they found a tribe of Indians, of whom they killed twenty or thirty. The cacique escaped in a manner which astonished every one. The chief Indians always have one or two picked horses, which they keep ready for any urgent occasion. On one of these, an old white horse, the cacique sprung, taking with him his little son. The horse had neither saddle nor bridle. To avoid the shots, the Indian rode in the peculiar method of his nation; namely, with an arm round the horse's neck, and one leg only on its back. Thus hanging on one side, he was seen patting the horse's head, and talking to him. The pursuers urged every effort in the chace; the Commandant three times changed his horse, but all in vain. The old Indian father and his son escaped and were free. What a fine picture one can form in one's mind,—the naked, bronze-like figure of the old man with his little boy, riding like a Mazeppa on the white horse, thus leaving far behind him the host of his pursuers!

I saw one day a soldier striking fire with a piece of flint, which I immediately recognized as having been a part of the head of an arrow. He told me it was found near the island of Cholechel, and that they are frequently picked up there. It was between two and three inches long, and therefore twice as large as those now used in Tierra del Fuego: it was made of opake cream-coloured flint, but the point and barbs had been intentionally broken off. It is well known that no Pampas Indians now use bows and arrows. I believe a small tribe in Banda Oriental must be excepted; but they are widely separated from the Pampas Indians, and border close on those tribes that inhabit the forest, and live on foot. It appears, therefore, that these arrow-heads are antiquarian relics of the Indians, before the great change in habits consequent on the introduction of the horse into South America.

SEPTEMBER 11TH.—Proceeded to the third posta in company with the lieutenant who commanded it. The distance is called fifteen leagues; but it is only guess-work, and is generally overstated. The road was uninteresting, over a dry grassy plain; and on our left hand at a greater or less distance there were some low hills; a continuation of which we crossed close to the posta. Before our arrival we met a large herd of cattle and horses, guarded by fifteen soldiers; but we were told many had been lost. It is very difficult to drive animals across the plains; for if in the night a puma, or even a fox, approaches, nothing can prevent the horses dispersing in every direction; and a storm will have the same effect.

A short time since, an officer left Buenos Ayres with five hundred horses, and when he arrived at the army he had under twenty.

Soon afterwards we perceived by the cloud of dust, that a party of horsemen were coming towards us; when far distant my companions knew them to be Indians, by their long hair streaming behind their backs. The Indians generally have a fillet round their heads, but never any covering; and their black hair blowing across their swarthy faces, heightens to an uncommon degree the wildness of their appearance. They turned out to be a party of Bernantio's friendly tribe, going to a salina for salt. The Indians eat much salt, their children sucking it like sugar. This habit is very different from that of the Spanish Gauchos, who, leading the same kind of life, eat scarcely any: according to Mungo Park, it is people who live on vegetable food who have an unconquerable desire for salt. The Indians gave us good-humoured nods as they passed at full gallop, driving before them a troop of horses, and followed by a train of lanky dogs.

SEPTEMBER 12TH AND 13TH.—I staid at this posta two days, waiting for a troop of soldiers, which General Rosas had the kindness to send to inform me, would shortly travel to Buenos Ayres; and he advised me to take the opportunity of the escort. In the morning we rode to some neighbouring hills to view the country, and to examine the geology. After dinner the soldiers divided themselves into two parties for a trial of skill with the bolas. Two spears were stuck in the ground thirty-five yards apart, but they were struck and entangled only once in four or five times. The balls can be thrown fifty or sixty yards, but with little certainty. This, however, does not apply to a man on horseback; for when the speed of the horse is added to the force of the arm, it is said, that they can be whirled with effect to the distance of eighty yards. As a proof of their force, I may mention, that at the Falkland Islands, when the Spaniards murdered some of their own countrymen and all the Englishmen, a young friendly Spaniard was running away, when a great tall man, by name Luciano, came at full gallop after him, shouting to him to stop, and saying that he only

wanted to speak to him. Just as the Spaniard was on the point of
reaching the boat, Luciano threw the balls: they struck him on
the legs with such a jerk, as to throw him down and to render him
for some time insensible. The man, after Luciano had had his talk,
was allowed to escape. He told us that his legs were marked by
great weals, where the thong had wound round, as if he had been
flogged with a whip. In the middle of the day two men arrived,
who brought a parcel from the next posta to be forwarded to the
general: so that besides these two, our party consisted this evening of my guide and self, the lieutenant, and his four soldiers.
The latter were strange beings; the first a fine young negro; the
second half Indian and negro; and the two others nondescripts;
namely, an old Chilian miner, the colour of mahogany, and another partly a mulatto; but two such mongrels, with such detest-
able expressions, I never saw before. At night, when they were
sitting round the fire, and playing at cards, I retired to view such
a Salvator Rosa scene. They were seated under a low cliff, so that
I could look down upon them; around the party were lying dogs,
arms, remnants of deer and ostriches; and their long spears were
stuck in the turf. Further in the dark background, their horses
were tied up, ready for any sudden danger. If the stillness of the
desolate plain was broken by one of the dogs barking, a soldier,
leaving the fire, would place his head close to the ground, and
thus slowly scan the horizon. Even if the noisy teru-teru uttered
its scream, there would be a pause in the conversation, and every
head, for a moment, a little inclined.

What a life of misery these men appear to us to lead! They were
at least ten leagues from the Sauce posta, and since the murder
committed by the Indians, twenty from another. The Indians are
supposed to have made their attack in the middle of the night; for
very early in the morning after the murder, they were luckily seen
approaching this posta. The whole party here, however, escaped,
together with the troop of horses; each one taking a line for himself, and driving with him as many animals as he was able to manage.

The little hovel, built of thistle-stalks, in which they slept, neither kept out the wind or rain; indeed in the latter case the only effect the roof had, was to condense it into larger drops. They had nothing to eat excepting what they could catch, such as ostriches, deer, armadilloes, etc., and their only fuel was the dry stalks of a small plant, somewhat resembling an aloe. The sole luxury which these men enjoyed was smoking the little paper cigars, and sucking maté. I used to think that the carrion vultures, man's constant attendants on these dreary plains, while seated on the little neighbouring cliffs, seemed by their very patience to say, "Ah! when the Indians come we shall have a feast."

In the morning we all sallied forth to hunt, and although we had not much success, there were some animated chaces. Soon after starting the party separated, and so arranged their plans, that at a certain time of the day (in guessing which they show much skill) they should all meet from different points of the compass on a plain piece of ground, and thus drive together the wild animals. One day I went out hunting at Bahia Blanca, but the men there merely rode in a crescent, each being about a quarter of a mile apart from the other. A fine male ostrich being turned by the headmost riders, tried to escape on one side. The Gauchos pursued at a reckless pace, twisting their horses about with the most admirable command, and each man whirling the balls round his head. At length the foremost threw them, revolving through the air: in an instant the ostrich rolled over and over, its legs fairly lashed together by the thong. . . .

SEPTEMBER 14TH.—As the soldiers belonging to the next posta meant to return, and we should together make a party of five, and all armed, I determined not to wait for the expected troops. My host, the lieutenant, pressed me much to stop. As he had been very obliging—not only providing me with food, but lending me his private horses—I wanted to make him some remuneration. I asked my guide whether I might do so, but he told me certainly not; that the only answer I should receive, probably would be, "We have meat for the dogs in our country, and therefore do not grudge it to a Christian." It must not be supposed that the rank of lieutenant in such an army would at all prevent the acceptance of payment: it was only the high sense of hospitality, which every traveller is bound to acknowledge as nearly universal throughout these provinces. After galloping some leagues, we came to a low swampy country, which extends for nearly eighty miles northward, as far as the Sierra Tapalguen. In some parts there were fine damp plains, covered with grass, while others had a soft, black, and peaty soil. There were also many extensive but shallow lakes, and large beds of reeds. The country on the whole resembled the better parts of the Cambridgeshire fens. At night we had some difficulty in finding amidst the swamps, a dry place for our bivouac.

SEPTEMBER 15TH.—Rose very early in the morning, and shortly after passed the posta where the Indians had murdered the five soldiers. The officer had eighteen chuzo wounds in his body. By the middle of the day, after a hard gallop, we reached the fifth posta: on account of some difficulty in procuring horses we stayed there the night. As this point was the most exposed on the whole line, twenty-one soldiers were stationed here; at sunset they returned from hunting, bringing with them seven deer, three ostriches, and many armadilloes and partridges. When riding through the country, it is a common pratice to set fire to the plain; and hence at night, as on this occasion, the horizon was illuminated in several places by brilliant conflagrations. This is done partly for the sake of puzzling any stray Indians, but chiefly for improving the pasture. In grassy plains unoccupied by the larger ruminating quadrupeds, it seems necessary to remove the superfluous vegetation by fire, so as to render the new year's growth serviceable. . . .

While changing horses at the guardia several people questioned us much about the army,—I never saw any thing like the enthusiasm for Rosas, and for the success of the "most just of all wars, because against barbarians." This expression, it must be confessed, is very natural, for till lately, neither man, woman, nor horse, was safe from the attacks of the Indians. We had a long day's ride over the same rich green plain, abounding with various flocks, and with here and there a solitary estancia, and its one *ombu* tree. In the evening it rained heavily: on arriving at a post-house we were told by the owner that if we had not a regular passport we must pass on, for there were so many robbers he would trust no one. When he read, however, my passport, which began with "El Naturalista Don Carlos," his respect and civility were as unbounded as his suspicions had been before. What a naturalist might be, neither he nor his countrymen, I suspect, had any idea; but probably my title lost nothing of its alure from that cause. . . .

OCTOBER 3RD AND 4TH.—I was confined for these two days to my bed by a headache. A good-natured old woman, who attended me, wished me to try many odd remedies. A common practice is, to bind an orange-leaf or a bit of black plaster to each temple: and a still more general plan is, to split a bean into halves, moisten them, and place one on each temple, where they will easily adhere. It is not thought proper ever to remove the beans or plaster, but to allow them to drop off; and sometimes, if a man, with patches on his head, is asked, what is the matter? he will answer, "I had a headache the day before yesterday." Many of the remedies used by the people of the country are ludicrously strange, but too disgusting to be mentioned. One of the least nasty is to kill and cut open two puppies and bind them on each side of a broken limb. Little hairless dogs are in great request to sleep at the feet of invalids.

St. Fé is a quiet little town, and is kept clean and in good order. The governor, Lopez, was a common soldier at the time of the revolution; but has now been seventeen years in power. . . .

OCT. 18TH AND 19TH.—We continued slowly to sail down the noble stream: the current helped us but little. We met, during our descent, very few vessels. One of the best gifts of nature, in so grand a channel of communication, seems here wilfully thrown away—a river in which ships might navigate from a temperate country, as surprisingly abundant in certain productions as destitute of others, to another possessing a tropical climate, and a soil which, according to the best of judges, Mr. Bonpland, is perhaps unequalled in fertility in any part of the world. How different would have been the aspect of this river if English colonists had by good fortune first sailed up the Plata! What noble towns would now have occupied its shores! Till the death of Francia, the Dictator of Paraguay, these two countries must remain distinct, as if placed on opposite sides of the globe. And when the old bloody-minded tyrant is gone to his long account, Paraguay will be torn by revolutions, violent in proportion to the previous unnatural calm. That country will have to learn, like every other South American state, that a republic cannot succeed till it contains a certain body of men imbued with the principles of justice and honor.

OCTOBER 20TH.—Being arrived at the mouth of the Parana, and as I was very anxious to reach Buenos Ayres, I went on shore at Las Conchas, with the intention of riding there. Upon landing, I found to my great surprise that I was to a certain degree a prisoner. A violent revolution having broken out, all the ports were laid under an embargo. . . .

This revolution was supported by scarcely any pretext of grievances: but in a state which, in the course of nine months (from February to October 1820), underwent fifteen changes in its government—each governor, according to the constitution, being elected for three years—it would be very unreasonable to ask for pretexts. In this case, a party of men—who, being attached to Rosas, were disgusted with the governor of Balcarce—to the number of seventy left the city, and with the cry of Rosas the whole country took arms. The city was then blockaded, no provisions, cattle or horses, were allowed to enter; besides this there was only a little skirmishing, and a few men daily killed. The outside party well knew that by stopping the supply of meat they would certainly be victorious. General Rosas could not have known of this rising; but it appears to be quite consonant with the plans of his party. A year ago he was elected governor, but he refused it, unless the Sala would also confer on him extraordinary powers. This was refused and since then his party have shown that no other governor can keep his place. The warfare on both sides was avowedly protracted till it was possible to hear from Rosas. A note arrived a few days after I left Buenos Ayres, which stated that the General disapproved of peace having been broken, but that he thought the outside party had justice on their side. On the bare reception of this, the Governor, ministers, and part of the military, to the number of some hundreds, fled from the city. The rebels entered, elected a new governor, and were paid for their services to the number of 5500 men. From these proceedings, it was clear that Rosas ultimately would become the dictator: to the term king, the people in this, as in other republics, have a particular dislike. Since leaving South America, we have heard that Rosas has been elected with powers and for a time altogether opposed to the constitutional principles of the republic. . . .

NOVEMBER 22ND.—. . . While staying at this estancia, I was amused with what I saw and heard of the shepherd-dogs of the country. When riding it is a common thing to meet a large flock of sheep guarded by one or two dogs, at the distance of some miles from any house or man. I often wondered how so firm a friendship had been established. The method of education consists in separating the puppy, while very young, from the bitch, and in accustoming it to its future companions. An ewe is held three or four times a day for the little thing to suck, and a nest of wool is made for it in the sheep-pen; at no time is it allowed to associate with other dogs, or with the children of the family. The puppy is, moreover, generally castrated; so that, when grown up, it can scarcely have any feelings in common with the rest of its kind. From this education it has no wish to leave the flock, and just as another dog will defend its master, man, so will these the sheep. It is amusing to observe, when approaching a flock, how the dog immediately advances barking, and the sheep all close in his rear, as if round the oldest ram. These dogs are also easily taught to bring home the flock, at a certain hour in the evening. Their most troublesome fault, when young, is their desire of playing with the sheep; for in their sport they sometimes gallop their poor subjects most unmercifully.

The shepherd-dog comes to the house every day for some meat, and as soon as it is given him, he skulks away as if ashamed of himself. On these occasions the house-dogs are very tyrannical, and the least of them will attack and pursue the stranger. The

minute, however, the latter has reached the flock, he turns round
and begins to bark, and then all the house-dogs take very quickly
to their heels. In a similar manner a whole pack of the hungry
wild dogs will scarcely ever (and I was told by some never) ven-
ture to attack a flock guarded by even one of these faithful shep-
herds. The whole account appears to me a curious instance of the
pliability of the affections in the dog; and yet, whether wild or
however educated, he has a feeling of respect or fear for those
that are fulfilling their instinct of association. . . .

One evening a "domidor" (a subduer of horses) came for the
purpose of breaking-in some colts. I will describe the preparatory
steps, for I believe they have not been mentioned by other travellers. A group of wild young horses is driven into the corral, or
large enclosure of stakes, and the door is shut. We will suppose
that one man alone has to catch and mount a horse, which as yet
had never felt bridle or saddle. I conceive, except by a Gaucho,
such a feat would be utterly impracticable. The Gaucho picks out
a full-grown colt; and as the beast rushes round the circus, he
throws his lazo so as to catch both the front legs. Instantly the
horse rolls over with a heavy shock, and whilst struggling on the
ground, the Gaucho, holding the lazo tight, makes a circle, so as
to catch one of the hind legs, just beneath the fetlock, and draws
it close to the two front legs: he then hitches the lazo, so that the
three are bound together. Then sitting on the horse's neck, he
fixes a strong bridle, without a bit, to the lower jaw: this he does
by passing a narrow thong through the eye-holes at the end of the
reins, and several times round both jaw and tongue. The two front
legs are now tied closely together with a strong leathern thong,
fastened by a slip-knot. The lazo, which bound the three together, being then loosed, the horse rises with difficulty. The
Gaucho now holding fast the bridle fixed to the lower jaw, leads
the horse outside the corral. If a second man is present (otherwise
the trouble is much greater) he holds the animal's head, whilst
the first puts on the horsecloths and saddle, and girths the whole
together. During this operation, the horse, from dread and astonishment at thus being bound round the waist, throws himself over

and over again on the ground, and, till beaten, is unwilling to rise. At last, when the saddling is finished, the poor animal can hardly breathe from fear, and is white with foam and sweat. The man now prepares to mount by pressing heavily on the stirrup, so that the horse may not lose its balance; and at the moment that he throws his leg over the animal's back, he pulls the slip-knot binding the front legs, and the beast is free. Some "domidors" pull the knot while the animal is lying on the ground, and, standing over the saddle, allow him to rise beneath them. The horse, wild with dread, gives a few most violent bounds, and then starts off at a full gallop: when quite exhausted, the man, by patience, brings him back to the corral, where, reeking hot and scarcely alive, the poor beast is let free. Those animals which will not gallop away, but obstinately throw themselves on the ground, are by far the most troublesome. This process is tremendously severe, but in two or three trials the horse is tamed. It is not, however, for some weeks that the animal is ridden with the iron bit and solid ring, for it must learn to associate the will of its rider with the feel of the rein, before the most powerful bridle can be of any service.

Animals are so abundant in these countries, that humanity and self-interest are not closely united; therefore I fear it is that the former is here scarcely known. One day, riding in the Pampas with a very respectable, "Estanciero," my horse, being tired, lagged behind. The man often shouted to me to spur him. When I remonstrated that it was a pity, for the horse was quite exhausted, he cried out, "Why not?—never mind—spur him—it is *my* horse." I had then some difficulty in making him comprehend that it was for the horse's sake, and not on his account, that I did not choose to use my spurs. He exclaimed, with a look of great surprise, "Ah, Don Carlos, que cosa!" It was clear that such an idea had never before entered his head.

The Gauchos are well known to be perfect riders. The idea of being thrown, let the horse do what it likes, never enters their head. Their criterion of a good rider is, a man who can manage an untamed colt, or who, if his horse falls, alights on his own feet, or can perform other such exploits. I have heard of a man betting that he would throw his horse down twenty times, and that nine-teen times he would not fall himself. I recollect seeing a Gaucho riding a very stubborn horse, which three times successively reared so high as to fall backwards with great violence. The man judged with uncommon coolness the proper moment for slipping off, not an instant before or after the right time; and as soon as the horse got up, the man jumped on his back, and at last they started at a gallop. The Gaucho never appears to exert any muscular force. I was one day watching a good rider, as we were galloping along at a rapid pace, and thought to my self, "surely if the horse starts, you appear so careless on your mount you must fall." At this mo-ment, a male ostrich sprang from its nest right beneath the horse's nose: the young colt bounded on one side like a stag; but as for the man, all that could be said was, that he started and took fright with his horse.

In Chile and Peru more pains are taken with the mouth of the horse than in La Plata, and this is evidently a consequence of the more intricate nature of the country. In Chile a horse is not con-sidered perfectly broken, till he can be brought up standing, in the midst of his full speed, on any particular spot,—for instance, on a cloak thrown on the ground: or, again, he will charge a wall, and rearing, scrape the surface with his hoofs. I have seen an an-imal bounding with spirit, yet merely reined by a fore-finger and thumb, taken at full gallop across a courtyard, and then made to wheel round the post of a veranda with great speed, but at so equal a distance, that the rider, with outstretched arm, all the while kept one finger rubbing the post. Then making a demi-volte in the air, with the other arm outstretched in a like manner, he wheeled round, with astonishing force, in an opposite direction.

Such a horse is well broken; and although this at first may ap-pear useless, it is far otherwise. It is only carrying that which is daily necessary into perfection. When a bullock is checked and caught by the lazo, it will sometimes gallop round and round in a circle, and the horse being alarmed at the great strain, if not well broken, will not readily turn like the pivot of a wheel. In conse-quence many men have been killed; for if the lazo once takes a twist round a man's body, it will instantly, from the power of the two opposed animals, almost cut him in twain. On the same principle the races are managed; the course is only two or three hundred yards long, the wish being to have horses that can make a rapid dash. The racehorses are trained not only to stand with their hoofs touching a line, but to draw all four feet together, so as at the first spring to bring into play the full action of the hindquarters. In Chile I was told an anecdote, which I believe was true; and it offers a good illustration of the use of a well-broken animal. A respectable man riding one day met two others, one of whom was mounted on a horse, which he knew to have been stolen from himself. He challenged them; they answered him by drawing their sabres and giving chace. The man, on his good and fleet beast, kept just ahead: as he passed a thick bush he wheeled round it, and brought up his horse to a dead check. The pursuers were obliged to shoot on one side and ahead. Then instantly dashing on, right behind them, he buried his knife in the back of one, wounded the other, recovered his horse from the dying robber, and rode home. For these feats of horsemanship two things are necessary: a most severe bit, like the Mameluke, the power of which, though seldom used, the horse knows full well; and large blunt spurs, that can be applied either as a mere touch, or as an instrument of extreme pain. I conceive that with English spurs, the slightest touch of which pricks the skin, it would be impossible to break in a horse after the South American fashion.

At an estancia near Las Vacas large numbers of mares are weekly slaughtered for the sake of their hides, although worth only five paper dollars, or about half-a-crown apiece. It seems at first strange that it can answer to kill mares for such a trifle; but as it is thought ridiculous in this country ever to break in or ride a mare, they are of no value except for breeding. The only thing for which I ever saw mares used, was to tread out wheat from the ear; for which purpose they were driven round a circular enclosure, where the wheat-sheaves were strewed. The man employed for slaughtering the mares happened to be celebrated for his dexterity with the lazo. Standing at the distance of twelve yards from the mouth of

the corral, he has laid a wager that he would catch by the legs
every animal, without missing one, as it rushed past him. There
was another man who said he would enter the corral on foot, catch
a mare, fasten the front legs together, drive her out, throw her
down, kill, skin, and stake the hide for drying (which latter is a
tedious job); and he engaged that he could perform this whole operation on twenty-two animals in one day. Or he would kill and
take the skin off fifty in the same time. This would have been a
prodigious task, for it is considered a good day's work to skin and
stake the hides of fifteen or sixteen animals.

NOVEMBER 26TH.—. . . During the last six months I have had
an opportunity of seeing a little of the character of the inhabitants
of these provinces. The Gauchos, or countrymen, are very superior to those who reside in the towns. The Gaucho is invariably
most obliging, polite, and hospitable: I did not meet with even
one instance of rudeness or inhospitality. He is modest, both respecting himself and country, but at the same time a spirited, bold
fellow. On the other hand, many robberies are committed, and
there is much bloodshed: the habit of constantly wearing the knife
is the chief cause of the latter. It is lamentable to hear how many
lives are lost in trifling quarrels. In fighting, each party tries to
mark the face of his adversary by slashing his nose or eyes; as is
often attested by deep and horrid-looking scars. Robberies are a
natural consequence of universal gambling, much drinking, and
extreme indolence. At Mercedes I asked two men why they did
not work. One gravely said the days were too long; the other that
he was too poor. The number of horses and the profusion of food
are the destruction of all industry. Moreover, there are so many
feast-days; and again, nothing can succeed without it be begun when
the moon is on the increase; so that half the month is lost from
these two causes.

Police and justice are quite inefficient. If a man who is poor
commits murder and is taken, he will be imprisoned, and perhaps
even shot; but if he is rich and has friends, he may rely on it no
very severe consequences will ensue. It is curious that the most

respectable inhabitants of the country invariably assist a murderer to escape: they seem to think that the individual sins against the government, and not against the people. A traveller has no protection besides his fire-arms; and the constant habit of carrying them is the main check to more frequent robberies.

The character of the higher and more educated classes who reside in the towns, partakes, but perhaps in a lesser degree, of the good parts of the Gaucho, but is, I fear, stained by many vices of which he is free. Sensuality, mockery of all religion, and the grossest corruption, are far from uncommon. Nearly every public officer can be bribed. The head man in the post-office sold forged government franks. The governor and prime minister openly combined to plunder the state. Justice, where gold came into play, was hardly expected by any one. I knew an Englishman, who went to the Chief Justice (he told me, that not then understanding the ways of the place, he trembled as he entered the room), and said, "Sir, I have come to offer you two hundred (paper) dollars (value about five pounds sterling) if you will arrest before a certain time a man who has cheated me. I know it is against the law, but my lawyer (naming him) recommended me to take this step." The Chief Justice smiled acquiescence, thanked him, and the man before night was safe in prison. With this entire want of principle in many of the leading men, with the country full of ill-paid turbulent officers, the people yet hope that a democratic form of government can succeed!

On first entering society in these countries, two or three features strike one as particularly remarkable. The polite and dignified manners pervading every rank of life, the excellent taste displayed by the women in their dresses, and the equality amongst all ranks. At the Rio Colorado some men who kept the humblest shops used to dine with General Rosas. A son of a major at Bahia Blanca gained his livelyhood by making paper cigars, and he wished to accompany me, as guide or servant, to Buenos Ayres, but his father objected on the score of the danger alone. Many officers in the army can neither read nor write, yet all meet in society as equals. In Entre Rios, the Sala consisted of only six representatives. One of them kept a common shop, and evidently was not degraded by the office. All this is what would be expected in a new country; nevertheless the absence of gentlemen by profession appears to an Englishman something strange.

When speaking of these countries, the manner in which they have been brought up by their unnatural parent, Spain, should always be borne in mind. On the whole, perhaps, more credit is due for what has been done, than blame for that which may be deficient. It is impossible to doubt but that the extreme liberalism of these countries must ultimately lead to good results. The very general toleration of foreign religions, the regard paid to the means of education, the freedom of the press, the facilities offered to all foreigners, and especially, as I am bound to add, to every one professing the humblest pretentions to science, should be recollected with gratitude by those who have visited Spanish South America. . . .

JANUARY 1834. [DAY NOT SPECIFIED]—. . . The second day after our return to the anchorage, a party of officers and myself went to ransack an old Indian grave, which I had found on the summit of a neighbouring hill. Two immense stones, each probably weighing at least a couple of tons, had been placed in front of a ledge of rock about six feet high. At the bottom of the grave on the hard rock there was a layer of earth about a foot deep, which must have been brought up from the plain below. Above it a pavement of flat stones was placed, on which others were piled, so as to fill up the space between the ledge and the two great blocks. To complete the grave, the Indians had contrived to detach from the ledge a huge fragment, and to throw it over the pile so as to rest on the two blocks. We undermined the grave on both sides, but could not find any relics, or even bones. The latter probably had decayed long since (in which case the grave must have been of extreme antiquity), for I found in another place some smaller heaps, beneath which a very few crumbling fragments could yet be distinguished as having belonged to a man. Falconer states, that where an Indian dies he is buried, but that subsequently his bones are carefully taken up and carried, let the distance be ever so great, to be deposited near the sea-coast. This custom, I think, may be accounted for by recollecting, that before the introduction of horses, these Indians must have led nearly the same life as the Fuegians now do, and therefore generally have resided in the neighborhood of the sea. The common prejudice of lying where one's ancestors have lain, would make the now roaming Indians bring the less perishable part of their dead to their ancient burial-ground on the coast.

MARCH 19TH, 1834.—Each morning, from not having ridden for some time previously, I was very stiff. I was surprised to hear the Gauchos, who have from infancy almost lived on horseback, say that, under similar circumstances, they always suffer. St. Jago told me, that having been confined for three months by illness, he went out hunting wild cattle, and in consequence, for the next two days, his thighs were so stiff that he was obliged to lie in bed. This shows that the Gauchos, although they do not appear to do so, yet really must exert much muscular effort in riding. The hunting of wild cattle, in a country so difficult to pass as this is on account of the swampy ground, must be very hard work. The Gauchos say they often pass at full speed over ground which would be impassable at a slower pace; in the same manner as a man is able to skate over thin ice. When hunting, the party endeavours to get as close as possible to the herd without being discovered. Each man carries four or five pair of the bolas; these he throws one after the other at as many cattle, which, when once entangled, are left for some days, till they become a little exhausted by hunger and struggling. They are then let free and driven towards a small herd of tame animals, which have been brought to the spot on purpose. From their previous treatment being too much terrified to leave the herd, they are easily driven, if their strength last out, to the settlement.

DECEMBER 17TH, 1832.—having now finished with Patagonia and the Falkland Islands, I will describe our first arrival in Tierra del Fuego. A little after noon we doubled cape St. Diego, and entered the famous strait of Le Maire. We kept close to the Fuegian shore, but the outline of the rugged, inhospitable Staten-land was visible amidst the clouds. In the afternoon we anchored in the Bay of Good Success. While entering we were saluted in a manner becoming the inhabitants of this savage land. A group of Fuegians partly concealed by the entangled forest, were perched on a wild point overhanging the sea; and as we passed by, they sprang up and waving their tattered cloaks sent forth a loud and sonorous shout. The savages followed the ship, and just before dark we saw their fire, and again heard their wild cry. The harbour consists of a fine piece of water half surrounded by low rounded mountains of clay-slate, which are covered to the water's edge by one dense gloomy forest. A single glance at the landscape was sufficient to show me how widely different it was from any thing I had ever beheld. At night it blew a gale of wind, and heavy squalls from the mountains swept past us. It would have been a bad time out at sea, and we, as well as others, may call this Good Success Bay.

In the morning the Captain sent a party to communicate with the Fuegians. When we came within hail, one of the four natives who were present advanced to receive us, and began to shout most vehemently, wishing to direct us where to land. When we were on shore the party looked rather alarmed, but contined talking and making gestures with great rapidity. It was without exception the most curious and interesting spectacle I ever beheld: I could not have believed how wide was the difference between savage and civilized man: it is greater than between a wild and domesticated animal, inasmuch as in man there is a greater power of improvement. The chief spokesman was old, and appeared to be the head of the family; the three others were powerful young men about six feet high. The women and children had been sent away. These Fuegians are a very different race from the stunted, miserable wretches farther westward; and they seem closely allied to the famous Paagonians of the Strait of Magellan. Their only garment consists of a mantle made of guanaco skin, with the wool outside; this they wear just thrown over their shoulders, leaving their persons as often exposed as covered. Their skin is of a dirty coppery red colour.

The old man had a fillet of white feathers tied round his head, which partly confined his black, coarse, and entangled hair. His face was crossed by two broad transverse bars; one, painted bright red, reached from ear to ear and included the upper lip; the other, white like chalk, extended above and parallel to the first, so that even his eyelids were thus coloured. The other two men were ornamented by streaks of black powder, made of charcoal. The party altogether closely resembled the devils which come on the stage in plays like Der Freischutz.

Their very attitudes were abject, and the expression of their countenances distrustful, surprised, and startled. After we had presented them with some scarlet cloth, which they immediately tied round their necks, they became good friends. This was shown by the old man patting our breasts, and making a chuckling kind of noise, as people do when feeding chickens. I walked with the old man, and this demonstration of friendship was repeated several times; it was concluded by three hard slaps, which were given me on the breast and back at the same time. He then bared his bosom for me to return the compliment, which being done, he seemed highly pleased. The language of these people, according to our notions, scarcely deserves to be called articulate. Captain Cook has compared it to a man clearing his throat, but certainly no European ever cleared his throat with so many hoarse, guttural, and clicking sounds.

They are excellent mimics: as often as we coughed or yawned, or made any odd motion, they immediately imitated us. Some of our party began to squint and look awry; but one of the young Fuegians (whose whole face was painted black, excepting a white band across his eyes) succeeded in making far more hideous grimaces. They could repeat with perfect correctness each word in any sentence we addressed them, and they remembered such words for some time. Yet we Europeans all know how difficult it is to distinguish apart the sounds in a foreign language. Which of us, for instance, could follow an American Indian through a sentence of more than three words? All savages appear to possess, to an uncommon degree, this power of mimicry. I was told, almost in the same words, of the same ludicrous habit among the Caffres: the Australians, likewise, have long been notorious for being able to imitate and describe the gait of any man, so that he may be recognized. How can this faculty be explained? is it a consequence of the more practised habits of perception and keener senses, common to all men in a savage state, as compared with those long civilized?

When a song was struck up by our party, I thought the Fuegians would have fallen down with astonishment. With equal surprise they viewed our dancing; but one of the young men, when asked, had no objection to a little walzing. Little accustomed to Europeans as they appeared to be, yet they knew and dreaded our fire-arms; nothing would tempt them to take a gun in their hands. They begged for knives, calling by the Spanish word "cuchilla." They explained also what they wanted, by acting as if they had a piece of blubber in their mouth, and then pretending to cut instead of tearing it.

I have not as yet noticed the Fuegians whom we had on board. During the former voyage of the Adventure and Beagle in 1826 to 1830, Captain Fitz Roy seized on a party of natives, as hostages for the loss of a boat, which had been stolen, to the great jeopardy of a party employed on the survey; and some of these natives, as well as a child whom he bought for a pearl-button, he took with him to England, determining to educate them and instruct them in religion at his own expense. To settle these natives in their own country, was one chief inducement to Captain Fitz Roy to undertake our present voyage; and before the Admiralty had resolved to send out this expedition, Captain Fitz Roy had generously chartered a vessel, and would himself have taken them back. The natives were accompanied by a missionary, R. Matthews; of whom and of the natives, Captain Fitz Roy has published a full and excellent account. Two men, one of whom died in England of the small-pox, a boy and a little girl, were originally taken; and we had now on board, York Minster, Jemmy Button (whose name expresses his purchase-money), and Fuegia Basket. York Minster was a full-grown, short, thick, powerful man: his disposition was reserved, taciturn, morose, and when excited violently passionate; his affections were very strong towards a few friends on board; his intellect good. Jemmy Button was a universal favourite, but likewise passionate; the expression of his face at once showed his nice disposition. He was merry and often laughed, and was remarkably sympathetic with any one in pain: when the water was rough, I was often a little sea-sick, and he used to come to me and say in a plaintive voice, "Poor, poor fellow!" but the notion, after his aquatic life, of a man being sea-sick, was too ludicrous, and he was generally obliged to turn on one side to hide a smile or laugh, and then he would repeat his "Poor, poor fellow!" He was of a patriotic disposition; and he liked to praise his own tribe and country, in which he truly said there were "plenty of trees," and he abused all the other tribes: he stoutly declared that there was no Devil in his land. Jemmy was short, thick, and fat, but vain of his personal appearance; he used always to wear gloves, his hair was neatly cut, and he was distressed if his well-polished shoes were dirtied. He was fond of admiring himself in a looking-glass; and a merry faced little Indian boy from the Rio Negro, whom we had for some months on board soon perceived this, and used to mock him: Jemmy, who was always rather jealous of the attention paid to this little boy, did not at all like this, and used to say, with rather a contemptuous twist of his head, "too much skylark." It seems yet wonderful to me when I think over all his many good qualities, that he should have been of the same race, and doubtless partaken of the same character, with the miserable, degraded savages whom we first met here. Lastly Fuegia Basket was a nice, modest, reserved young girl, with a rather pleasing but sometimes sullen expression, and very quick in learning anything, especially languages. This she showed in picking up some Portuguese and Spanish, when left on shore for only a short time at Rio de Janeiro and Monte Video, and in her knowledge of English. York Minster was very jealous of any attention paid to her; for it was clear he determined to marry her as soon as they were settled on shore.

Although all three could both speak and understand a good deal of English, it was singularly difficult to obtain much information from them, concerning the habits of their countrymen: this was partly owing to their apparent difficulty in understanding the simplest alternative. Every one accustomed to very young children, knows how seldom one can get an answer even to do simple a question as whether a thing is black *or* white; the idea of black or white seems alternately to fill their minds. So it was with these Fuegians, and hence it was generally impossible to find out, by cross-questioning, whether one had rightly understood anything which they had asserted. Their sight was remarkably acute: it is well known that sailors, from long practice, can make out a distant object much better than a landsman; but both York and Jemmy were much superior to any sailor on board: several times they have declared what some distant object has been, and though doubted by every one, they have proved right, when it has been examined through a telescope. They were quite conscious of this power; and Jemmy, when he had any little quarrel with the officer on watch, would say, "Me see ship, me no tell."

It was interesting to watch the conduct of the savages, when we landed, towards Jemmy Button: they immediately perceived the difference between him and ourselves, and held much conversation one with another on the subject. The old man addressed a long harangue to Jemmy, which it seems was to invite him to stay with them. But Jemmy understood very little of their language, and was, moreover, thoroughly ashamed of his countrymen. When York Minster afterwards come on shore, they noticed him in the same way, and told him he ought to shave; yet he had not twenty dwarf hairs on his face whilst we all wore our untrimmed beards. They examined the colour of his skin, and compared it with ours. One of our arms being bared, they expressed the liveliest surprise and admiration at its whiteness, just in the same way in which I have seen the ourangoutang do at the Zoological Gardens. We thought that they mistook two or three of the officers, who were rather shorter and fairer, though adorned with large beards, for the ladies of our party. The tallest amongst the Fuegians was evidently much pleased at his height being noticed. When placed back to back with the tallest of the boat's crew, he tried his best to edge on higher ground, and to stand on tiptoe. He opened his mouth to show his teeth, and turned his face for a side view; and all this was done with such alacrity, that I dare say he thought himself the handsomest man in Tierra del Fuego. After our first feeling of grave astonishment was over, nothing could be more ludicrous than the odd mixture of surprise and imitation which these savages every moment exhibited.

DECEMBER 25TH.—. . . The Fuegian wigwam resembles, in size and dimensions, a haycock. It merely consists of a few broken branches stuck in the ground, and very imperfectly thatched on one side with a few tufts of grass and rushes. The whole cannot be the work of an hour, and it is only used for a few days. At Goeree Roads I saw a place where one of these naked men had slept, which absolutely offered no more cover than the form of a hare. The man was evidently living by himself, and York Minster said he was "very bad man," and that probably he had stolen something. On the west coast, however, the wigwams are rather better, for they are covered with seal-skins. We were detained here several days by the bad weather. The climate is certainly wretched: the summer solstice was now passed, yet every day snow fell on the hills, and in the valleys there was rain, accompanied by sleet. The thermometer generally stood about 45°, but in the night fell to 38° or 40°. From the damp and boisterous state of the atmosphere, not cheered by a gleem of sunshine, one fancied the climate even worse than it really was.

While going one day on shore near Wollanston Island, we pulled alongside a canoe with six Fuegians. These were the most abject and miserable creatures I anywhere beheld. On the east coast the natives, as we have seen, have guanaco cloaks, and on the west, they possess seal-skins. Amongst these central tribes the men generally have an otter-skin, or some small scrap about as large as a pocket-handkerchief, which is barely sufficient to cover their backs

as low down as their loins. It is laced across the breast by strings,
and according as the wind blows, it is shifted from side to side.
But these Fuegians in the canoe were quite naked and even one
full-grown woman was absolutely so. It was raining heavily, and
the fresh water, together with the spray, trickled down her body.
In another harbour not far distant, a woman, who was suckling a
recently-born child, came one day alongside the vessel, and remained there out of mere curiosity, whilst the sleet fell and thawed
on her naked bosom, and on the skin of her naked baby! These
poor wretches were stunted in their growth, their hideous faces
bedaubed with white paint, their skins filthy and greasy, their hair
entangled, their voices discordant, and their gestures violent.
Viewing such men, one can hardly make oneself believe that they
are fellow-creatures, and inhabitants of the same world. It is a
common subject of conjecture what pleasure in life some of the
lower animals can enjoy: how much more reasonably the same
question may be asked with respect to these barbarians! At night,
five or six human beings, naked and scarcely protected from the
wind and rain of this tempestuous climate, sleep on their wet
ground coiled up like animals. Whenever it is low water, winter
or summer, night or day, they must rise to pick shellfish from the
rocks; and the women either dive to collect sea-eggs, or sit pa-
tiently in their canoes, and with a baited hair-line without any hook,
jerk out little fish. If a seal is killed, or the floating carcass of a
putrid whale discovered, it is a feast; and such miserable food is
assisted by a few tasteless berries and fungi.

They often suffer from famine: I heard Mr. Low, a sealing-mas-
ter intimately acquainted with the natives of this country, give a
curious account of the state of a party of one hundred and fifty
natives on the west coast, who were very thin and in great distress. A succession of gales prevented the women from getting shell-
fish on the rocks, and they could not go out in their canoes to
catch seal. A small party of these men one morning set out, and
the other Indians explained to him, that they were going a four
days' journey for food: on their return, Low went to meet them,
and he found them excessively tired, each man carrying a great

square piece of putrid whales-blubber with a hole in the middle, through which they put their heads, like the Gauchos do through their ponchos or cloaks. As soon as the blubber was brought into a wigwam, an old man cut off thin slices, and muttering over them, broiled them for a minute, and distributed them to the famished party, who during this time preserved a profound silence. Mr. Low believes that whenever a whale is cast on shore, the natives bury large pieces of it in the sand, as a resource in time of famine; and a native boy, whom he had on board, once found a stock thus buried. The different tribes when at war are cannibals. From the concurrent, but quite independent evidence of the boy taken by Mr. Low, and of Jemmy Button, it is certainly true, that when pressed in winter by hunger, they kill and devour their old women before they kill their dogs: the boy, being asked by Mr. Low why they did this, answered, "Doggies catch otters, old women no." This boy described the manner in which they are killed by being held over smoke and thus choked; he imitated their screams as a joke, and described the parts of their bodies which are considered best to eat. Horrid as such a death by the hands of their friends and relatives must be, the fears of the old women, when hunger begins to press, are more painful to think of; we were told that they then often run away into the mountains, but that they are pursued by the men and brought back to the slaughter-house at their own fire-sides!

Captain Fitz Roy could never ascertain that the Fuegians have any distinct belief in a future life. They sometimes bury their dead in caves, and sometimes in the mountain forests; we do not know what ceremonies they perform. Jemmy Button would not eat landbirds, because "eat dead men:" they are unwilling even to mention their dead friends. We have no reason to believe that they perform any sort of religious worship; though perhaps the muttering of the old man before he distributed the putrid blubber to his famished party, may be of this nature. Each family or tribe has a wizard or conjuring doctor, whose office we could never clearly ascertain. Jemmy believed in dreams, though not, as I have said, in the devil: I do not think that our Fuegians were much more superstitious than some of the sailors; for an old quarter-master firmly believed that the successive heavy gales, which we encounted off Cape Horn, were caused by our having the Fuegians on board. The nearest approach to religious feeling which I heard of, was shown by York Minster, who, when Mr. Bynoe shot some very young ducklings as specimens, declared in the most solemn manner, "Oh Mr. Bynoe, much rain, snow, blow much." This was evidently a retributive punishment for wasting human food. In a wild and excited manner he also related, that his brother, one day whilst returning to pick up some dead birds which he had left on the coast, observed some feathers blown by the wind. His brother said (York imitating his manner), "What that?" and crawling onwards, he peeped over the cliff, and saw "wild man" picking his birds; he crawled a little nearer and then hurled down a great stone and killed him. York declared for a long time afterwards storms raged, and much rain and snow fell. As far as we could make out, he seemed to consider the elements themselves as the avenging agents: it is evident in this case, how naturally, in a race a little more advanced in culture, the elements would become personified. What the "bad wild men" were, has always appeared to me most mysterious: from what York said, when we found the place like the form of a hare, where a single man had slept the night before, I should have thought that they were thieves who had been driven from their tribes; but other obscure speeches made me doubt this; I have sometimes imagined that the most probable explanation was that they were insane.

The different tribes have no government or chief; yet each is surrounded by other hostile tribes, speaking different dialects, and separated from each other only by a deserted border or neutral territory: the cause of their warfare appears to be the means of subsistence. Their country is a broken mass of wild rocks, lofty hills, and useless forests: and these are viewed through mists and endless storms. The habitable land is reduced to the stones on the beach; in search of food they are compelled unceasingly to wander from spot to spot, and so steep is the coast, that they can only move about in their wretched canoes. They cannot know the feeling of having a home, and still less that of domestic affection; for the husband is to the wife a brutal master to a laborious slave. Was a more horrid deed ever perpetrated, than that witnessed on the west coast by Byron, who saw a wretched mother pick up her bleeding dying infant-boy, whom her husband had mercilessly dashed on the stones for dropping a basket of sea-eggs! How little can the higher powers of the mind be brought into play: what is there for imagination to picture, for reason to compare, for judgment to decide upon? to knock a limpet from the rock does not require even cunning, that lowest power of the mind. Their skill in some respects may be compared to the instinct of animals; for it is not improved by experience: the canoe, their most ingenious work, poor as it is, has remained the same, as we know from Drake, for the last two hundred and fifty years.

Whilst beholding these savages, one asks, whence have they come? What could have tempted, or what change compelled a tribe of men, to leave the fine regions of the north, to travel down the Cordillera or backbone of America, to invent and build canoes, which are not used by the tribes of Chile, Peru, and Brazil, and then to enter on one of the most inhospitable countries within the limits of the globe? Although such reflections must at first seize on the mind, yet we may feel sure that they are partly erroneous. There is no reason to believe that the Fuegians decrease in number; therefore we must suppose they they enjoy a sufficient share of happiness, of what ever kind it may be, to render life worth having. Nature by making habit omnipotent, and its effects hereditary, has fitted the Fuegians to the climate and the productions of this miserable country.

JANUARY 15TH, 1833.—The Beagle anchored in Goeree Roads. Captain Fitz Roy having resolved to settle the Fuegians, according to their wishes, in Ponsonby Sound, four boats were equipped to carry them there through the Beagle Channel. This channel, which was discovered by Captain Fitz Roy during the last voyage, is a most remarkable feature in the geography of this, or indeed of any other country: it may be compared to the valley of Loch-

ness in Scotland, with its chain of lakes and firths. It is about one
hundred and twenty miles long, with an average breadth, not
subject to any very great variation, of about two miles; and is
throughout the great part so perfectly straight, that the view,
bounded on each side by a line of mountains, gradually becomes
indistinct in the long distance. It crosses the southern part of Tierra
del Fuego in an east and west line, and in the middle is joined at
right angles on the south side by an irregular channel, which has
been called Ponsonby Sound. This is the residence of Jemmy Button's tribe and family.

JANUARY 19TH.—Three whale-boats and the yawl, with a party
of twenty-eight, started under the command of Captain Fitz Roy.
In the afternoon we entered the eastern mouth of the channel,
and shortly afterwards found a snug little cove concealed by some
surrounding islets. Here we pitched our tents and lighted our fires.
Nothing could look more comfortable than this scene. The glassy
water of the little harbour, with the branches of the trees hanging
over the rocky beach, the boats at anchor, the tents supported by
the crossed oars, and the smoke curling up the wooded valley,
formed a picture of quiet retirement. The next day (20th) we
smoothly glided onwards in our little fleet, and came to a more
inhabited district. Few if any of these natives could ever have seen
a white man; certainly nothing could exceed their astonishment at
the apparition of the four boats. Fires were lighted on every point
(hence the name of Tierra del Fuego, or the land of fire), both to
attract our attention and to spread far and wide the news. Some
of the men ran for miles along the shore. I shall never forget how
wild and savage one group appeared: suddenly four or five men
came to the edge of an overhanging cliff; they were absolutely naked, and their long hair streamed about their faces; they held rugged staffs in their hands, and, springing from the ground, they
waved their arms round their heads, and sent forth the most hideous yells.

At dinner-time we landed among a party of Fuegians. At first
they were not inclined to be friendly; for until the captain pulled
in ahead of the other boats, they kept their slings in their hands.

We soon, however, delighted them by trifling presents, such as tying red tape round their heads. They liked our biscuit: but one of the savages touched with his finger some of the meat preserved in tin cases which I was eating, and feeling it soft and cold, showed as much disgust at it, as I should have done at putrid blubber. Jemmy was thoroughly ashamed of his countrymen, and declared his own tribe were quite different, in which he was wofully mistaken. It was as easy to please as it was difficult to satisfy these savages. Young and old, men and children, never ceased repeating the word "Yammerschooner," which means "give me." After pointing to almost every object, one after the other, even to the buttons on our coats, and saying their favourite word in as many intonations as possible, they would then use it in a neuter sense, and vacantly repeat "Yammerschooner." After yammerschoonering for any article very eagerly, they would by a simple artifice point to their young women or little children, as much as to say, "if you will not give it me, surely you will to such as these."

At night we endeavoured in vain to find an uninhabited cove; and at last were obliged to bivouac not far from a party of natives. They were very inoffensive as long as they were few in numbers, but in the morning (21st) being joined by others they showed symptoms of hostility, and we thought that we should have come to a skirmish. An European labours under great disadvantages when treating with savages like these, who have not the least idea of the power of fire-arms. In the very act of levelling his musket he appears to the savage far inferior to a man armed with a bow and arrow, a spear, or even a sling. Nor is it easy to teach them our superiority except by striking a fatal blow. Like wild beasts, they do not appear to compare numbers; for each individual, if attacked, instead of retiring, will endeavour to dash your brains out with a stone, as certainly as a tiger under similar circumstances would tear you. Captain Fitz Roy on one occasion being very anxious, from good reasons, to frighten away a small party, first flourished a cutlass near them, at which they only laughed; he then twice fired his pistol close to a native. The man both times looked astounded, and carefully but quickly rubbed his head; he then stared awhile, and gabbled to his companions, but he never seemed to think of running away. We can hardly put ourselves in the position of these savages, and understand their actions. In the case of this Fuegian, the possibility of such a sound as the report of a gun close to his ear could never have entered his mind. He perhaps literally did not for a second know whether it was a sound or a blow, and therefore very naturally rubbed his head. In a similar manner, when a savage sees a mark struck by a bullet, it may be some time before he is able at all to understand how it is effected; for the fact of a body being invisible from its velocity would perhaps be to him an idea totally inconceivable. Moreover, the extreme force of a bullet, that penetrates a hard substance without tearing it, may convince the savage that it has no force at all. Certainly I believe that many savages of the lowest grade, such as these of Tierra del Fuego, have seen objects struck, and even small animals killed by the musket, without being in the least aware how deadly an instrument it is.

JANUARY 22D.—After having passed an unmolested night, in what would appear to be neutral territory between Jemmy's tribe and the people whom we saw yesterday, we sailed pleasantly along. I do not know anything which shows more clearly the hostile state of the different tribes, than these wide border or neutral tracts. Although Jemmy Button well knew the force of our party, he was, at first, unwilling to land amidst the hostile tribe nearest to his own. He often told us how the savage Oens men "when the leaf red," crossed the mountains from the eastern coast of Tierra del Fuego, and made inroads on the natives of this part of the country. It was most curious to watch him when thus talking, and see his eyes gleaming and his whole face assume a new and wild expression. As we preceeded along the Beagle Channel, the scenery assumed a peculiar and very magnificent character; but the effect was much lessened from the lowness of the point of view in a boat, and from looking along the valley, and thus losing all the beauty of a succession of ridges. The mountains were here about three thousand feet high, and terminated in sharp and jagged points. They rose in one unbroken sweep from the water's edge, and were covered to the height of fourteen or fifteen hundred feet by the dusky-coloured forest. It was most curious to observe, as far as the eye could range, how level and truly horizontal the line on the mountain side was, at which trees ceased to grow: it precisely resembled the high-water mark of drift-weed on a sea-beach.

At night we slept close to the junction of Ponsonby Sound with the Beagle Channel. A small family of Fuegians, who were living in the cove, were quiet and inoffensive, and soon joined our party round a blazing fire. We were well clothed, and though sitting close to the fire were far from too warm; yet these naked savages, though further off, were observed, to our great surprise, to be streaming with perspiration at undergoing such a roasting. They seemed, however, very well pleased, and all joined in the chorus of the seamen's songs: but the manner in which they were invariably a little behindhand was quite ludicrous.

During the night the news had spread, and early in the morning (23d) a fresh party arrived, belonging to the Tekenika, or Jemmy's tribe. Several of them had run so fast that their noses were bleeding, and their mouths frothed from the rapidity with which they talked; and with their naked bodies all dedaubed with black, white, and red, they looked like so many demoniacs who had been fighting. We then proceeded (accompanied by twelve canoes, each holding four or five people) down Ponsonby Sound to the spot where poor Jemmy expected to find his mother and relatives. He had already heard that his father was dead; but as he had had a "dream in his head" to that effect, he did not seem to care much about it, and repeatedly comforted himself with the very natural reflection—"Me no help it." He was not able to learn any particulars regarding his father's death, as his relations would not speak about it.

Jemmy was now in a district well known to him, and guided the boats to a quiet pretty cove named Woollya, surrounded by islets, every one of which and every point had its proper native name. We found here a family of Jemmy's tribe but not his relations: we made friends with them; and in the evening they sent a canoe to inform Jemmy's mother and brothers. The cove was bordered by some acres of good sloping land, not covered (as elsewhere) either by peat or by forest-trees. Captain Fitz Roy originally intended, as before stated, to have taken York Minster and Fuegia to their own tribe on the west coast; but as they expressed a wish to remain here, and as the spot was singularly favourable, Captain Fitz Roy determined to settle here the whole party, including Matthews, the missionary. Five days were spent in building for them three large wigwams, in landing their goods, in digging two gardens, and sowing seeds.

The next morning after our arrival (the 24th) the Fuegians began to pour in, and Jemmy's mother and brothers arrived. Jemmy recognized the stentorian voice of one of his brothers at a prodigious distance. The meeting was less interesting than that between a horse, turned out into a field, when he joins an old companion. There was no demonstration of affection; they simply stared for a short time at each other; and the mother immediately went to look after her canoe. We heard, however, through York that the mother had been inconsolable for the loss of Jemmy, and had searched everywhere for him, thinking that he might have been left after having been taken in the boat. The women took much notice of and were very kind to Fuegia. We had already perceived that Jemmy had almost forgotten his own language. I should think that there was scarcely another human being with so small a stock of language, for his English was very imperfect. It was laughable, but almost pitiable, to hear him speak to his wild brother in English, and then ask him in Spanish ("no sabe?") whether he did not understand him.

Everything went on peaceably during the three next days, whilst the gardens were digging and wigwams building. We estimated the number of natives at about one hundred and twenty. The women worked hard, whilst the men lounged about all day long, watching us. They asked for everything they saw, and stole what they could. They were delighted at our dancing and singing, and were particularly interested at seeing us wash in a neighbouring brook; they did not pay much attention to anything else, not even to our boats. Of all the things which York saw, during his absence from his country, nothing seems more to have astonished him than an ostrich, near Maldonado: breathless with astonishment he came running to Mr. Bynoe, with whom he was out walking—"Oh, Mr. Bynoe, oh, bird all same horse!" Much as our white skins surprised the natives, by Mr. Low's account a negro-cook to a sealing vessel, did so more effectually; and the poor fellow was so mobbed and shouted at that he would never go on shore again. Everything went on so quietly, that some of the officers and myself took long walks in the surrounding hills and woods. Suddenly, however, on the 27th, every woman and child disappeared. We were all uneasy at this, as neither York nor Jemmy could make out the cause. It was thought by some that they had been frightened by our cleaning and firing off our muskets on the previous evening: by others, that it was owing to offence taken by an old savage, who, when told to keep further off, had cooly spit in the sentry's face, and had then, by gestures acted over a sleeping Fuegian, plainly showed, as it was said, that he should like to cut up and eat our man. Captain Fitz Roy, to avoid the chance of an encounter, which would have been fatal to so many Fuegians, thought it advisable for us to sleep at a cove a few miles distant. Matthews, with his usual quiet fortitude (remarkable in a man apparently possessing little energy of character), determined to stay with the Fuegians, who evinced no alarm for themselves; and so we left them to pass their first awful night.

On our return in the morning (28th) we were delighted to find all quiet, and the men employed in their canoes spearing fish. Captain Fitz Roy determined to send the yawl and one whale-boat back to the ship; and to proceed with the two other boats, one under his own command (in which he most kindly allowed me to accompany him), and one under Mr. Hammond, to survey the western parts of the Beagle Channel, and afterwards to return and visit the settlement. The day to our astonishment was overpoweringly hot, so that our skins were scorched: with this beautiful weather, the view in the middle of the Beagle Channel was very remarkable. Looking towards either hand, no object intercepted the vanishing points of this long canal between the mountains. The circumstance of its being an arm of the sea was rendered very evident by several huge whales spouting in different directions. On one occasion I saw two of these monsters, probably male and female, slowly swimming one after the other, within less than a stone's throw of the shore, over which the beech-tree extended its branches.

We sailed on till it was dark, and then pitched our tents in a quiet creek. The greatest luxury was to find for our beds a beach of pebbles, for they were dry and yielded to the body. Peaty soil is damp; rock is uneven and hard; sand gets into one's meat, when cooked and eaten boat-fashion; but when lying in our blanket-bags, on a good bed of smooth pebbles, we passed most comfortable nights.

FEBUARY 6TH.—We arrived at Woollya. Matthews gave so bad an account of the conduct of the Fuegians, that Captian Fitz Roy determined to take him back to the Beagle; and ultimately he was left at New Zealand, where his brother was a missionary. From the time of our leaving, a regular system of plunder commenced; fresh parties of the natives kept arriving: York and Jemmy lost many things, and Matthews almost every thing which had not been concealed underground. Every article seemed to have been torn up and divided by the natives. Matthews described the watch he was obliged always to keep as most harassing; night and day he was surrounded by the natives, who tired to tire him out by making an incessant noise close to his head. One day an old man, whom Matthews asked to leave his wigwam, immediately returned with a large stone in his hand: another day a whole party came armed with stones and stakes, and some of the younger men and Jemmy's brother were crying: Matthews met them with presents. Another party showed by signs that they wished to strip him naked and pluck all the hairs out of his face and body. I think we arrived just in time to save his life. Jemmy's relatives had been so vain and foolish, that they had showed to strangers their plunder, and their manner of obtaining it. It was quite melancholy leaving the three Fuegians with their savage countrymen; but it was a great comfort that had no personal fears. York, being a powerful resolute man, was pretty sure to get on well, together with his wife Fuegia. Poor Jemmy looked rather disconsolate, and would then, I have little doubt, have been glad to have returned with us. His own brother had stolen many things from him; and as he remarked, 'what fashion call that:' he abused his countryman, 'all bad men, no sabe (know) nothing,' and, though I never heard him swear before, 'damned fools.' Our three Fuegians, though they had been only three years with civilized men, would, I am sure, have been glad to have retained their new habits; but this was obviously impossible. I fear it is more than doubtful, whether their visit will have been of any use to them. . . .

On the last day of Febuary in the succeeding year (1834), the Beagle anchored in a beautiful little cove at the eastern entrance of the Beagle Channel. Captain Fitz Roy determined on the bold, and as it proved successful, attempt to beat against the westerly winds by the same route, which we had followed in the boats to the settlement at Woollya. We did not see many natives until we were near Ponsonby Sound, where we were followed by ten or twelve canoes. The natives did not at all understand the reason of our tacking, and instead of meeting us at each tack, vainly strove to follow us in our zig-zag course. I was amused at finding what a difference the circumstance of being quite superior in force made, in the interest of beholding these savages. While in the boats I got to hate the very sound of their voices, so much trouble they did give us. The first and last word was "yammerschooner." When, entering some quiet little cove, we have looked round and thought to pass a quiet night, the odious word "yammerschooner" had shrilly sounded from some gloomy nook, and then the little signal-smoke has curled up to spread the news far and wide. On leaving some place we have said to each other, 'Thank Heaven, we have at last fairly left these wretches!' when one more faint halloo from an all-powerful voice, heard at a prodigious distance, would reach our ears, and clearly could we distinguish—"Yammerschooner." But now, the more Fuegians the merrier; and very merry work it was. Both parties laughing, wondering, gaping at each other; we pitying them, for giving us good fish and crabs for rags, etc.; they grasping at the chance of finding people so foolish as to exchange such splendid ornaments for a good supper. It was most amusing to see the undisguised smile of satisfaction with which one young woman with her face painted black, tied several bits of scarlet cloth around her head with rushes. Her husband, who enjoyed the very universal privilege in this country of possessing two wives, evidently became jealous of all the attention paid to his young wife; and, after a consultation with his naked beauties, was paddled away by them.

Some of the Fuegians plainly showed that they had a fair notion of barter. I gave one man a large nail (a most valuable present) without making any signs for a return; but he immediately picked out two fish, and handed them up on the point of his spear. If any present was designed for one canoe, and it fell near another, it was invariably given to the right owner. The Fuegian boy, whom Mr. Low had on board, showed, by going into the most violent passion, that he quite understood the reproach of being called a liar, which in truth he was. We were this time, as on all former occasions, much surprised at the little notice, or rather none whatever, which was taken of many things, the use of which must have been evident to the natives. Simple circumstances—such as the beauty of scarlet cloth or blue beads, the absence of women, our care in washing ourselves,—excited their admiration far more than any grand or complicated object, such as our ship. Bougainville has well remarked concerning these people, that they treat the "chef-d'oeuvres de l'industrie humaine, comme ils traitent les loix de la nature et ses phénomènes."

On the 5th of March, we anchored in the cove at Woollya, but we saw not a soul there. We were alarmed at this, for the natives in Ponsonby Sound showed by gestures, that there had been fighting; and we afterwards heard that the dreaded Oens men had made a descent. Soon a canoe, with a little flag flying was seen approaching, with one of the men in it washing the paint off his face. This man was poor Jemmy,—now a thin haggard savage, with long disordered hair, and naked, except a bit of a blanket round his waist. We did not recognise him till he was close to us; for he was ashamed of himself, and turned his back to the ship. We had left him plump, fat, clean, and well dressed;—I never saw so complete and grievous a change. As soon however as he was clothed, and the first flurry was over, things wore a good appearance. He dined with Captain Fitz Roy, and ate his dinner as tidily as formerly. He told us he had 'too much' (meaning enough) to eat, that he was not cold, that his relations were very good people, and that he did not wish to go back to England: in the evening we found out the cause of this great change in Jemmy's feelings, in the arrival of his young and nice-looking wife. With his usual good feeling, he brought two beautiful otter-skins for two of his best friends, and some spear-heads and arrows made with his own hands for the Captain. He said he had built a canoe for himself, and he boasted that he could talk a little of his own language! But it is a most signular fact, that he appears to have taught all his tribe some English: an old man spontaneously announced 'Jemmy Button's wife.' Jemmy had lost all his property. He told us that York Minster had built a large canoe, and with his wife Fuegia, had several months since gone to his own country, and had taken farewell by an act of consummate villainy; he persuaded Jemmy and his mother to come with him, and then on the way deserted them by night, stealing every article of their property.

Jemmy went to sleep on shore, and in the morning returned, and remained on board till the ship got under weigh, which frightened his wife, who continued crying violently till he got into his canoe. He returned loaded with valuable property. Every soul on board was heartily sorry to shake hands with him for the last time. I do not now doubt that he will be as happy as, perhaps happier than, if he had never left his own country. Every one must sincerely hope that Captain Fitz Roy's noble hope may be fulfilled, of being rewarded for the many generous sacrifices which he made for these Fuegians, by some shipwrecked sailor being protected by the descendants of Jemmy Button and his tribe! When Jemmy reached the shore, he lighted a signal fire, and the smoke curled up, bidding us a last and long farewell, as the ship stood on her course into the open sea.

The perfect equality among the individuals composing the Fuegian tribes, must for a long time retard their civilization. As we see those animals, whose instinct compels them to live in society and obey a chief, are most capable of improvement, so is it with the races of mankind. Whether we look at it as a cause or a consequence, the more civilized always have the most artificial governments. For instance, the inhabitants of Otaheite, who, when first discovered, were governed by hereditary kings, had arrived at a far higher grade than another branch of the same people, the New Zealanders,—who, although benefited by being compelled to turn their attention to agriculture, were republicans in the most absolute sense. In Tierra del Fuego until some chief shall arise with power sufficient to secure any acquired advantage, such as the domesticated animals, it seems scarcely possible that the political state of the country can be improved. At present, even a piece of cloth given to one is torn into shreds and distributed; and no one individual becomes richer than another. On the other hand, it is difficult to understand how a chief can arise till there is property of some sort by which he might manifest his superiority and increase his power.

I believe in this extreme part of South America, man exists in a lower state of improvement than in any other part of the world. The South Sea islanders of the two races inhabiting the Pacific, are comparatively civilized. The Esquimaux, in his subterranean hut, enjoys some of the comforts of life, and in his canoe, when fully equipped, manifests much skill. Some of the tribes of Southern Africa, prowling about in search of roots, and living concealed on the wild and arid plains, are sufficiently wretched. The Australian, in the simplicity of the arts of life, comes nearest the Fuegian: he can, however, boast of his boomerang, his spear and throwing-stick, his method of climbing trees, of tracking animals, and of hunting. Although the Australian may be superior in acquirements, it by no means follows that he is likewise superior in mental capacity: indeed, from what I saw of the Fuegians when on board, and from what I have read of the Australians, I should think the case was exactly the reverse.

In the end of May, 1834, we entered for the second time the eastern mouth of the Strait of Magellan. . . .

During our previous visit (in January), we had an interview at Cape Gregory with the famous so-called Gigantic Patagonians, who gave us all a cordial reception. Their height appears greater than it really is, from their large guanaco mantles, their long flowing hair, and general figure: on an average their height is about six feet, with some men taller and only a few shorter; and the women are also tall; altogether they are certainly the tallest race which we anywhere saw. In features they strikingly resemble the more northern Indians whom I saw with Rosas, but they have a wilder and more formidable appearance: their faces were much painted with red and black, and one man was ringed and dotted with white like a Fuegian. Capt. Fitz Roy offered to take any three of them on board, and all seemed determined to be of the three. It was long before we could clear the boat; at last we got on board with our three giants, who dined with the Captain, and behaved quite like gentlemen, helping themselves with knives, forks, and spoons: nothing was so much relished as sugar. This tribe has had so much communication with sealers and whalers, that most of the men can speak a little English and Spanish; and they are half civilized, and proportionately demoralised.

The next morning a large party went on shore, to barter for skins and ostrich-feathers; fire-arms being refused, tobacco was in greatest request, far more so than axes or tools. The whole population of the toldos, men, women, and children were arranged on a bank. It was an amusing scene, and it was impossible not to like the so-called giants, they were so thoroughly good-humoured and unsuspecting; they asked us to come again. They seem to like to have Europeans to live with them; and old Maria, an important woman in the tribe, once begged Mr. Low to leave any one of his sailors with them. They spend the greater part of the year here; but in summer they hunt along the foot of the Cordillera: sometimes they travel as far as the Rio Negro, 750 miles to the north. They are well stocked with horses, each man having according to Mr. Low, six or seven, and all the women, and even children, their one own horse. In the time of Sarmiento (1580), these Indians had bows and arrows, now long since disused; they then also possessed some horses. This is a very curious fact, showing the extraordinarily rapid multiplication of horses in South America. The horse was first landed at Buenos Ayres in 1537, and the colony being then for a time deserted, the horse ran wild; in 1580, only forty-three years afterwards, we hear of them at the Strait of Magellan! Mr. Low informs me, that a neighbouring tribe of foot-Indians is now changing into horse-Indians: the tribe at Gregory Bay giving them their worn-out horses, and sending in winter a few of their best skilled men to hunt for them.

JUNE 1ST.—We anchored in the fine bay of Port famine. . . .

Before reaching Port Famine, two men were seen running along the shore and hailing the ship. A boat was sent for them. They turned out to be two sailors who had run away from a sealing-vessel, and had joined the Patagonians. These Indians had treated them with the usual disinterested hospitality. They had parted company through accident, and were then proceeding to Port Famine in hopes of finding some ship. . . .

During our stay at Port Famine, the Fuegians twice came and plagued us. As there were many instruments, clothes, and men on shore, it was thought necessary to frighten them away. The first time a few great guns were fired, when they were far distant. It was most ludicrous to watch through a glass the Indians, as often as the shot struck the water, take up stones, and as a bold defiance, throw them towards the ship, though about a mile and a-half distant! A boat was then sent with orders to fire a few musket-shots wide of them. The Fuegians hid themselves behind the trees, and for every discharge of the muskets they fired their arrows; all, however, fell short of the boat, and the officer as he pointed at them laughed. This made the Fuegians frantic with passion, and they shook their mantles in vain rage. At last, seeing the balls cut and strike the trees, they ran away, and we were left in peace and quietness. During the former voyage the Fuegians were here very troublesome, and to frighten them a rocket was fired at night over their wigwams: it answered effectually, and one of the officers told me that the clamour first raised, and the barking of the dogs, was quite ludicrous in contrast with the profound silence which in a minute or two afterwards prevailed. The next morning not a single Fuegian was in the neighbourhood. . . .

AUGUST 17TH.—[In the mountains of central Chile]
. . . Almost every part of the hill had been drilled by attempts to open gold-mines: the rage for mining has left scarcely a spot in Chile unexamined. I spent the evening as before, talking round the fire with my two companions. The Guasos of Chile, who correspond to the Gauchos of the Pampas, are, however, a very different set of beings. Chile is the more civilized of the two countries, and the inhabitants, in consequence, have lost much individual character. Gradations in rank are much more strongly marked: the Guaso does not by any means consider every man his equal; and I was quite surprised to find that my companions did not like to eat at the same time with myself. This feeling of inequality is a necessary consequence of the existence of an aristocracy of wealth. It is said that some few of the greater landowners possess from five to ten thousand pounds sterling per annum: an inequality of riches which I believe is not met with, in any of the cattle-breeding countries eastward of the Andes. A traveller does not here meet that unbounded hospitality which refuses all payment, but yet is so kindly offered that no scruples can be raised in accepting it. Almost every house in Chile will receive you for the night, but a trifle is expected to be given in the morning; even a rich man will accept two or three shillings. The Gaucho, although he may be a cut-throat, is a gentleman; the Guaso is in few respects better, but at the same time a vulgar, ordinary fellow. The two men, although employed much in the same manner, are different in their habits and attire; and the peculiarities of each are universal in their respective countries. The Gaucho seems part of his horse, and scorns to exert himself excepting when

on its back; the Guaso may be hired to work as a labourer in the fields. The former lives entirely on animal food; the latter almost wholly on vegetables. We do not here see the white boots, the broad drawers, and scarlet chilipa; the picturesque costume of the Pampas. Here, common trowsers are protected by black and green worsted leggings. The poncho, however, is common to both. The chief pride of the Guaso lies in his spurs; which are absurdly large. I measured one which was six inches in the *diameter* of the rowel, and the rowel itself contained upwards of thirty points. The stirrups are on the same scale, each consisting of a square, carved block of wood, hollowed out, yet weighing three or four pounds. The Guaso is perhaps more expert with the lazo than the Gaucho; but, from the nature of the country, he does not know the use of the bolas.

AUGUST 18TH.—. . . In the evening we reached the mines of Jajuel, situated in a ravine at the flank of the great chain. I stayed here five days. My host the superintendent of the mine, was a shrewd but rather ignorant Cornish miner. He had married a Spanish woman, and did not mean to return home; but his admiration for the mines of Cornwall remained unbounded. Amongst many other questions he asked me, "Now that George Rex is dead, how many more of the family of Rexes are yet alive?" This Rex certainly must be a relation of the great author Finis, who wrote all books!

These mines are of copper, and the ore is all shipped to Swansea to be smelted. Hence the mines have an aspect singularly quiet, as compared to those in England: here no smoke, furnaces, or great steam—engines disturb the solitude of the surrounding mountains.

The Chilian government, or rather the old Spanish law, encourages by every method the searching for mines. The discoverer may work a mine on any ground, by paying five shillings; and before paying this he may try, even in the garden of another man, for twenty days.

It is now well known that the Chilian method of mining is the cheapest. My host says that the two principal improvements introduced by foreigners have been, first, reducing by previous roasting the copper pyrites—which, being the common ore in Cornwall, the English miners were astounded on their arrival to find thrown away as useless: secondly, stamping and washing the scoriae from the old furnaces—by which process particles of metal are recovered in abundance. I have actually seen mules carrying to the coast, for transportation to England, a cargo of such cinders. But the first case is the most curious. The Chilian miners were so convinced that copper pyriates contained not a particle of copper, that they laughed at the Englishmen for their ignorance, who laughed in turn, and bought their richest veins for a few dollars. It is very odd that, in a country where mining had been extensively carried on for many years, so simple a process as gently roasting the ore to expel the sulphur previous to smelting it, had never been discovered. a few improvements have likewise been introduced in some of the simple machinery; but even to the present day, water is removed from some mines by men carrying it up the shaft in leathern bags!

The labouring men work very hard. They have little time allowed for their meals, and during summer and winter they begin when it is light, and leave off at dark. They are paid one pound sterling a month, and their food is given them: this for breakfast consists of sixteen figs and two small loaves of bread; for dinner, boiled beans; for supper, broken roasted wheat grain. They scarcely ever taste meat; as, with the twelve pounds per annum, they have to clothe themselves, and support their families. The miners who work in the mine itself have twenty-five shillings per month, and are allowed a little charqui. But these men come down from their bleak habitations only once in every fortnight or three weeks. . . .

SEPTEMBER 13TH.—We left the baths of Cauquenes, and rejoining the main road slept at the Rio Claro. From this place we rode to the town of S. Fernando. . . . We slept at the gold-mines of Yaquil, which are worked by Mr. Nixon, an American gentleman, to whose kindness I was much indebted during the four days

I stayed at his house. The next morning we rode to the mines, which are situated at the distance of some leagues, near the summit of a lofty hill. . . .

When we arrived at the mine, I was struck by the pale appearance of many of the men, and inquired from Mr. Nixon respecting their condition. The mine is 450 feet deep, and each man brings up about 200 pounds of weight of stone. With this load they have to climb up the alternate notches cut in the trunks of trees, placed in a zigzag line up the shaft. Even beardless young men, eighteen and twenty years old, with little muscular development of their bodies (they are quite naked excepting drawers) ascend with this great load from nearly the same depth. A strong man, who is not accustomed to this labour, perspires most profusely, with merely carrying up his own body. With this very severe labour, they live entirely on boiled beans and bread. They would prefer having bread alone; but their masters, finding that they cannot work so hard upon this, treat them like horses, and make them eat the beans. Their pay is here rather more than at the mines of Jajuel, being from 24 to 28 shillings per month. They leave the mine only once in three weeks; when they stay with their families for two days. One of the rules in this mine sounds very harsh, but answers pretty well for the master. The only method of stealing gold is to secrete pieces of ore, and take them out as occasion may offer. Whenever the major-domo finds a lump thus hidden, its full value is stopped out of the wages of all the men; who thus, without they all combine, are obliged to keep watch over each other.

When the ore is brought to the mill, it is ground into an impalpable powder; the process of washing removes all the lighter particles, and amalgamation finally secures the gold-dust. The washing, when described, sounds a very simple process; but it is beautiful to see how the exact adaptation of the current of water to the specific gravity of the gold, so easily separates the powdered matrix from the metal. The mud which passes from the mills is collected into pools, where it subsides, and every now and then is clearaed out, and thrown into a common heap. A great deal of chemical action then commences, salts of various kinds effloresce on the surface, and the mass becomes hard. After having been left for a year or two, and then rewashed, it yields gold; and this process may be repeated even six or seven times; but the gold each time becomes less in quantity, and the intervals required (as the inhabitants say, to generate the metal) are longer. There can be no doubt that the chemical action, already mentioned, each time liberates fresh gold from some combination. The discovery of a method to effect this before the first grinding, would without doubt raise the value of gold-ores many fold. It is curious to find how the minute particles of gold, being scattered about and not corroding, at last accumulate in some quantity. A short time since a few miners, being out of work, obtained permission to scrape the ground round the house and mill: they washed the earth thus got together, and so procured thirty dollars worth of gold. . . .

Bad as the above treatment of the miners appears, it is gladly accepted of by them; for the condition of the labouring agriculturists is much worse. Their wages are lower, and they live almost exclusively on beans. This poverty must be chiefly owing to the feudal-like system on which the land is tilled: the landowner gives a small plot of ground to the labourer, for building on and cultivating, and in return has his services (or those of a proxy) for every day of his life, without any wages. Until a father has a grown-up son, who can by his labour pay the rent, there is no one, except on occasional days, to take care of his own patch of ground. Hence extreme poverty is very common among the labouring classes in this country.

NOVEMBER 10TH.—The Beagle sailed from Valparaiso to the south, for the purpose of surveying the southern part of Chile, the island of Chiloe, and the broken land called the Chonos Archipelago, as far south as the Peninsula of Tres Montes. On the 21st we anchored in the bay of S. Carlos, the capital of Chiloe. . . .

The inhabitants, from their complexion and low stature, appear to have three-fourths of Indian blood in their veins. They are an humble, quiet, industrious set of men. Although the fertile soil, resulting from the decomposition of the volcanic rocks, supports

a rank vegetation, yet the climate is not favourable to any produc-
tion which requires much sunshine to ripen it. There is very little
pasture for the larger quadrupeds; and in consequence, the staple
articles of food are pigs, potatoes, and fish. The people all dress
in strong woollen garments, which each family makes for itself,
and dyes with indigo of a dark blue colour. The arts, however, are
in the rudest state;—as may be seen in their strange fashion of
ploughing, their method of spinning, grinding corn, and in the
construction of their boats. The forests are so impenetrable, that
the land is nowhere cultivated except near the coast and on the
adjoining islets. Even where paths exist, they are scarcely passa-
ble from the soft and swampy state of the soil. The inhabitants,
like those of Tierra del Fuego, move about chiefly on the beach
or in boats. Although with plenty to eat, the people are very poor:
there is no demand for labour, and consequently the lower orders
cannot scrape together money sufficient to purchase even the
smallest luxuries. There is also a great deficiency of a circulating
medium. I have seen a man bringing on his back a bag of charcoal, with which to buy some trifle, and another carrying a plank
to exchange for a bottle of wine. Hence every tradesman must also
be a merchant, and again sell the goods which he takes in exchange. . . .

NOVEMBER 24TH.—. . . Chacao was formerly the principal port
in the island; but many vessels having been lost, owing to the
dangerous currents and rocks in the straits, the Spanish government burnt the church, and thus arbitrarily compelled the greater
number of inhabitants to migrate to S. Carlos. We had not long
bivouacked, before the barefooted son of the governor came down
to reconnoitre us. Seeing the English flag hoisted at the yawl's
mast-head, he asked, with the utmost indifference, whether it was
always to fly at Chacao. In several places, the inhabitants were
much astonished at the appearance of men-of-war's boats, and
hoped and believed it was the forerunner of a Spanish fleet, coming to recover the island from the patriot government of Chile.
All the men in power, however, had been informed of our intended visit, and were exceedingly civil. While we were eating

our supper, the governor paid us a visit. He had been a lieuten-
ant-colonel in the Spanish service, but now was miserably poor.
He gave us two sheep, and accepted in return two cotton handkerchiefs, some brass trinkets, and a little tobacco. . . .

NOVEMBER 26TH.—. . . Landing at midday, we saw a family of
pure Indian extraction. The father was singularly like York Minster; and some of the younger boys, with their ruddy complexions,
might have been mistaken for Pampas Indians. Everything I have
seen, convinces me of the close connexion of the different American tribes, who nevertheless speak distinct languages. The party
could muster but little Spanish, and talked to each other in their
own tongue. It is a pleasant thing to see the aborigines advanced
to the same degree of civilization, however low that may be, which
their white conquerors have attained. More to the south we saw
many pure Indians: indeed, all the inhabitants of some of the islets retain their Indian surnames. In the census of 1832, there were
in Chiloe and its dependencies forty-two thousand souls: the greater
number of these appear to be of mixed blood. Eleven thousand
retain their Indian surnames, but it is probable that not nearly all
of these are of pure breed. Their manner of life is the same with
that of the other poor inhabitants, and they are all Christians; but
it is said that they yet retain some strange superstitious ceremonies, and that they pretend to hold communication with the devil
in certain caves. Formerly, every one convicted of this offence was
sent to the Inquisition at Lima. Many of the inhabitants who are
not included in the eleven thousand with Indian surnames, cannot be distinguished by their appearance from Indians. Gomez,
the governor of Lemuy, is descended from Noblemen of Spain on
both sides; but by constant intermarriages with the natives the
present man is an Indian. On the other hand, the governor of
Quinchao boasts much of his purely kept Spanish blood. . . .

The two succeeding days were fine, and at night we reached
the island of Quinchao. This neighbourhood is the most cultivated
part of the Archipelago; for a broad strip of land on the coast of
the main island, as well as on many of the smaller adjoining ones,
is almost completely cleared. Some of the farm-houses seemed very

comfortable. I was curious to ascertain how rich any of these people might be, but Mr. Douglas says that no one can be considered as possessing a regular income. One of the richest landowners might possibly accumulate; in a long industrious life, as much as 1000 L sterling, but should this happen, it would all be stowed away in some secret corner, for it is the custom of almost every family to have a jar or treasure-chest buried in the ground.

NOVEMBER 30TH.—Early on Sunday morning we reached Castro, the ancient capital of Chiloe, but now a most forlorn and deserted place. The usual quadrangular arrangement of Spanish towns could be traced, but the streets and plaza were coated with fine green turf, on which sheep were browsing. The church, which stands in the middle, is entirely built of plank, and has a picturesque and venerable appearance. The poverty of the place may be conceived from the fact, that although containing some hundreds of inhabitants, one of our party was unable anywhere to purchase either a pound of sugar or an ordinary knife. No individual possessed either a watch or a clock; and an old man, who was supposed to have a good idea of time, was employed to strike the church bell by guess. The arrival of our boats was a rare event in this quiet retired corner of the world; and nearly all the inhabitants came down to the beach to see us pitch our tents. They were very civil, and offered us a house; and one man even sent us a cask of cider as a present. In the afternoon we paid our respects to the governor—a quiet old man, who, in his appearance and manner of life, was scarcely superior to an English cottager. At night heavy rain set in, which was hardly sufficient to drive away from our tents the large circle of lookers on. An Indian family, who had come to trade in a canoe from Caylen, bivouacked near us. They had no shelter during the rain. In the morning I asked a young Indian, who was wet to the skin, how he had passed the night. He seemed perfectly content, and answered, "Muy bien, senor."

DECEMBER 1ST.—We steered for the island of Lemuy. I was anxious to examine a reported coal-mine, which turned out to be lignite of little value, in the sandstone (probably of an ancient tertiary epoch) of which these islands are composed. When we reached Lemuy we had much difficulty in finding any place to pitch our tents, for it was spring-tide, and the land was wooded down to the water's edge. In a short time we were surrounded by a large group of the nearly pure Indian inhabitants. They were much surprised at our arrival, and said one to the other, "This is the reason we have seen so many parrots lately; the cheucau (an odd red-breasted little bird, which inhabits the thick forest, and utters very peculiar noises) has not cried 'beware' for nothing." They were soon anxious for barter. Money was scarcely worth anything, but their eagerness for tobacco was something quite extraordinary. After tobacco, indigo came next in value; then capsicum, old clothes, and gunpowder. The latter article was required for a very innocent purpose: each parish has a public musket, and the gunpowder was wanted for making a noise on their saint or feast days.

The people here live chiefly on shell-fish and potatoes. At certain seasons they catch also, in "corrales," or hedges under water, many fish which are left on the mud-banks as the tide falls. They occasionally possess fowls, sheep, goats, pigs, horses, and cattle; the order in which they are here mentioned, expressing their respective numbers. I never saw anything more obliging and humble than the manner of these people. They generally began with stating, that they were poor natives of the place, and not Spaniards, and that they were in sad want of tobacco and other comforts. At Caylen, the most southern island, the sailors bought with a stick of tobacco, of the value of three-halfpence, two fowls, one of which, the Indian stated, had skin between its toes, and turned out to be a fine duck; and with some cotton handkerchiefs, worth three shillings, three sheep and a large bunch of onions were procured. The yawl at this place was anchored some way from the shore, and we had fears for her safety from robbers during the night. Our pilot, Mr. Douglas, accordingly told the constable of the district that we always placed sentinels with loaded arms, and not understanding Spanish, if we saw any person in the dark, we should assuredly shoot him. The constable, with much humility, agreed to the perfect propriety of this arrangement, and promised us that no one should stir out of his house during that night.

DECEMBER 18TH.—. . . A strong desire is always felt to ascertain whether any human being has previously visited an unfrequented spot. A bit of wood with a nail in it, is picked up and studied as if it were covered with hieroglyphics. Possessed with this feeling, I was much interested by finding, on a wild part of th coast, a bed made of grass beneath a ledge of rock. Close by it there had been a fire, and the man had used an axe. The fire, bed and situation showed the dexterity of an Indian; but he could scarcely have been an Indian, for the race is in this part extinct, owing to the Catholic desire of making at one blow Christians and Slaves. I had at the same time some misgivings that the solitary man who had made his bed on this wild spot, must have been some poor shipwrecked sailor, who, in trying to travel up the coast, had here laid himself down for his dreary night.

DECEMBER 28TH.—The weather continued very bad, but it at last permitted us to proceed with the survey. The time hung heavy on our hands, as it always did when we were delayed from day to day by successive gales of wind. In the evening another harbour was discovered, where we anchored. Directly afterwards a man was seen waving his shirt, and a boat was sent which brought back two seamen. A party of six had run away from an American whaling vessel, and had landed a little to the southward in a boat, which was shortly afterwards knocked to pieces by the surf. They had now been wandering up and down the coast for fifteen months, without knowing which way to go, or where they were. What a singluar piece of good fortune it was that this harbour was now discovered! Had it not been for this one chance, they might have wandered till they had grown old men, and at last have perished on this wild coast. Their sufferings had been very great, and one of their party had lost his life by falling from the cliffs. They were sometimes obliged to separate in search of food, and this explained the bed of the solitary man. Considering what they had undergone, I think they had kept a very good reckoning of time, for they had lost only four days.

JANUARY 23RD, 1835.—. . . The district of Cucao is the only inhabited part on the whole west coast of Chiloe. It contains about thirty or forty Indian families, who are scattered along four or five miles of the shore. They are very much secluded from the rest of Chiloe, and have scarcely any sort of commerce, except sometimes in a little oil, which they get from seal-blubber. They are tolerably dressed in clothes of their own manufacture, and they have plenty to eat. They seemed, however, discontented, yet humble to a degree which it was quite painful to witness. These feelings are, I think, chiefly to be attributed to the harsh and authoritative manner in which they are treated by their rulers. Our companions, although so very civil to us, behaved to the poor Indians as if they had been slaves, rather than free men. They ordered provisions and the use of their horses, without ever condescending to say how much, or indeed whether the owners should be paid at all. In the morning, being left alone with these poor people, we soon ingratiated ourselves by presents of cigars and mate. A lump of white sugar was divided between all present, and tasted with the greatest curiosity. The Indians ended all their complaints by saying, "And it is only because we are poor Indians, and know nothing, but it was not so when we had a King."

FEBURARY 12TH.—[MAINLAND CHILE] We continued to ride through the uncleared forest; only occasionally meeting an Indian on horseback, or a troop of fine mules bringing alerce-planks and corn from the southern plains. In the afternoon one of the horses knocked up: we were then on the brow of a hill, which commanded a fine view of the Llanos. The view of these open plains was very refreshing, after being hemmed in and buried in the wilderness of trees. The uniformity of a forest soon becomes very wearisome. This west coast makes me remember with pleasure the free, unbounded plains of Patagonia; yet, with the true spirit of contradiction, I cannot forget how sublime is the silence of the forest. The Llanos are the most fertile and thickly peopled parts of the country; as they possess the immense advantage of being nearly free from trees. Before leaving the forest we crossed some flat little lawns, around which single trees stood, as in an English park: I have often noticed with surprise, in wooded undulatory districts, that the quite level parts have been destitute of trees. On account of the tired horse, I determined to stop at the Mission of Cudico, to the friar of which I had a letter of introduction. Cudico is an intermediate district between the forest and the Llanos. There are a good many cottages, with patches of corn and potatoes, nearly all belonging to Indians. The tribes dependent on Valdivia are "reducidos y cristianos." The Indians farther northward, about Arauco and Imperial, are still very wild, and not converted; but they have all much intercourse with the Spaniards. The padre said that the Christian Indians did not much like coming to mass, but that otherwise they showed respect for religion. The greatest difficulty is in making them observe the ceremonies of marriage. The wild Indians take as many wives as they can support, and a cacique will sometimes have more than ten: on entering his house, the number may be told by that of the separate fires. Each wife lives a week in turn with the cacique; but all are employed in weaving ponchos, etc. for his profit. To be the wife of a cacique, is an honour much sought after by the Indian women.

The men of all these tribes wear a coarse woollen poncho: those south of Valdivia wear short trowsers, and those north of it a petticoat, like the chilipa of the Gauchos. All have their long hair bound by a scarlet fillet, but with no other covering on their heads. These Indians are good-sized men; their cheekbones are prominent, and in general appearance they resemble the great American family to which they belong; but their physiognomy seemed to me to be slightly different from that of any other tribe which I had before seen. Their expression is generally grave, and even austere, and possesses much character: this may pass either for honest bluntness or fierce determination. The long black hair, the grave and much-lined features, and the dark complexion, called to my mind old portraits of James I. On the road we met with none of that humble politeness so universal in Chiloe. Some gave their "mari-

mari" (good morning) with promptness, but the greater number did not seem inclined to offer any salute. This independence of manners is probably a consequence of their long wars, and the repeated victories which they alone of all the tribes in America, have gained over the Spaniards.

I spent the evening very pleasantly, talking with the padre. He was exceedingly kind and hospitable; and coming from Santiago, had contrived to surround himself with some few comforts. Being a man of some little education, he bitterly complained of the total want of society. With no particular zeal for religion, no business or pursuit, how completely must this man's life be wasted! The next day, on our return, we met seven very wild-looking Indians, of whom some were caciques that had just received from the Chilian government, their yearly small stipend for having long remained faithful. They were fine-looking men, and they rode one after the other, with most gloomy faces. An old cacique, who headed them, had been, I suppose, more excessively drunk than the rest, for he seemed both extremely grave and very crabbed. Shortly before this, two Indians joined us, who were travelling from a distant mission to Valdivia concerning some lawsuit. One was a good-humoured old man, but from his wrinkled beardless face looked more like an old woman than a man. I frequently presented both of them with cigars; and though ready to receive them, and I dare say gratefully, they would hardly condescend to thank me. A Chilotan Indian would have taken off his hat, and given his "Dios le page!" The traveling was very tedious, both from the badness of the roads, and from the number of great fallen trees, which it was necessary either to leap over or to avoid by making long circuits. We slept on the road, and next morning reached Valdivia, whence I proceeded on board. . . .

MAY 4TH.—Finding the coast-road devoid of interest of any kind, we turned inland towards the mining district and valley of Illapel. This valley, like every other in Chile, is level, broad, and very fertile: it is bordered on each side, either by cliffs of stratified shingle, or by bare rocky mountains. Above the straight line of the uppermost irrigating ditch, all is brown as on a high road; while

all below is of as bright a green as verdigris, from the beds of al-
farfa, a kind of clover. We proceeded to Los Hornos, another
mining district, where the principal hill was drilled with holes,
like a great ants'-nest. The Chilian miners are a peculiar race of
men in their habits. Living for weeks together in the most desolate spots, when they descend to the villages on feast-days, there
is no excess or extravagance into which they do not run. They
sometimes gain a considerable sum, and then, like sailors with
prize-money, they try how soon they can contrive to squander it.
They drink excessively, buy quantities of clothes, and in a few days
return penniless to their miserable abodes, there to work harder
than beasts of burden. This thoughtlessness, as with sailors, is evidently the result of a similar manner of life. Their daily food is
found them, and they acquire no habits of carefulness; moreover,
temptation and the means of yielding to it are placed in their power
at the same time. On the other hand, in Cornwall, and some other
parts of England, where the system of selling part of the vein is
followed, the miners, from being obliged to act and think for
themselves, are a singularly intelligent and well-conducted set of
men.

The dress of the Chilian miner is peculiar and rather picturesque. He wears a very long shirt of some dark-coloured baize,
with a leathern apron; the whole being fastened round his waist
by a bright-coloured sash. His trowsers are very broad, and his
small cap of scarlet cloth is made to fit the head closely. We met
a party of these miners in full costume, carrying the body of one
of their companions to be buried. They marched at a very quick
trot, four men supporting the corpse. One set having run as hard
as they could for about two hundred yards, were relieved by four
others, who had previously dashed on ahead on horseback. Thus
they proceeded, encouraging each other by wild cries: altogether
the scene formed a most strange funeral.

We continued travelling northward, in a zigzag line; sometimes
stopping a day to geologise. The country was so thinly inhabited,
and the track so obscure, that we often had difficulty in finding
our way. On the 12th I stayed at some mines. The one in this case

was not considered particularly good, but from being abundant it was supposed the mine would sell for about thirty or forty thousand dollars (that is, 6000 or 8000 pounds sterling); yet it had been bought by one of the English Associations for an ounce of gold (3L. 8s.). The ore is yellow pyrites, which, as I have already remarked, before the arrival of the English, was not supposed to contain a particle of copper. On a scale of profits nearly as great as in the above instance, piles of cinders, abounding with minute globules of metallic copper, were purchased; yet with these advantages, the mining associations, as is well known, contrived to lose immense sums of money. The folly of the greater number of the commissioners and shareholders amounted to infatuation;—a thousand pounds per annum given in some cases to entertain the Chilian authorities; libaries of well-bound geological books; miners brought out for particular metals, as tin, which are not found in Chile; contracts to supply the miners with milk, in parts where there are no cows; machinery, where it could not possibly be used; and a hundred similar arrangements, bore witness to our absurdity, and to this day afford amusement to the natives. Yet there can be no doubt, that the same capital well employed in these mines would have yielded an immense return: a confidential man of business, a practical miner and assayer, would have been all that was required.

Captain Head has described the wonderful load which the "Apires," truly beasts of burden, carry up from the deepest mines. I confess I thought the account exaggerated; so that I was glad to take an opportunity of weighing one of the loads, which I picked out by hazard. It required considerable exertion on my part, when standing directly over it, to lift it from the ground. The load was considered under weight when found to be 197 pounds. The apire had carried this up eighty perpendicular yards,—part of the way by a steep passage, but the greater part up notched poles, placed in a zigzag line up the shaft. According to the general regulation, the apire is not allowed to halt for breath, except the mine is six hundred feet deep. The average load is considered as rather more than 200 pounds, and I have been assured that one of 300 pounds (twenty-two stone and a half) by way of a trial has been brought up from the deepest mine! At this time the apires were bringing up the usual load twelve times in the day; that is, 2400 pounds from eighty yards deep; and they were employed in the intervals in breaking and picking ore.

These men, excepting from accidents, are healthy, and appear cheerful. Their bodies are not very muscular. They rarely eat meat once a week, and never oftener, and then only the hard dry charqui. Although with a knowledge that the labour was volontary, it was nevertheless quite revolting to see the state in which they reached the mouth of the mine; their bodies bent forward, leaning with the arms on the steps, their legs bowed, their muscles quivering, the perspiration streaming from their faces over their breasts, their nostrils distended, the corners of their mouth forcibly drawn back, and the explusion of their breath most laborious. Each time they draw their breath, they utter an articulate cry of "ay-ay," which ends in a sound rising from deep in the chest, but shrill like the note of a fife. After staggering to the pile of ore, they emptied the "carpacho;" in two or three seconds recovering their breath, they wiped the sweat from their brows, and apparently quite fresh descended the mine again at a quick pace. This appears to me a wonderful instance of the amount of labour which habit, for it can be nothing else, will enable a man to endure.

In the evening, talking with the *mayor-domo* of these mines, about the number of foreigners now scattered over the whole country, he told me that, though quite a young man, he remembers when he was a boy at school at Coquimbo, a holiday being given to see the captain of an English ship, who was brought to the city to speak to the governor. He believes that nothing would have induced any boy in the school, himself included, to have gone close to the Englishman; so deeply had they been impressed with an idea of the heresy, contamination, and evil to be derived from contact with such a person. To this day they relate the atrocious actions of the bucaniers; and especially of one man, who took away the figure of the Virgin Mary, and returned the year after for that of St. Joseph, saying it was a pity the lady should not have a husband. I heard also of an old lady who, at a dinner in Coquimbo, remarked how wonderfully strange it was that she should have lived to dine in the same room with an Englishman; for she remembered as a girl, that twice, at the mere cry of "Los Ingleses," every soul, carrying what valuables they could, had taken to the mountains. . . .

JUNE 26TH.—. . . I observed Indian ruins in several parts of the Cordillera: the most perfect, which I saw, were the Ruinas de Tambillos, in the Uspallata Pass. Small square rooms were there huddled together in separate groups: some of the doorways were yet standing; they were formed by a cross slab of stone only about three feet high. Uloa has remarked on the lowness of the doors in the ancient Peruvian dwellings. These houses, when perfect, must have been capable of containing a considerable number of persons. Tradition says, that they were used as halting places for the Incas, when they crossed the mountains. Traces of Indian habitations have been discovered in many other parts, where it does not appear probable that they were used as mere resting-places, but yet where the land is as utterly unfit for any kind of cultivation as it is near the Tambillos or at the Incas Bridge, or in the Portillo Pass, at all which places I saw ruins. In the ravine of Jajuel, near Aconcagua, where there is no pass, I heard of remains of houses situated at a great height, where it is extremely cold and sterile. At first I imagined that these buildings had been places of refuge, built by the Indians on the first arrival of the Spaniards; but I have since been inclined to speculate on the probability of a small change of climate.

In this northern part of Chile, within the Cordillera, old Indian houses are said to be especially numerous: by digging amongst the ruins, bits of woollen articles, instruments of precious metals, and heads of Indian corn, are not unfrequently discovered: an arrowhead made of agate, and of precisely the same form with those now used in Tierra del Fuego, was given me. I am aware that the Peruvian Indians now frequently inhabit most lofty and bleak situations; but at Copiapó I was assured by men who had spent their lives in travelling through the Andes, that there were very many (*muchisimas*) buildings at heights so great as almost to border on the perpetual snow, and in parts where there exist no passes, and where the land produces absolutely nothing, and what is still more extraordinary, where there is no water. Nevertheless it is the opinion of the people of the country (although they are much puzzled by the circumstance), that, from the appearance of the houses, the Indians must have used them as places of residence. In this valley, at Punta Gorda, the remains consisted of seven or eight square little rooms, which were of a similar form with those at Tambillos, but built chiefly of mud, which the present inhabitants cannot, either here or, according to Ulloa, in Peru, imitate in durability. They were situated in the most conspicuous and defenceless position, at the bottom of the flat broad valley. There was no water nearer than three or four leagues, and that only very small quantity; and bad: the soil was absolutely sterile; I looked in vain even for a lichen adhering to the rocks. At the present day, with the advantage of beasts of burden, a mine, unless it were very rich, could scarcely be worked here with profit. Yet the Indians formerly chose it as a place of residence! If at the present time two or three showers of rain were to fall annually, instead of one, as now is the case, during as many years, a small rill of water would probably be formed in this great valley; and then, by irrigation (which was formerly so well understood by the Indians), the soil would easily be rendered sufficiently productive to support a few families.

JULY 19TH.—. . . No state in South America, since the declaration of independence, has suffered more from anarchy than Peru. At the time of our visit, there were four chiefs in arms contending for supremacy in the government: if one succeeded in becoming for a time very powerful, the others coalesced against him; but no sooner were they victorious, than they were again hostile to each other. The other day, at the Anniversary of the Independence, high mass was performed, the President partaking of the sacrament: during the *Te Deum laudamus,* instead of each regiment displaying the Peruvian flag a black one with the death's head was unfurled. Imagine a government under which such a scene could be ordered on such an occasion, to be typical of their determination of fighting to death! This state of affairs happened at a time very unfortunately for me, as I was precluded from taking any excursion much beyond the limits of the town. The barren island of S. Lorenzo, which forms the harbour, was nearly the only place where one could walk securely. The upper part, which is upwards of 1000 feet in height, during this season of the year (winter), comes within the lower limit of the clouds; and in consequence, an abundant cryptogamic vegetation, and a few flowers, cover the summit. . . .

Callao is a filthy, ill-built, small seaport. The inhabitants, both here and at Lima, present every imaginable shade of mixture between European, Negro, and Indian blood. They appear a depraved, drunken set of people. The atmosphere is loaded with foul smells, and that peculiar one, which may be perceived in almost every town within the tropics, was here very strong. The fortress, which withstood Lord Cochrane's long siege, has an imposing appearance. But the president, during our stay, sold the brass guns, and proceeded to dismantle part of it. The reason assigned was, that he had not an officer to whom he could trust so important a charge. He himself had good reasons for thinking so, as he had obtained the presidentship by rebelling while in charge of this same fortress. After we left South America, he paid the penalty in the usual manner, by being conquered, taken prisoner, and shot. . . .

The city of Lima is now in a wretched state of decay: the streets are nearly unpaved; and heaps of filth are piled up in all directions, where the black gallinazos, tame as poultry, pick up bits of carrion. The houses have generally an upper story, built, on account of the earthquakes, of plastered woodwork; but some of the old ones, which are now used by several families, are immensely large, and would rival in suites of apartments the most magnificient in any place. Lima, the City of Kings, must formerly have been a splendid town. The extraordinary number of churches gives it, even at the present day, a peculiar and striking character, especially when viewed from a short distance.

Tahiti and New Zealand

NOVEMBER 15TH. [1835]—At daylight, Tahiti, an island which must for ever remain classical to the voyager in the South Sea, was in view. At a distance the appearance was not attractive. The luxuriant vegetation of the lower part could not yet be seen, and as the clouds rolled past, the wildest and most precipitous peaks showed themselves towards the centre of the island. As soon as we anchored in Matavai Bay, we were surrounded by Canoes. This was our Sunday, but the Monday of Tahiti: if the case had been reversed, we should not have received a single visit; for the injunction not to launch a canoe on the sabbath is rigidly obeyed. After dinner we landed to enjoy all the delights produced by the first impression of a new country, and that country the charming Tahiti. A crowd of men, women, and children, was collected on the memorable Point Venus, ready to receive us with laughing, merry faces. They marshalled us towards the house of Mr. Wilson, the missionary of the district, who met us on the road, and gave us a very friendly reception. After sitting a short time in his house, we separated to walk about, but returned there in the evening.

The land capable of cultivation, is scarcely in any part more than a fringe of low alluvial soil, accumulated round the base of the mountains, and protected from the waves of the sea by a coral reef, which encircles the entire line of coast. Within the reef there is an expanse of smooth water, like that of a lake, where the canoes of the natives can ply with safety and where ships anchor. The low land which comes down to the beach of coral-sand, is covered by the most beautiful productions of the intertropical regions. In the midst of bananas, orange, cocoa-nut, and bread-fruit trees, spots are cleared where yams, sweet potatoes, the sugar-cane, and pineapples, are cultivated. Even the brushwood is an imported fruit-tree, namely, the guava, which from its abundance has become as noxious as a weed. In Brazil I have often admired the varied beauty of the bananas, palms, and the orange-trees contrasted together; and here we also have the bread-fruit, conspicuous from its large, glossy, and deeply digitated leaf. It is admirable to behold groves of a tree, sending forth its branches with the vigour of an English oak, loaded with large and most nutritious fruit. However seldom the usefulness of an object can account for the pleasure of beholding it, in the case of these beautiful woods, the knowledge of their high productiveness no doubt enters largely into the feeling of admiration. The little winding paths, cool from the surrounding shade, led to the scattered houses; the owners of which every where gave us a cheerful and most hospitable reception.

I was pleased with nothing so much as with the inhabitants. There is a mildness in the expression of their countenances which at once banishes the idea of a savage; and an intelligence which shows that they are advancing in civilization. The common people, when working, keep the upper part of their bodies quite naked; and it is then that the Tahitians are seen to advantage. They are very tall, broad-shouldered, athletic, and well proportioned. It has been remarked, that it requires little habit to make a dark skin more pleasing and natural to the eye of an European than his own colour. A white man bathing by the side of a Tahitian, was like a plant bleached by the gardener's art compared with a fine dark green one growing vigorously in the open fields. Most of the men tattooed, and the ornaments follow the curvature of the body so gracefully, that they have a very elegant effect. One common pattern, varying in its details, is somewhat like the crown of a palm tree. It springs from the central line of the back, and gracefully curls round both sides. The simile may be a fanciful one, but I thought the body of a man thus ornamented was like the trunk of a noble tree embraced by a delicate creeper.

Many of the elder people had their feet covered with small figures, so placed as to resemble a sock. This fashion, however, is partly gone by, and has been succeeded by others. Here, although fashion is far from immutable, every one must abide by that prevailing in his youth. An old man has thus his age for ever stamped on his body, and he cannot assume the airs of a young dandy. The women are tattooed in the same manner as the men, and very commonly on their fingers. One unbecoming fashion is now almost universal: namely, shaving the hair from the upper part of the head, in a circular form, so as to leave only an outer ring. The missionaries have tried to persuade the people to change this habit; but it is the fashion, and that is a sufficient answer at Tahiti, as at Paris. I was much disappointed in the personal appearance of the women: they are far inferior in every respect to the men. The custom of wearing a white or scarlet flower in the back of the head, or through a small hole in each ear, is pretty. A crown of woven cocoa-nut leaves is also worn as a shade for the eyes. The women appear to be in greater want of some becoming costume even than the men.

Nearly all the natives understand a little English—that is, they know the names of common things; and by the aid of this, together with signs, a lame sort of conversation could be carried on. In returning in the evening to the boat, we stopped to witness a very pretty scene. Numbers of children were playing on the beach, and had lighted bonfires which illuminated the placid sea and surrounding trees; others, in circles, were singing Tahitian verses. We seated ourselves on the sand, and joined their party. The songs were impromptu, and I believe related to our arrival: one little girl sang a line, which the rest took up in parts, forming a very pretty chorus. The whole scene made us unequivocally aware that we were seated on the shores of an island in the far-famed South Sea.

NOVEMBER 17TH.—This day is reckoned in the log-book as Tuesday the 17th, instead of Monday the 16th, owing to our, so far, successful chase of the sun. Before breakfast the ship was hemmed in by a flotilla of canoes; and when the natives were allowed to come on board, I suppose there could not have been less than two hundred. It was the opinion of every one that it would have been difficult to have picked out an equal number from any other nation, who would have given so little trouble. Everybody brought something for sale: shells were the main article of trade. The Tahitians now fully understand the value of money, and prefer it to old clothes or other articles. The various coins, however, of English and Spanish denomination puzzle them, and they never seemed to think the small silver quite secure until changed into dollars. Some of the chiefs have accumulated considerable sums of money. One chief, not long since, offered 800 dollars (about 160£. sterling) for a small vessel; and frequently they purchase whale-boats and horses at the rate of from 50 to 100 dollars.

NOVEMBER 18TH.—. . . The Tahitians have the dexterity of amphibious animals in the water. An anecdote mentioned by Ellis shows how much they feel at home in this element. When a horse was landing for Pomarre in 1817, the slings broke, and it fell into the water: immediately the natives jumped overboard, and by their cries and vain efforts at assistance almost drowned it. As soon, however, as it reached the shore, the whole population took to flight, and tried to hide themselves from the man-carrying pig, as they christened the horse. . . .

They then proceeded to make a fire, and cook our evening meal. A light was procured, by rubbing a blunt-pointed stick in a groove made in another, as if with intention of deepening it, until by the friction the dust became ignited. A peculiarly white and very light wood (the Hibiscus tilaceus) is alone used for this purpose: it is the same which serves for poles to carry any burden, and for the floating outriggers to their canoes. The fire was produced in few seconds: but to a person who does not understand the art, it requires, as I found, the greatest exertion; but at last, to my great pride, I succeeded in igniting the dust. The Gaucho in the Pampas uses a different method: taking an elastic stick about eighteen inches long, he presses one end on his breast, and the other pointed end into a hole in a piece of wood, and then rapidly turns the curved part, like a carpenter's centre-bit. The Tahitians having made a small fire of sticks placed a score of stones, of about the size of cricket balls, on the burning wood. In about ten minutes the sticks were consumed, and the stones hot. They had previously folded up in small parcels of leaves, pieces of beef, fish, ripe and unripe bananas, and the tops of the wild arum. These green parcels were laid in a layer between two layers of the hot stones, and the whole then covered up with earth, so that no smoke or steam could escape. In about a quarter of an hour, the whole was most deliciously cooked. The choice green parcels were now laid on a cloth of banana leaves, and with a cocoa-nut shell we drank the cool water of the running stream; and thus we enjoyed our rustic meal. . . .

Before we laid ourselves down to sleep, the elder Tahitian fell on his knees, and with closed eyes repeated a long prayer in his native tongue. He prayed as a Christian should do, with fitting reverence, and without the fear of ridicule or any ostentation of piety. At our meals neither of the men would taste food, without saying beforehand a short grace. Those travellers who think that a Tahitian prays only when the eyes of the missionary are fixed on him, should have slept with us that night on the mountainside. . . .

November 19th.—At daylight my friends, after their morning prayer, prepared an excellent breakfast in the same manner as in the evening. They themselves certainly partook of it largely; indeed I never saw any men eat near so much. I suppose such enormously capacious stomachs must be the effect of a large part of their diet consisting of fruit and vegetables, which contain, in a given bulk, a comparatively small portion of nutriment. Unwittingly, I was the means of my companions breaking, as I afterwards learned, one of their own laws and resolutions: I took with me a flask of spirits, which they could not refuse to partake of; but as often as they drank a little, they put their fingers before their mouths, and uttered the word "Missionary." About two years ago, although the use of the ava was prevented, drunkenness from the introduction of spirits became very prevalent. The missionaries prevailed on a few good men, who saw that their country was rapidly going to ruin, to join with them in a Temperance Society. From good sense or shame, all the chiefs and the queen were at last persuaded to join. Immediately a law was passed, that no spirits should be allowed to be introduced into the island, and that he who sold and he who bought the forbidden article should be punished by a fine. With remarkable justice, a certain period was allowed for stock in hand to be sold, before the law came into effect. But when it did, a general search was made, in which even the houses of the missionaries were not exempted, and all the ava (as the natives call all ardent spirits) was poured on the ground. When one reflects on the effect of intemperance on the aborigines of the two Americas, I think it will be acknowledged that every well-wisher of Tahiti owes no common debt of gratitude to the missionaries. As long as the little island of St. Helena remained under the government of the East India Company, spirits, owing to the great injury they had produced, were not allowed to be imported; but wine was supplied from the Cape of Good Hope. It is rather a striking, and not very gratifying fact, that in the same year that spirits were allowed to be sold in St. Helena, their use was banished from Tahiti by the free will of the people.

NOVEMBER 20TH—. . . From the varying accounts which I had read before reaching these islands, I was very anxious to form, from my own observation, a judgment of their moral state,—although such judgment would necessarily be very imperfect. First impressions at all times very much depend on one's previously-acquired ideas. My notions were drawn from Ellis's 'Polynesian Researches'—an admirable and most interesting work, but naturally looking at everything under a favourable point of view; from Beechey's Voyage; and from that of Kotzebue, which is strongly adverse to the whole missionary system. He who compares these three accounts will, I think, form a tolerably accurate conception of the present state of Tahiti. One of my impressions, which I took from the two last authorities, was decidedly incorrect; viz., that the Tahitians had become a gloomy race, and lived in fear of the missionaries. Of the latter feeling I saw no trace, unless, indeed, fear and respect be confounded under one name. Instead of discontent being a common feeling, it would be difficult in Europe to pick out of a crowd half so many merry and happy faces. The prohibition of the flute and dancing is inveighed against as wrong and foolish;—the more than presbyterian manner of keeping the sabbath is looked at in a similar light. On these points I will not pretend to offer any opinion, in opposition to men who have resided as many years as I was days on the island.

On the whole it appears to me that the morality and religion of the inhabitants are highly creditable. There are many who attack, even more acrimoniously than Kotzebue, both the missionaries, their system, and the effects produced by it. Such reasoners never compare the present state with that of the island only twenty years ago; nor even with that of Europe at this day; but they compare it with the high standard of Gospel perfection. They expect the missionaries to effect that which the Apostles themselves failed to do. In as much as the condition of the people falls short of this high standard, blame is attached to the missionary, instead of credit for that which he has effected. They forget, or will not remember, that human sacrifices, and the power of an idolatrous priesthood—a system of profligacy unparalleled in any other part of the world—infanticide a consequence of that system—bloody wars, where the conquerors spared neither women nor children—that all these have been abolished; and that dishonesty, intemperance, and licentiousness have been greatly reduced by the introduction of Christianity. In a voyager to forget these things is base ingratitude; for should he chance to be at the point of shipwreck on some unknown coast, he will most devoutly pray that the lesson of the missionary may have extended thus far.

In point of morality, the virtue of the women, it has been often said, is most open to exception. But before they are blamed too severely, it will be well distinctly to call to mind the scenes described by Captain Cook and Mr. Banks, in which the grandmothers and mothers of the present race played a part. Those who are most severe, should consider how much of the morality of the women in Europe, is owing to the system early impressed by mothers on their daughters, and how much in each individual case to the precepts of religion. But it is useless to argue against such reasoners;—I believe that, disappointed in not finding the field of licentiousness quite so open as formerly, they will not give credit to a morality which they do not wish to practise, or to a religion which they undervalue, if not despise.

SUNDAY 22ND.—The harbour of Papiéte, where the queen resides, may be considered as the capital of the island: it is also the seat of government, and the chief resort of shipping. Captain Fitz Roy took a party there this day to hear divine service, first in the Tahitian language, and afterwards in our own. Mr. Prichard, the leading missionary in the island, performed the service. The chapel consisted of a large airy framework of wood; and it was filled to excess by tidy, clean people, of all ages and both sexes. I was rather disappointed in the apparent degree of attention; but I believe my expectations were raised too high. At all events the appearance was quite equal to that in a country church in England. The singing of the hymns was decidedly very pleasing; but the language from the pulpit, although fluently delivered, did not sound well: a constant repetition of the words, like "*tata ta, mata mai,*" rendered it montonous. After English service, a party returned on foot to Matavai. It was a pleasant walk, sometimes along the sea-beach and sometimes under the shade of the many beautiful trees.

About two years ago, a small vessel under English colours was plundered by some of the inhabitants of the Low Islands, which were then under the dominion of the Queen of Tahiti. It was believed that the perpetrators were instigated to this act by some indiscreet laws issued by her majesty. The British government demanded compensation; which was acceded to, and a sum of nearly three thousand dollars was agreed to be paid on the first of last September. The Commodore at Lima ordered Captain Fitz Roy to inquire concerning this debt, and to demand satisfaction if it were not paid. Captain Fitz Roy accordingly requested an interview with the Queen Pomarre, since famous from the ill-treatment she has received from the French; and a parliament was held to consider the question, at which all the principal chiefs of the island, and the queen, were assembled. I will not attempt to describe what took place, after the interesting account given by Captain Fitz Roy. The money, it appeared, had not been paid;

perhaps the alleged reasons were rather equivocal; but otherwise I cannot sufficiently express our general surprise at the extreme good sense, the reasoning power, moderation, candour, and prompt resolution, which were displayed on all sides. I believe we all left the meeting with a very different opinion of the Tahitians, from what we entertained when we entered. The chiefs and people resolved to subscribe and complete the sum which was wanting; Captain Fitz Roy urged that it was hard that their private property should be sacrificed for the crimes of distant islanders. They replied, that they were grateful for his consideration, but that Pomarre was their Queen, and that they were determined to help her in this her difficulty. This resolution and its prompt execution, for a book was opened early the next morning, made a perfect conclusion to this very remarkable scene of loyalty and good feeling.

After the main discussion was ended, several of the chiefs took the opportunity of asking Captain Fitz Roy many intelligent questions on international customs and laws, relating to the treatment of ships and foreigners. On some points, as soon as the decision was made, the law was issued verbally on the spot. This Tahitian parliament lasted for several hours; and when it was over Captain Fitz Roy invited Queen Pomarre to pay the Beagle a visit.

November 25th.—In the evening four boats were sent for her majesty; the ship was dressed with flags, and the yards manned on her coming on board. She was accompanied by most of the chiefs. The behaviour of all was very proper: they begged for nothing, and seemed much pleased with captain Fitz Roy's presents. The Queen is a large awkward woman, without any beauty, grace, or dignity. She has only one royal attribute: a perfect immoveability of expression under all circumstances, and that rather a sullen one. The rockets were most admired; and a deep "Oh!" could be heard from the shore, all round the dark bay, after each explosion. The sailors's songs were also much admired; and the queen said she thought that one of the most boisterous ones certainly could not be a hymn! The royal party did not return on shore till past midnight.

NOVEMBER 26TH.—In the evening, with a gentle land-breeze, a course was steered for New Zealand; and as the sun set, we had a farewell view of the mountains of Tahiti—the island to which every voyager has offered up his tribute of admiration.

DECEMBER 19TH.—In the evening we saw in the distance New Zealand. . . .

DECEMBER 21ST.—Early in the morning we entered the Bay of Islands, . . . In several parts of the bay, little villages of square tidy-looking houses are scattered close down to the water's edge. Three whaling-ships were lying at anchor, and a canoe every now and then crossed from shore to shore; with these exceptions, an air of extreme quietness reigned over the whole district. Only a single canoe came alongside. This, and the aspect of the whole scene, afforded a remarkable, and not very pleasing contrast, with our joyful and boisterous welcome at Tahiti. . . .

DECEMBER 22ND.—In the morning I went out walking; but I soon found that the country was very impracticable. . . . I afterwards observed that the principal hills inland . . . showed an artificial outline. These are the Pas, so frequently mentioned by Captain Cook under the name of "hippah;" the difference of sound owing to the prefixed article.

That the Pas had formerly been much used, was evident from the piles of shells, and the pits in which, as I was informed, sweet potatoes used to be kept as a reserve. As there was no water on these hills, the defenders could never have anticipated a long siege, but only a hurried attack for plunder, against which the successive terraces would have afforded good protection. The general introduction of fire-arms has changed the whole system of warfare; and an exposed situation on the top of a hill is now worse than useless. The Pas in consequence are, at the present day, always built on a level piece of ground. They consist of a double stockade of thick and tall posts, placed in a zigzag line, so that every part can be flanked. Within the stockade a mound of earth is thrown up, behind which the defenders can rest in safety, or use their fire-arms over it. On the level of the ground little archways sometime pass through this breastwork, by which means the defenders can crawl out to the stockade to reconnoitre their enemies. . . .

These Pas are considered by the New Zealanders as very perfect means of defence: for the attacking force is never so well disciplined as to rush in a body to the stockade, cut it down, and effect their entry. When a tribe goes to war, the chief cannot order one party to go here and another there; but every man fights in the manner which best pleases himself; and to each separate individual to approach a stockade defended by fire-arms must appear certain death. I should think a more warlike race of inhabitants could not be found in any part of the world than the New Zealanders. Their conduct on first seeing a ship, as described by Captain Cook, strongly illustrates this: the act of throwing volleys of stones at so great and novel an object, and their defiance of "Come on shore and we will kill and eat you all," shows uncommon boldness. This warlike spirit is evident in many of their customs, and even in their smallest actions. If a New Zealander is struck, although but in joke, the blow must be returned; and of this I saw an instance with one of our officers.

At the present day, from the progress of civilization, there is much less warfare, except among some of the southern tribes. I heard a characteristic anecdote of what took place some time ago in the south. A missionary found a chief and his tribe in preparation for war;—their muskets clean and bright, and their ammunition ready. He reasoned long on the inutility of the war, and the little provocation which had been given for it. The chief was much shaken in his resolution, and seemed in doubt: but at length it occurred to him that a barrel of his gunpowder was in a bad state and that it would not keep much longer. This was brought forward as an unanswerable argument for the necessity of immediately declaring war: the idea of allowing so much good gunpowder to spoil was not to be thought of; and this settled the point. I was told by the missionaries that in the life of Shongi, the chief who visited England, the love of war was the one lasting spring of every action. The tribe in which he was a principal chief, had at one time been much oppressed by another tribe, from the Thames River. A solemn oath was taken by the men, that when their boys should grow up, and they should be powerful enough, they would never forget or forgive these injuries. To fulfil this oath appears to have been Shongi's chief motive for going to England; and when there it was his sole object. Presents were valued only as they could be converted into arms; of the arts, those alone interested him which were connected with the manufacture of arms. When at Sydney, Shongi, by a strange coincidence, met the hostile chief of the Thames River at the house of Mr. Marsden: their conduct was civil to each other; but Shongi told him that when again in New Zealand he would never cease to carry war into his country. The challenge was accepted; and Shongi on his return fulfilled the threat to the utmost letter. The tribe on the Thames River was utterly overthrown, and the chief to whom the challenge had been given was himself killed. Shongi, although harbouring such deep feelings of hatred and revenge, is described as having been a goodnatured person.

In the evening I went with Captain Fitz Roy and Mr. Baker, one of the missionaries, to pay a visit to Kororadika: we wandered about the village, and saw and conversed with many of the people, both men, women, and children. Looking at the New Zealander, one naturally compares him with the Tahitian; both belonging to the same family of mankind. The comparision, however, tells heavily against the New Zealander. He may, perhaps, be superior in energy, but in every other respect his character is of a much lower order. One glance at their respective expressions brings conviction to the mind that one is a savage, the other a civilized man. It would be vain to seek in the whole of New Zealand a person with the face and mien of the old Tahitian Chief Utamme. No doubt the extraordinary manner in which tattooing is here practised, gives a disagreeable expression to their countenances. The complicated but symmetrical figures covering the whole face, puzzle and mislead an unaccustomed eye: it is moreover probable, that the deep incisions, by destroying the play of the superficial muscles, give an air of rigid inflexibility. But, besides this, there is a twinkling in the eye, which cannot indicate any thing but cunning and ferocity. Their figures are tall and bulky; but not comparable in elegance with those of the working-classes in Tahiti.

Both their persons and houses are filthy dirty and offensive: the idea of washing either their bodies or their clothes never seems to enter their heads. I saw a chief, who was wearing a shirt black and matted with filth, and when asked how it came to be so dirty, he replied, with surprise, "Do not you see it is an old one?" Some of the men have shirts; but the common dress is one or two large blankets, generally black with dirt, which are thrown over the shoulders in a very inconvenient and awkward fashion. A few of the principal chiefs have decent suits of English clothes; but these are only worn on great occasions.

DECEMBER 23RD.—At a place called Waimate, about fifteen miles from the Bay of Islands, and midway between the eastern and western coasts, the missionaries have purchased some land for agricultural purposes. I had been introduced to the Rev. W. Williams, who, upon my expressing a wish, invited me to pay him a visit there. Mr. Bushby, the British resident, offered to take me in his boat by a creek, where I should see a pretty waterfall, and by which means my walk would be shortened. He likewise procured for me a guide. Upon asking a neighbouring chief to recommend a man, the chief himself offered to go; but his ignorance of the value of money was so complete, that at first he asked how many pounds I would give him, but afterwards was well contented with two dollars. When I showed the chief a very small bundle, which I wanted carried, it became absolutely necessary for him to take a slave. These feelings of pride are beginning to wear away; but formerly a leading man would sooner have died, than undergone the indignity of carrying the smallest burden. My companion was a light active man, dressed in a dirty blanket, and with his face completely tatooed. He had formerly been a great warrior. He appeared to be on very cordial terms with Mr. Bushby; but at various time they had quarrelled violently. Mr. Bushby remarked that a little quiet irony would frequently silence any one of these natives in their most blustering moments. This chief has come and harangued Mr. Bushby in a hectoring manner, saying, "A great chief, a great man, a friend of mine, has come to pay me a visit—you must give him something good to eat, some fine presents, etc." Mr. Bushby has allowed him to finish his discourse, and then has quietly replied by some such answer as, "What else shall your slave do for you?" The man would then instantly, with a very comical expression, cease his braggadocio.

Some time ago, Mr. Bushby suffered a far more serious attack. A chief and a party of men tried to break into his house in the middle of the night, and not finding this so easy, commenced a brisk firing with their muskets. Mr. Bushby was slightly wounded; but the party was at length driven away. Shortly afterwards it was discovered who was the aggressor; and a general meeting of the chiefs was convened to consider the case. It was considered by the New Zealanders as very atrocious, inasmuch as it was a night attack, and that Mrs. Bushby was lying ill in the house: this latter circumstance, much to their honour, being considered in all cases as a protection. The chiefs agreed to confiscate the land of the aggressor to the King of England. The whole proceeding, however, in thus trying and punishing a chief was entirely without precedent. The aggressor, moreover, lost caste in the estimation of his equals; and this was considered by the British as of more consequence than the confiscation of his land.

As the boat was shoving off, a second chief stepped into her, who only wanted the amusement of the passage up and down the creek. I never saw a more horrid and ferocious expression than this man had. It immediately struck me I had somewhere seen his likeness: it will be found in Retzch's outlines to Schiller's ballad of Fridolin, where two men are pushing Robert into the burning iron furnace. It is the man who has his arm on Robert's beast. Physiognomy here spoke the truth; this chief had been a notorious murderer, and was an arrant coward to boot. At the point where the boat landed Mr. Bushby accompanied me a few hundred yards on the road: I could not help admiring the cool impudence of the hoary old villain, whom we left lying in the boat, when he shouted to Mr. Bushby, "do not you stay long. I shall be tired of waiting here."

We now commenced our walk. The road lay along a well-beaten path, bordered on each side by the tall fern, which covers the whole country. After travelling some miles, we came to a little country village, where a few hovels were collected together, and some patches of ground cultivated with potatoes. The introduction of the potato has been the most essential benefit to the island; it is now much more used than any native vegetable. New Zealand is favoured by one great natural advantage; namely, that the inhabitants can never perish from famine. The whole country abounds with fern; and the roots of this plant, if not very palatable, yet contain much nutriment. A native can always subsist on these, and on the shell-fish, which are abundant on all parts of the sea-coast. The villages are chiefly conspicuous by the platforms which are raised on four posts ten or twelve feet above the ground, and on which the produce of the fields is kept secure from all accidents.

On coming near one of the huts I was much amused by seeing in due form the ceremony of rubbing, or, as it ought to be called, pressing noses. The women, on our first approach, began uttering something in a most dolorous voice; they then squatted themselves down and held up their faces; my companion standing over them, one after another, placed the bridge of his nose at right angles to theirs, and commenced pressing. This lasted rather longer than a cordial shake of the hand with us; and as we vary the force of the grasp of the hand in shaking, so do they in pressing. During the process they uttered comfortable little grunts, very much in the same manner as two pigs do, when rubbing against each other. I noticed that the slave would press noses with any one he met, indifferently either before or after his master the chief. Although among these savages, the chief has absolute power of life and death over his slave, yet there is an entire absence of ceremony between them. Mr. Burchell has remarked the same thing in Southern Africa, with the rude Bachapins. Where civilization has arrived at a certain point, complex formalities soon arise be-

tween the different grades of society: thus at Tahiti all were formerly obliged to uncover themselves as low as the waist in presence of the king.

The ceremony of pressing noses having been duly completed
with all present, we seated ourselves in a circle in the front of one
of the hovels, and rested there half-an-hour. All the hovels have
nearly the same form and dimensions, and all agree in being fil-
thily dirty. They resemble a cow-shed with one end open, but
having a partition a little way within, with a square hole in it,
making a small gloomy chamber. In this the inhabitants keep all
their property, and when the weather is cold they sleep there.
They eat, however, and pass their time in the open part in front.
My guides having finished their pipes, we continued our walk. The
path led through the same undulating country, the whole uni-
formly clothed as before with fern. On our right had we had a
serpentine river, the banks of which were fringed with trees, and
here and there on the hill sides there was a clump of wood. The
whole scene, in spite of its green colour, had rather a desolate
aspect. The sight of so much fern impresses the mind with a idea
of sterility: this, however, is not correct; for wherever the fern grows
thick and breast-high, the land by tillage becomes productive. Some
of the residents think that all this extensive open country originally was covered with forests, and that it has been cleared by
fire. It is said, that by digging in the barest spots, lumps of the
kind of resin which flows from the kauri pine are frequently found.
The natives had an evident motive in clearing the country; for the
fern, formerly a staple article of food, flourishes only in the open
cleared tracks. The almost entire absence of associated grasses,
which forms so remarkable a feature in the vegetation of this island, may perhaps be acounted for the land having been aboriginally covered with forest-trees.

The soil is volcanic; in several parts we passed over slaggy la-
vas, and craters could clearly be distinguished on several of the
neighbouring hills. Although the scenery is nowhere beautiful, and
only occasionally pretty, I enjoyed my walk. I should have enjoyed it more, if my companion, the chief, had not possessed ex-

traordinary conversational powers. I knew only three words; "good," "bad," and "yes:" and with these I answered all his remarks, without of course having understood one word he said. This, however, was quite sufficient: I was a good listener, an agreeable person, and he never ceased talking to me.

At length we reached Waimate. After having passed over so many miles of an uninhabited useless country, the sudden appearance of an English farm-house, and its well-dressed fields, placed there as if by an enchanter's wand, was exceedingly pleasant. Mr. Williams not being at home, I received in Mr. Davies's house, a cordial welcome. After drinking tea with his family party, we took a stroll about the farm. At Waimate there are three large houses, where the missionary gentlemen Messrs. Williams, Davies, and Clarke, reside; and near them are the huts of the native labourers. On an adjoining slope, fine crops of barley and wheat were standing in full ear; and in another part, fields of potatoes and clover. But I cannot attempt to describe all I saw; there were large gardens, with every fruit and vegetable which England produces; and many belonging to a warmer clime. I may instance asparagus, kidney beans, cucumbers, rhubarb, apples, pears, figs, peaches, apricots, grapes, olives, gooseberries, currants, hops, gorse for fences, and English oaks; also many kinds of flowers. Around the farm-yard there were stables, a thrashing-barn with its winnowing machine, and blacksmith's forge, and on the ground ploughshares and other tools: in the middle was that happy mixture of pigs and poultry, laying comfortably together, as in every English farm-yard. At the distance of a few hundred yards, where the water of a little rill had been dammed up into a pool, there was a large and substantial water-mill.

All this is very surprising, when it is considered that five years ago, nothing but the fern flourished here. Moreover, native workmanship, taught by the missionaries, has effected this change;— the lesson of the missionary is the enchanter's wand. The house had been built, the windows framed, the fields ploughed, and even the trees grafted by the New Zealander. At the mill, a New Zealander was seen powdered white with flour, like his brother miller in England. When I looked at this whole scene, I thought it admirable. It was not merely that England was brought vividly before my mind; yet, as the evening drew to a close, the domestic sounds, the fields of corn, the distant undulating country with its trees might well have been mistaken for our father-land: nor was it the triumphant feeling at seeing what Englishmen could effect; but rather the high hopes thus inspired for the future progress of this fine island.

Several young men, redeemed by the missionaries from slavery, were employed on the farm. They were dressed in a shirt, jacket, and trousers, and had a respectable appearance. Judging from one trifling anecdote, I should think they must be honest. When walking in the fields, a young labourer came up to Mr. Davies, and gave him a knife and gimlet, saying that he had found them on the road and did not know to whom they belonged! These young men and boys appeared very merry and good-humoured. In the evening I saw a party of them at cricket: when I thought of the austerity of which the missionaries have been accused, I was amused by observing one of their own sons taking an active part in the game. A more decided and pleasing change was manifested in the young women, who acted as servants within the houses. Their clean, tidy, and healthy appearance, like that of dairymaids in England, formed a wonderful contrast with the women of the filthy hovels in Kororadika. The wives of the missionaries tried to perusade them not to be tattooed; but a famous operator having arrived from the south, they said, "we really must just have a few lines on our lips; else when we grow old, our lips will shrivel, and we shall be so very ugly." There is not nearly so much tattooing as formerly; but as it is a badge of distinction between the chief and the slave, it will probably long be practised. So soon does any train of ideas become habitual, that the missionaries told me that even in their eyes a plain face looked mean, and not like that of a New Zealand gentleman.

Late in the evening I went to Mr. Williams's house, where I passed the night. I found there a large party of children, collected together for Christmas-day, and all sitting round a table at tea. I never saw a nicer or more merry group; and to think that this was in the centre of the land of cannibalism, murder, and all atrocious crimes! The cordiality and happiness so plainly pictured in the faces of the little circle, appeared equally felt by the older persons of the mission.

DECEMBER 24TH.—In the morning, prayers were read in the native tongue to the whole family. After breakfast I rambled about the gardens and farm. This was a market-day, when the natives of the surrounding hamlets bring their potatoes, Indian corn, or pigs, to exchange for blankets, tobacco, and sometimes, through the persuasions of the missionaries, for soap. Mr. Davies's eldest son, who manages a farm of his own, is the man of business in the market. The children of the missionaries, who came while young to the island, understand the language better than their parents, and can get anything more readily done by the natives. . . .

CHRISTMAS-DAY.—In a few more days the fourth year of our absence from England will be completed. Our first Christmas-day was spent at Plymouth; the second at St. Martin's Cove, near Cape Horn; the third at Port Desire, in Patagonia; the fourth at anchor in a wild harbour in the peninsula of Tres Montes; this fifth here; and the next, I trust in Providence, will be in England. We attended divine service in the chapel of Pahia; part of the service being read in English, and part in the native language. Whilst at New Zealand we did not hear of any recent acts of cannibalism; but Mr. Stokes found burnt human bones strewed round a fireplace on a small island near the anchorage; but these remains of a comfortable banquet might have been lying there for several years. It is probable that the moral state of the people will rapidly improve. Mr. Bushby mentioned one pleasing anecdote as a proof of the sincerity of some, at least, of those who profess Christianity. One of his young men left him, who had been accustomed to read prayers to the rest of the servants. Some weeks afterwards, happening to pass late in the evening by an outhouse, he saw and heard one of his men reading the Bible with difficulty by the light of the fire, to the others. After this the party knelt and prayed: in their prayers they mentioned Mr. Bushby and his family, and the missionaries, each separately in his respective district.

DECEMBER 26TH.—Mr. Bushby offered to take Mr. Sulivan and myself in his boat some miles up the river to Cawa-Cawa; and proposed afterwards to walk on to the village of Waiomio, where there are some curious rocks. Following one of the arms of the bay, we enjoyed a pleasant row, and passed through pretty scenery, until we came to a village, beyond which the boat could not pass. From this place a chief and a party of men volunteered to walk with us to Waiomio, a distance of four miles. The chief was at this time rather notorious from having lately hung one of his wives and a slave for adultery. When one of the missionaries remonstrated with him he seemed surprised, and said he thought he was exactly following the English method. Old Shongi, who happened to be in England during the Queen's trial, expressed great disapprobation at the whole proceeding: he said he had five wives, and he would rather cut off all their heads than be so much troubled about one. Leaving this village, we crossed over to another, seated on a hill-side at a little distance. The daughter of a chief, who was still a heathen, had died there five days before. The hovel in which she had expired had been burnt to the ground: her body being enclosed between two small canoes, was placed upright on the ground, and protected by an enclosure bearing wooden images of their gods, and the whole was painted bright red, so as to be conspicuous from afar. Her gown was fastened to the coffin, and her hair being cut off was cast at its foot. The relatives of the family had torn the flesh of their arms, bodies, and faces, so that they were covered with clotted blood; and the old women looked most filthy, disgusting objects. On the following day some of the officers visited this place, and found the women still howling and cutting themselves.

We continued our walk, and soon reached Waiomio. Here there are some singular masses of limestone, resembling ruined castles. These rocks have long served for burial-places, and in consequence are held too sacred to be approached. One of the young men, however, cried out, "Let us all be brave," and ran on ahead; but when within a hundred yards, the whole party thought better of it, and stopped short. With perfect indifference, however, they allowed us to examine the whole place. At this village we rested some hours, during which time there was a long discussion with Mr. Bushby, concerning the right of sale of certain lands. One old man, who appeared a perfect genealogist, illustrated the successive possessors by bits of stick driven into the ground. Before leaving the houses a little basketful of roasted sweet potatoes was given to each of our party; and we all, according to the custom, carried them away to eat on the road. I noticed that among the women employed in cooking, there was a man-slave: it must be a humiliating thing for a man in this warlike country to be employed in doing that which is considered as the lowest woman's work. Slaves are not allowed to go to war; but this perhaps can hardly be considered as a hardship. I heard of one poor wretch who, during hostilities, ran away to the opposite party; being met by two men, he was immediately seized; but as they could not agree to whom he should belong, each stood over him with a stone hatchet, and seemed determined that the other at least should not take him away alive. The poor man, almost dead with fright, was only saved by the address of a chief's wife. We afterwards enjoyed a pleasant walk back to the boat, but did not reach the ship till late in the evening.

DECEMBER 30TH.—In the afternoon we stood out of the Bay of Islands, on our course to Sidney. I believe we were all glad to leave New Zealand. It is not a pleasant place. Amongst the natives there is absent that charming simplicity which is found at Tahiti; and the greater part of the English are the very refuse of society. Neither is the country attractive. I look back but to one bright spot, and that is Waimate, with its Christian inhabitants.

Australia

JANUARY 12TH. 1836.—. . . At sunset, a party of a score of the black aborigines passed by, each carrying, in their accustomed manner, a bundle of spears and other weapons. By giving a leading young man a shilling, they were easily detained, and threw their spears for my amusement. They were all partly clothed, and several could speak a little English: their countenances were good-humoured and pleasant, and they appeared far from being such utterly degraded beings as they have usually been represented. In their own arts they are admirable. A cap being fixed at thirty yards distance, they transfixed it with a spear, delivered by the throwing-stick with the rapidity of an arrow from the bow of a practiced archer. In tracking animals or men they show most wonderful sagacity; and I heard of several of their remarks which manifested considerable acuteness. They will not, however, cultivate the ground, or build houses and remain stationary, or even take the trouble of tending a flock of sheep when given to them. On the whole they appear to me to stand some few degress higher in the scale of civilization than the Fuegians.

It is very curious thus to see in the midst of a civilized people, a set of harmless savages wandering about without knowing where they shall sleep at night, and gaining their livelihood by hunting in the woods. As the white man has travelled onwards, he has spread over the country belonging to several tribes. These, although thus enclosed by one common people, keep up their ancient distinctions, and sometimes go to war with each other. In an engagement which took place lately, the two parties most singularly chose the centre of the village of Bathurst for the field of battle. This was of service to the defeated side, for the runaway warriors took refuge in the barracks.

The number of aborigines is rapidly decreasing. In my whole ride, with the exception of some boys brought up by Englishmen, I saw only one other party. This decrease, no doubt, must be partly owing to the introduction of spirits, to European diseases (even the milder ones of which, such as the measles, prove very destructive), and to the gradual extinction of the wild animals. It is said that numbers of their children invariably perish in very early infancy from the effects of their wandering life; and as the difficulty of procuring food increases, so must their wandering habits increase; and hence the population, without any apparent deaths from famine, is repressed in a manner extremely sudden compared to what happens in civilized countries, where the father, though in adding to his labour he may injure himself, does not destroy his off-spring.

Besides these several evident causes of destruction, there appears to be some more mysterious agency generally at work. Wherever the European has trod, death seems to pursue the aboriginal. We may look to the wide extent of the Americas, Polynesia, the Cape of Good Hope, and Australia, and we find the same result. Nor is it the white man alone that thus acts the destroyer; the Polynesian of Malay extraction has in parts of the East Indian archipelago, thus driven before him the dark-coloured native. The varieties of man seem to act on each other in the same way as different species of animals—the stronger always extirpating the weaker. It was melancholy at New Zealand to hear the fine energetic natives saying, that they knew the land was doomed to pass from their children. Every one has heard of the inexplicable reduction of the population in the beautiful and healthy island of Tahiti since the date of Captain Cook's voyages: although in that case we might have expected that it would have been increased; for infanticide, which formerly prevailed to so extraordinary a degree, has ceased, profligacy has greatly diminished, and the murderous wars become less frequent.

The Rev. J. Williams, in his interesing work, says, that the first intercourse between natives and Europeans, "is invariably attended with the introduction of fever, dysentery, or some other disease, which carries off numbers of the people." Again he affirms, "It is certainly a fact, which cannot be controverted, that most of the diseases which have raged in the islands during my residence there, have been introduced by ships; and what renders this fact remarkable is, that there might be no appearance of disease among the crew of the ship which conveyed this destructive importation." This statement is not quite so extraordinary as it at first appears; for several cases are on record of the most malignant fevers having broken out, although the parties themselves, who were the cause, were not affected. In the early part of the reign of George III., a prisoner who had been confined in a dungeon, was taken in a coach with four constables before a magistrate; and, although the man himself was not ill, the four constables died from a short putrid fever; but the contagion extended to no others. From these facts it would almost appear as if the effluvium of one set of men shut up for some time together was poisonous when inhaled by others, and possibly more so, if the men be of different races. Mysterious as this circumstance appears to be, it is not more surprising than that the body of one's fellow-creature, directly after death, and before putrefaction has commenced, should often be of so deleterious a quality, that the mere puncture from an instrument used in its dissection should prove fatal. . . .

JANUARY 22ND.—. . . The rapid prosperity and future prospects of this colony are to me, not understanding these subjects, very puzzling. The two main exports are wool and whale-oil, and to both of these productions there is a limit. The country is totally unfit for canals, therefore there is not a very distant point, beyond which the land-carriage of wool will not repay the expense of shearing and tending sheep. Pasture everywhere is so thin that settlers have already pushed far into the interior: moreover, the country further inland becomes extremely poor. Agriculture, on account of the droughts, can never succeed on an extended scale: therefore, so far as I can see, Australia must ultimately depend upon being the centre of commerce for the southern hemisphere, and perhaps on her future manufactories. Possessing coal, she always has the moving power at hand. From the habitable country extending along the coast, and from her English extraction, she is sure to be a maritime nation. I formerly imagined that Australia would rise to be as grand and powerful a country as North America, but now it appears to me that such future grandeur is rather problematical.

With respect to the state of the convicts, I had still fewer opportunities of judging than on the other points. The first question is, whether their condition is at all one of punishment: no one will maintain that it is a very severe one. This, however, I suppose, is of little consequence as long as it continues to be an object of dread to criminals at home. The corporeal wants of the convicts are tolerably well supplied: their prospect of future liberty and comfort is not distant, and after good conduct certain. A "ticket of leave," which, as long as a man keeps clear of suspicion as well as of crime, makes him free within a certain district, is given upon good conduct, after years proportional to the length of the sentence; yet with all this, and overlooking the previous imprisonment and wretched passage out, I believe the years of assignment are passed away with discontent and unhappiness. As an intelligent man remarked to me, the convicts know no pleasure beyond sensuality, and in this they are not gratified. The enormous bribe which Government possesses in offering free pardons, together with the deep horror of the secluded penal settlements, destroys confidence between the convicts, and so prevents crime. As to a sense of shame, such a feeling does not appear to be known, and of this I witnessed some very singular proofs. Though it is a curious fact, I was universally told that the character of the convict population is one of arrant cowardice: not unfrequently some become desperate and quite indifferent as to life, yet a plan requiring cool or continued courage is seldom put into execution. The worst feature in the whole case is, that although there exists what may be called a legal reform, and comparatively little is committed which the law can touch, yet that any moral reform should take place appears to be quite out of the question. I was assured by well-informed people, that a man who should try to improve, could not while living with other assigned servants;—his life would be one of intolerable misery and persecution. Nor must the contamination of the convict-ships and prisons, both here and in England be forgotten. On the whole, as a place of punishment, the object is scarcely gained; as a real system of reform it has failed, as perhaps would every other plan; but as a means of making men outwardly honest,—of converting vagabonds, most useless in one hemisphere, into active citizens of another, and thus giving birth to a new and splendid country—a grand centre of civilization—it has succeeded to a degree perhaps unparalleled in history.

JANUARY 30TH.—The Beagle sailed for Hobart Town in Van Diemen's Land [Tasmania]. On the 5th of February after a six days' passage, of which the first part was fine, and the latter very cold and squally, we entered the mouth of Storm Bay: the weather justified this awful name. The bay should rather be called an estuary, for it receives at its head the waters of the Derwent. . . .

All the aborigines have been removed to an island in Bass's Straits, so that Van Diemen's Land enjoys the great advantage of being free from a native population. This most cruel step seems to have been quite unavoidable, as the only means of stopping a fearful succession of robberies, burnings, and murders, committed by the blacks; and which sooner or later would have ended in their utter destruction. I fear there is no doubt, that this train of evil and its consequences, originated in the infamous conduct of some of our countrymen. Thrity years is a short period, in which to have banished the last aboriginal from his native island,—and that island nearly as large as Ireland. The correspondence on this subject, which took place between the government at home and that of Van Diemen's Land, is very interesting. Although numbers of natives were shot and taken prisoners in the skirmishing, which was going on at intervals for several years; nothing seems fully to have impressed them with the idea of our overwhelming power, until the whole island, in 1830, was put under martial law, and by proclamation the whole population commanded to assist in one great attempt to secure the entire race. The plan adopted was nearly similar to that of the great hunting-matches in India: A line was formed reaching across the island, with the intention of driving the natives into a *cul-de sac* on Tasman's peninsula. The attempt failed; the natives, having tied up their dogs, stole during one night through the lines. This is far from surprising, when their practised senses, and usual manner of crawling after wild animals is considered. I have been assured that they can conceal themselves on almost bare ground, in a manner which until witnessed is scarcely credible; their dusky bodies being easily mistaken for the blackened stumps which are scattered all over the country. I was told of a trial between a party of Englishmen and a native, who was to stand in full view on the side of a bare hill; if the Englishmen closed their eyes for less than a minute, he would squat down, and then they were never able to distinguish him from the surrounding stumps. But to return to the hunting-match; the natives understanding this kind of warfare, were terribly alarmed, for they at once perceived the power and numbers of the whites. Shortly afterwards a party of thirteen belonging to two tribes came in; and, conscious of their unprotected condition, delivered themselves up in despair. Subsequently by the intrepid exertions of Mr. Robinson, an active and benevolent man, who fearlessly visited by himself the most hostile of the natives, the whole were induced to act in a similar manner. They were then removed to an island, where food and clothes were provided them. Count Strzelecki states, that "at the epoch of their deportation in 1835, the number of natives amounted to 210. In 1842, that is after the interval of seven years, they mustered only fifty-four individuals; and, while each family of the interior of New South Wales, uncontaminated by contact with the whites, swarms with children, those of Flinders' Island had during eight years, an accession of only fourteen in number!". . .

FEBURARY 7TH.—[Australia] . . . A large tribe of natives, called the White Cockatoo men, happened to pay the settlement a visit while we were there. These men, as well as those of the tribe belonging to King George's Sound, being tempted by the offer of some tubs of rice and sugar, were persuaded to hold a 'corrobery," or great dancing-party. As soon as it grew dark, small fires were lighted, and the men commenced their toilet, which consisted in painting themselves white in spots and lines. As soon as all was ready, large fires were kept blazing, round which the women and children were collected as spectators; the Cockatoo and King George's men formed two distinct parties, and generally danced in answer to each other. The dancing consisted in their running either sideways or in Indian file into an open space, and stamping the ground with great force as they marched together. Their heavy footsteps were accompanied by a kind of grunt, by beating their clubs and spears together, and by various other gesticulations, such as extending their arms and wriggling their bodies. It was a most rude, barbarous scene, and, to our ideas, without any sort of meaning; but we observed that the black women and children watched it with the greatest pleasure. Perhaps these dances originally represented actions, such as wars and victories; there was one called the Emu dance, in which each man extended his arm in a bent manner, like the neck of that bird. In another dance, one man imitated the movements of a kangaroo grazing in the woods, whilst a second crawled up, and pretended to spear him. When both tribes mingled in the dance, the ground trembled with the heaviness of their steps, and the air resounded with their wild cries. Every one appeared in high spirits, and the group of nearly naked figures, viewed by the light of the blazing fires, all moving in hideous harmony, formed a perfect display of a festival amongst the lowest barbarians. In Tierra del Fuego, we have beheld many curious scenes in savage life, but never, I think, one where the natives were in such high spirits, and so perfectly at their ease. After the dancing was over, the whole party formed a great circle on the ground, and the boiled rice and sugar was distributed, to the delight of all.

After several tedious delays from clouded weather, on the 14th of March, we gladly stood out of King George's Sound on our course to Keeling Island. Farewell, Australia! you are a rising child, and doubtless some day will reign a great princess in the South: but you are too great and ambitious for affection, yet not great enough for respect. I leave your shore without sorrow or regret.

On the 19th of August we finally left the shores of Brazil. I thank God, I shall never again visit a slave-country. To this day, if I hear a distant scream, it recalls with painful vividness my feelings, when passing a house near Pernambuco, I heard the most pitiable moans, and could not but suspect that some poor slave was being tortured, yet knew that I was as powerless as a child even to remonstrate. I suspected that these moans were from a tortured slave, for I was told that this was the case in another instance. Near Rio de Janeiro I lived opposite to an old lady, who kept screws to crush the fingers of her female slaves. I have staid in a house where a young household mulatto, daily and hourly, was reviled, beaten, and persecuted enough to break the spirit of the lowest animal. I have seen a little boy, six or seven years old, struck thrice with a horse-whip (before I could interfere) on his naked head, for having handed me a glass of water not quite clean; I saw his father tremble at a mere glance from his master's eye. These latter cruelties were witnessed by me in a Spanish colony, in which it has always been said, that slaves are better treated than by the Portuguese, English, or other European nations. I have seen at Rio Janeiro a powerful negro afraid to ward off a blow directed, as he thought, at his face. I was present when a kind-hearted man was on the point of separating forever the men, women, and little children of a large number of families who had long lived together. I will not even allude to the many heart-sickening atrocities which I authentically heard of;—nor would I have mentioned the above revolting details, had I not met with several people, so blinded by the constitutional gaiety of the negro, as to speak of slavery as a tolerable evil. Such people have generally visited at the houses of the upper classes, where the domestic slaves are usually well treated; and they have not, like myself, lived amongst the lower classes. Such enquirers will ask slaves about their condition; they forget that the slave must indeed be dull, who does not calculate on the chance of his answer reaching his master's ear.

It is argued that self-interest will prevent excessive cruelty; as if self-interest protected our domestic animals, which are far less likely than degraded slaves, to stir up the rage of their savage masters. It is an argument long since protested against with noble feeling, and strikingly exemplified, by the ever illustrious Humboldt. It is often attempted to palliate slavery by comparing the state of slaves with our poorer countrymen: if the misery of our poor be caused not by the laws of nature, but by our institutions, great is our sin; but how this bears on slavery, I cannot see; as well might the use of the thumbscrew be defended in one land, by showing that men in another land suffered from some dreadful disease. Those who look tenderly at the slave-owner, and with a cold heart at the slave, never seem to put themselves into the position of the latter;—what a cheerless prospect, with not even a hope of change! Picture to yourself the chance, ever hanging over you, of your wife and your little children—those objects which nature urges even the slave to call his own—being torn from you and sold like beasts to the first bidder! And these deeds are done and palliated by men, who profess to love their neighbours as themselves, who believe in God, and pray that his Will be done on Earth! It makes one's blood boil, yet heart tremble, to think that we Englishmen and our American descendants, with their boastful cry of liberty, have been and are so guilty: but it is a consolation to reflect, that we at least have made a greater sacrifice, than ever made by any nation to expiate our sin.

THE DESCENT OF MAN

2. The sole object of this work is to consider, firstly, whether man, like every other species, is descended from some preexisting form; secondly, the manner of his development; and thirdly, the value of the differences between the so-called races of man.

3. During many years it has seemed to me highly probable that sexual selection has played an important part in differentiating the races of man; but in my 'Origin of Species' I contented myself by merely alluding to this belief. When I came to apply this view to man, I found it indispensable to treat the whole subject in full detail. Consequently the second part of the present work, treating of sexual selection, has extended to an inordinate length, compared with the first part; but this could not be avoided.

5–6. The enquirer would next come to the important point whether man tends to increase at so rapid a rate, as to lead to occasional severe struggles for existence; and consequently to beneficial variations, whether in body or mind, being preserved, and injurious ones eliminated. Do the races or species of men, whichever term may be applied, encroach on and replace one another, so that some finally become extinct? We shall see that all these questions, as indeed is obvious in respect to most of them, must be answered in the affirmative, in the same manner as with the lower animals.

27. The variability or diversity of the mental faculties in men of the same race, not to mention the greater differences between the men of distinct races, is so notorious that not a word need here be said.

28. . . . So in regard to mental qualities, their transmission is manifested in our dogs, horses, and other domestic animals. Be-

sides special tastes and habits, general intelligence, courage, bad
and good temper, etc., are certainly transmitted. With man we
see similar facts in almost every family; and we now know, through
the admirable labours of Mr. Galton, that genius which implies a
wonderfully complex combination of high faculties, tends to be inherited; and, on the other hand, it is too certain that insanity and
deteriorated mental powers likewise run in families.

With respect to the causes of variability, we are in all cases very
ignorant; but we can see that in man as in the lower animals, they
stand in some relation to the conditions to which each species has
been exposed, during several generations. Domesticated animals
vary more than those in a state of nature; and this is apparently
due to the diversified and changing nature of the conditions to
which they have been subjected. In this respect the different races
of man resemble domesticated animals, and so do the individuals
of the same race, when inhabiting a very wide area, like that of
America. We see the influence of diversified conditions in the more
civilized nations; for the members belonging to different grades of
rank, and following different occupations, present a greater range
of character than do the members of barbarous nations. But the
uniformity of savages has often been exaggerated, and in some cases
can hardly be said to exist. It is, nevertheless, an error to speak
of man, even if we look on to the conditions to which he has been
exposed, as "far more domesticated" than any other animal. Some
savage races, such as the Australians, are not exposed to more diversified conditions than are many species which have a wide range.
In another and much more important respect, man differs widely
from any strictly domesticated animal; for his breeding has never
long been controlled, either by methodical or unconscious selection. No race or body of men has been so completely subjugated
by other men, as that certain individuals should be preserved, and
thus unconsciously selected, from somehow excelling in utility to
their masters. Nor have certain male and female individuals been
intentionally picked out and matched, except in the well-known
case of the Prussian grenadiers; and in this case man obeyed, as
might have been expected, the law of methodical selection; for it

is asserted that many tall men were reared in the villages inhabited by the grenadiers and their tall wives. In Sparta, also, a form of selection was followed, for it was enacted that all children should be examined shortly after birth; the well-formed and vigorous being preserved, the others left to perish.

If we consider all the races of man as forming a single species, his range is enormous; but some separate races, as the Americans and Polynesians, have very wide ranges. It is a well-known law that widely-ranging species are much more variable than species with restricted ranges; and the variability of man may with more truth be compared with that of widely-ranging species, than with that of domesticated animals.

32. Whether the several foregoing modifications would become hereditary, if the same habits of life were followed during many generations, is not known, but it is probable.

33. It is familiar to every one that watchmakers and engravers are liable to be short-sighted, whilst men living much out of doors, and especially savages, are generally long-sighted. Short-sight and long-sight certainly tend to be inherited. The inferiority of Europeans, in comparison with savages, in eyesight and in the other senses, is no doubt the accumulated and transmitted effect of lessened use during many generations; for Rengger states that he has repeatedly observed Europeans, who had been brought up and spent their whole lives with the wild Indians, who nevertheless did not equal them in the sharpness of their senses.

35....Consequently we may infer that when at a remote epoch the progenitors of man were in a transitional state, and were changing from quadrupeds into bipeds, natural selection would probably have been greatly aided by the inherited effects of the increased or diminished use of the different parts of the body.

45. There is reason to suspect, as Malthus has remarked, that the reproductive power is actually less in barbarous, than in civilised races. We know nothing positively on this head, for with savages no census has been taken; but from the concurrent testimony of missionaries, and of others who have long resided with such people, it appears that their families are usually small, and large ones rare. This may be partly accounted for, as it is believed, by the women suckling their infants during a long time; but it is highly probable that savages, who often suffer much hardship, and who do not obtain so much nutritious food as civilized men, would be actually less prolific. . . . We might, therefore, expect that civilised men, who in one sense are highly domesticated, would be more prolific than wild men. It is also probable that the increased fertility of civilised nations would become, as with our domestic animals, an inherited character; it is at least known that with mankind a tendency to produce twins runs in families.

Notwithstanding that savages appear to be less prolific than civilised people, they would no doubt rapidly increase if their numbers were not by some means rigidly kept down. The Santali, or hill-tribes of India, have recently afforded a good illustration of this fact . . . [as] they have increased at an extraordinary rate since vaccination has been introduced, other pestilences mitigated, and war sternly repressed. This increase, however, would not have been possible had not these rude people spread into the adjoining districts, and worked for hire. Savages almost always marry; yet there is some prudential restraint, for they do not commonly marry at the earliest possible age. The young men are often required to shew that they can support a wife; and they generally have first to earn the price with which to purchase her from her parents. With savages the difficulty of obtaining subsistence occasionally limits their number in a much more direct manner than with civilized people, for all tribes periodically suffer from severe famines. . . .

Malthus had discussed these several checks, but he does not lay stress enough on what is probably the most important of all, namely infanticide, especially of female infants, and the habit of procuring abortion. . . . These practices appear to have originated in savages recognising the difficulty, or rather the impossibility of supporting all the infants that are born. Licentiousness may also be added to the forgoing checks; but this does not follow from failing means of subsistence; though there is reason to believe that in some cases (as in Japan) it has been intentionally encouraged as a means of keeping down the population. . . .

If we look back to an extremely remote epoch, before man had arrived at the dignity of manhood, he would have been guided more by instinct and less by reason than are the lowest savages at the present time. Our early semi-human progenitors would not have practiced infanticide or polyandry; for the instincts of the lower animals are never so perverted as to lead them regularly to destroy their own offspring, or to be quite devoid of jealousy. There would have been no prudential restraint from marriage, and the sexes would have freely united at an early age. Hence the progenitors of man would have tended to increase rapidly; but checks of some kind, either periodical or constant, must have kept down their numbers, even more severely than with existing savages.

47. *Natural Selection*—We have now seen that man is variable in body and mind; and that the variations induced, either directly or indirectly, by the same general causes, and obey the same general laws, as with the lower animals. Man has spread widely over the face of the earth, and must have been exposed, during his incessant migrations, to the most diversified conditions.

48. Man in the rudest state in which he now exists is the most dominant animal that has ever appeared on this earth. He has spread more widely that [sic] any other highly organised form: and all others have yielded before him. He manifestly owes this immense superiority to his intellectual faculties, to his social habits, which lead him to aid and defend his fellows, and to his corporeal structure. The supreme importance of these characters has been proved by the final arbitrament of the battle for life. Through his powers of intellect, articulate language has been evolved; and on this his wonderful advancement has mainly depended. . . . He has invented and is able to use various weapons, tools, traps, etc., with which he defends himself, kills or catches prey, and otherwise obtains food. He has made rafts or canoes for fishing or crossing over to neighbouring fertile islands. He has discovered the art of making fire, by which hard and stringy roots can be rendered digestible, and poisonous roots or herbs innocuous. This discovery of fire, probably the greatest ever made by man, excepting language, dates from before the dawn of history. These several inventions, by which man in the rudest state has become so preeminent, are the direct results of the development of his powers of observation, memory, curiosity, imagination, and reason. I cannot, therefore, understand how it is that Mr. Wallace maintains, that "natural selection could only have endowed the savage with a brain a little superior to that of an ape."

54. The belief that there exists in man some close relation between the size of the brain and the development of the intellectual faculties is supported by the comparision of the skulls of savage and civilised races, of ancient and modern people, and by the analogy of the whole vetebrate series. . . . Nevertheless, it must be admitted that some skulls of very high antiquity, such as the famous one of Neanderthal, are well developed and capacious. . . .

62. Judging from the habits of savages and of the greater number of the Quadrumana, primeval men, and even their ape-like progenitors, probably lived in society. With strictly social animals, natural selection sometimes acts on the individual, through the preservation of variations which are beneficial to the community. A community which includes a large number of well-endowed individuals increases in number, and is victorious over other less favoured ones; even although each separate member gains no advantage over the others of the same community. Associated insects have thus acquired many remarkable structures, which are of little or no service to the individual, such as the pollen-collecting apparatus, or the sting of the worker-bee, or the great jaws of soldier ants. With the higher social animals, I am not aware that any structure has been modified solely for the good of the community, though some are of secondary service to it. . . . In regard to certain mental powers the case . . . is wholly different; for these faculties have been chiefly, or even exclusively, gained for the benefit of the community, and the individuals thereof, have at the same time gained an advantage indirectly.

64. The small strength and speed of man, his want of natural weapons, etc., are more than counterbalanced, firstly, by his intellectual powers, through which he has formed for himself weapons, tools, etc., though still remaining in a barbarous state, and secondly, by his social qualities which lead him to give and recieve aid from his fellow-men. No country of the world abounds in a greater degree with dangerous beasts than Southern Africa; no country presents more fearful physical hardships than the Artic regions; yet one of the puniest of races, that of the Bushmen, maintains itself in Southern Africa, as do the dwarfed Esquimaux in the Arctic regions. The ancestors of man were, no doubt, inferior in intellect, and probably in social disposition, to the lowest existing savages; but it is quite conceivable that they might have existed, or even flourished, if they had advanced in intellect, whilst gradually losing their brute-like powers, such as that of climbing trees, etc. But these ancestors would not have been exposed to any special danger, even if far more helpless and defenceless than any existing savages, had they inhabited some warm continent or large island, such as Australia, New Guinea, or Borneo, which is now the home of the orang. And natural selection arising from competition of tribe with tribe, in some such large area as one of these, together with the inherited effects of habit, would, under favorable conditions, have sufficed to raise man to his present high position in the organic scale.

65. We have seen in the last two chapters that man bears in his bodily structure clear traces of his descent from some lower form; but it may be urged that, as man differs so greatly in his mental powers from all other animals, there must be some error in this conclusion. No doubt the difference in this respect is enormous, even if we compare the mind of one of the lowest savages, who has no words to express any number higher than four, and who uses hardly any abstract terms for common objects or for the affections, with that of the most highly organized ape. The difference would, no doubt, still remain immense, even if one of the higher apes had been improved or civilized as much as a dog has been in comparision with its parent-form, the wolf or jackal. The Fuegians rank amongst the lowest barbarians; but I was continually struck with surprise how closely the three natives on board H.M.S. "Beagle," who had lived some years in England and could talk a little English, resembled us in disposition and in most of our mental faculties. . . .

Nor is the difference slight in moral disposition between a barbarian, such as the man described by the old navigator Byron, who dashed his child on the rocks for dropping a basket of sea-urchins, and a Howard or a Clarkson; and in intellect, between a savage who uses hardly any abstract terms, and a Newton or a Shakespeare. Differences of this kind between the highest men of the highest races and the lowest savages, are connected by the finest gradations. Therefore it is possible they might pass and be developed into each other.

My object in this chapter is to shew that there is no fundamental difference between man and the higher mammals in their mental facilities. . . .

As man possesses the same sense as the lower animals, his fundamental intuitions must be the same. Man has also some few instincts in common, as that of self-preservation, sexual love, the love of a mother for her new-born offspring, the desire possessed by the latter to suck, and so forth. But man, perhaps, has somewhat fewer instincts than those possessed by the animals which come next to him in the series.

67. The fewness and the comparative simplicity of the instincts in the higher animals are remarkable in contrast with those of the lower animals. . . .

Although the first dawnings of intelligence, according to Mr. Herbert Spencer, have been developed through the multiplication and co-ordination of reflex actions, and although many of the simpler instincts graduate into reflex actions, and can hardly be distiguished from them, as in the case of young animals sucking, yet the more complex instincts seem to have originated independently of intelligence. I am, however, very far from wishing to deny that instinctive actions may lose their fixed and untaught character, and be replaced by others performed by the aid of the free will. On the other hand, some intelligent actions, after being performed during several generations, become converted into instincts and are inherited, as when birds on oceanic islands learn to avoid man. These actions may then be said to be degraded in character, for they are no longer performed through reason or from experience. But the greater number of the more complex instincts appear to have been gained in a wholly different manner, through the natural selection of variations of simpler instinctive actions. Such variations appear to arise from the same unknown causes acting on the cerebral organisation, which induce slight variations or individual differences in other parts of the body; these variations, owing to our ignorance are often said to arise spontaneously.

. . . [i]t is not improbable that there is a certain amount of interference between the development of free intelligence and of instinct,—which latter implies some inherited modification of the brain. Little is known about the functions of the brain, but we can perceive that as the intellectual powers become highly developed, the various parts of the brain must be connected by very intricate channels of the freest intercommunication; and as a consequence, each separate part would perhaps tend to be less well fitted to answer to particular sensations or associations in a definite and inherited—that is instinctive—manner. . . .

I have thought this digression worth giving, because we may easily underrate the mental powers of the higher animals, and especially of man, when we compare their actions founded on the memory of past events, on foresight, reason, and imagination, with exactly similar actions instinctively performed by the lower animals; in this latter case the capacity of performing such actions has been gained, step by step, through the variability of the mental organs and natural selection, without any conscious intelligence on the part of the animal during each successive generation. No doubt, as Mr. Wallace has argued, much of the intelligent work done by man is due to imitation and not to reason; but there is this great difference between his actions and many of those performed by the lower animals, namely, that man cannot, on his first trial, make for instance, a stone hatchet or a canoe, through his power of imitation. He has to learn his work by practice; a beaver, on the other hand, can make its dam or canal, and a bird its nest, as well, or nearly as well, and a spider its wonderful web, quite as well, the first time it tries, as when old and experienced.

69. The fact that the lower animals are excited by the same emotions as ourselves is so well established, that it will not be necessary to weary the reader by many details. Terror acts in the same manner on them as on us, causing the muscles to tremble, the heart to palpitate, the sphincters to be relaxed, and the hair to stand on end. Suspicion, the offspring of fear, is eminently characteristic of most wild animals. It is, I think, impossible to read the account given by Sir E. Tennent, of the behaviour of the female elephants, used as decoys, without admitting that they intentionally practise deceit, and well know what they are about. Courage and timidity are extremely variable qualities in the individuals of the same species, as is plainly seen in our dogs.

72. The principle of *Imitation* is strong in man, and especially, as I have myself observed, with savages. In certain morbid states of the brain this tendency is exaggerated to an extraordinary degree; some hemiplegic patients and others, at the commencement of inflammatory softening of the brain, unconsciously imitate every word which is uttered, whether in their own or in a foreign language, and every gesture or action which is performed near them. Desor has remarked that no animal voluntarily imitates an action performed by man, until in the ascending scale we come to monkeys, which are well known to be ridiculous mockers. Animals, however, sometimes imitate each other's actions: thus two species of wolves, which had been reared by dogs, learned to bark, as does sometimes the jackal, but whether this can be called voluntary imitation is another question. Birds imitate the songs of their parents, and sometimes of other birds; and parrots are notorious imitators of any sound which they often hear. . . .

The parents of many animals, trusting to the principle of imitation in their young, and more especially to their instinctive or inherited tendencies, may be said to educate them. We see this when a cat brings a live mouse to her kittens . . . .

73. Hardly any faculty is more important for the intellectual progress of man than *Attention*. Animals clearly manifest this power as when a cat watches a hole and prepares to spring on its prey. Wild animals sometimes become so absorbed when thus engaged, that they may be easily approached.

74. It is almost superflous to state that animals have excellent *Memories* for persons and places. A baboon at the Cape of Good Hope, as I have been informed by Sir Andrew Smith, recognized him with joy after an absence of nine months. I had a dog who was savage and averse to all strangers, and I purposely tried his memory after an absense of five years and two days. I went near the stable where he lived, and shouted to him in my old manner; he shewed no joy, but instantly followed me out walking and obeyed me, exactly as if I had parted with him only half an hour before.

The *Imagination* is one of the highest prerogatives of man. By this faculty he unites former images and ideas, independently of the will, and thus creates brilliant and novel results. A poet, as Jean Paul Richter remarks, "who must reflect whether he shall make a character say yes or no—to the devil with him; he is only a stupid corpse." Dreaming gives us the best notion of this power; as

Jean Paul again says, "The dream is an involuntary art of poetry." The value of the products of our imagination depends of course on the number, accuracy, and clearness of our impressions, on our judgment and taste in selecting or rejecting the involuntary combinations, and to a certain extent on our power of voluntarily combining them. As dogs, cats, horses, and probably all the higher animals, even birds have vivid dreams, and this is shewn by their movements and sounds uttered, we must admit that they possess some power of imagination. There must be something special, which causes dogs to howl in the night, and especially during moonlight, in that remarkable and melancholy manner called baying.

75. Of all the faculties of the human mind, it will, I presume, be admitted that *Reason* stands at the summit. Only a few persons now dispute that animals possess some power of reasoning. Animals may constantly be seen to pause, deliberate, and resolve. It is a significant fact, that the more the habits of any particular animal are studied by a naturalist, the more he attributes to reason and the less to unlearnt instincts. . . . No doubt it is often difficult to distinguish between the power of reason and that of instinct.

77. The savage and the dog have often found water at a low level, and the coincidence under such circumstances has become associated in their minds. A cultivated man would perhaps make some general proposition on the subject; but from all that we know of savages it is extremely doubtful whether they would do so, and a dog certainly would not. But a savage, as well as a dog would search in the same way, though frequently disappointed; and in both it seems to be equally an act of reason, whether or not any general proposition on the subject is consciously placed before the mind. The same would apply to the elephant and the bear making currents in the air or water. The savage would certainly neither know nor care by what law the desired movements were effected; yet his act would be guided by a rude process of reasoning, as surely as would a philosopher in his longest chain of deductions. There would no doubt be this difference between him and one of the higher animals, that he would take notice of much slighter circumstances and conditions, and would observe any connection between them after much less experience, and this would be of paramount importance. I kept a daily record of the actions of one of my infants, and when he was about eleven months old, and before he could speak a single word, I was continually struck with the greater quickness, with which all sorts of objects and sounds were associated together in his mind, compared with that of the most intelligent dogs I ever knew. But the higher animals differ in exactly the same way in this power of association from those low in the scale, such as the pike, as well as in that of drawing inferences and of observation.

81. It has often been said that no animal uses any tool; but the chimpanzee in a state of nature cracks a native fruit, somewhat like a walnut, with a stone. Rengger easily taught an American monkey thus to break open hard palm-nuts; and afterwards of its own accord, it used stones to open other kinds of nuts as well as boxes. It thus also removed the soft rind of fruit that had a disagreeable flavour. Another monkey was taught to open the lid of a large box with a stick, and afterwards it used the stick as a lever to move heavy bodies; and I have myself seen a young orang put a stick into a crevice, slip his hand to the other end, and use it in the proper manner as a lever. The tamed elephants in India are well known to break off branches of trees and use them to drive away the flies; and this same act has been observed in an elephant in a state of nature. I have seen a young orang, when she thought she was going to be whipped, cover and protect herself with a blanket or straw. In these several cases stones and sticks were employed as implements; but they are likewise used as weapons. Brehm states, on the authority of the well-known traveller Schimper, that in Abyssinia when the baboons belonging to one species (*C. gelada*) descend in troops from the mountains to plunder the fields, they sometimes encounter troops of another species (*C.*

hamadryas), and then a fight ensures. The Geladas roll down great stones, which the Hamadryas try to avoid, and then both species, making a great uproar, rush furiously against each other.

82. The Duke of Argyll remarks, that the fashioning of an implement for a special purpose is absolutely peculiar to man; and he considers that this forms an immeasurable gulf between him and the brutes. This is no doubt a very important distinction; but there appears to me much truth in Sir John Lubbock's suggestion, that when primeval man first used flint-stones for any purpose, he would have accidentally splintered them, and would then have used the sharp fragments. From this step it would be a small one to break the flints on purpose, and not a very wide step to fashion them rudely. This latter advance, however, may have taken long ages, if we may judge by the immense interval of time which elapsed before the men of the neolithic period took to grinding and polishing their stone tools. In breaking the flints, as Sir J. Lubbock likewise remarks, sparks would have been emitted, and in grinding them heat would also have been evolved: thus the two usual methods of "obtaining frie may have originated." The nature of fire would have been known in the many volcanic regions where lava occasionally flows through forests. The anthropomorphous apes, guided probably by instinct, build for themselves temporary platforms; but as many instincts are largely controlled by reason, the simpler ones, such as this of building a platform, might readily pass into a voluntary and conscious act. The orang is known to cover itself at night with the leaves of the Pandanus; and Brehm states that one of his baboons used to protect itself from the heat of the sun by throwing a straw-mat over its head. In these several habits, we probably see the first steps towards some of the simpler arts, such as rude architecture and dress, as they arose amongst the early progenitors of man.

Abstraction, General Conceptions, Self-consciousness, Mental Individuality.—It would be very difficult for any one with even much more knowledge than I possess, to determine how far animals exhibit any traces of these high mental powers. This difficulty arises from the impossibility of judging what passes through the mind of an animal; and again, the fact that writers differ to a great extent in the meaning which they attribute to the above terms, causes a further difficulty. If one may judge from various articles which have been published lately, the greatest stress seems to be laid on the supposed entire absence in animals of the power of abstraction, or of forming general concepts. But when a dog sees another dog at a distance, it is often clear that he perceives that it is a dog in the abstract; for when he gets nearer his whole manner suddenly changes, if the other dog be a friend. A recent writer remarks, that in all such cases it is a pure assumption to assert that the mental act is not essentially of the same nature in the animal as in man. If either refers what he perceives with his senses to a mental concept, then so do both. . . .

It may be freely admitted that no animal is self-conscious, if by this term it is implied that he reflects on such points, as whence he comes or whither he will go, or what is life and death, and so forth. But how can we feel sure that an old dog with an excellent memory and some power of imagination, as shewn by his dreams, never reflects on his past pleasures or pains in the chase? And this would be a form of self-consciousness. On the other hand, as Buchner has remarked, how little can the hard-worked wife of a degraded Australian savage, who uses very few abstract words, and cannot count above four, exert her self-consciousness, or reflect on the nature of her own existence. It is generally admitted, that the higher animals possess memory, attention, association, and even some imagination and reason. If these powers, which differ much in different animals, are capable of improvement, there seems no great improbability in more complex faculties, such as the higher forms of abstraction, and self-consciousness, etc., having been evolved through the development and combination of the simpler ones. It has been urged against the views here maintained, that it is impossible to say at what point in the ascending scale animals become capable of abstraction, etc.; but who can say at what age this occurs in our young children? We see at least that such powers are developed in children by imperceptible degrees.

84. *Language.*—This faculty has justly been considered as one of the chief distinctions between man and the lower animals. But man, as a highly competent judge, Archbishop Whately remarks, "is not the only animal that can make use of language to express what is passing in his mind, and can understand, more or less what is so expressed by another.". . .

85. The habitual use of articulate language is, however, peculiar to man; but he uses, in common with the lower animals, inarticulate cries to express his meaning aided by gestures and the movements of the muscles of the face. This especially holds good with the more simple and vivid feelings, which are but little connected with our higher intelligence. our cries of pain, fear, surprise, anger, together with their appropriate actions, and the murmur of a mother to her beloved child, are more expressive than any words. That which distinguishes man from the lower animals is not the understanding of articulate sounds, for, as every one knows, dogs understand many words and sentences. In this respect they are at the same stage of development as infants, between the ages of ten and twelve months, who understand many words and short sentences, but cannot yet utter a single word. It is not the mere articulation which is our distinguishing character, for parrots and other birds possess this power. Nor is it the mere capacity of connecting definite sounds with definite ideas; for it is certain that some parrots, which have been taught to speak, connect unerringly words with things, and persons with events. The lower animals differ from man solely in his almost infinitely larger power of associating together the most diversified sounds and ideas; and this obviously depends on the high development of his mental powers.

As Horn Took, one of the founders of the noble science of philology, observes, language is an art, like brewing or baking; but writing would have been a better simile. It certainly is not a true instinct, for every language has to be learnt. It differs, however, widely from all ordinary arts, for man has an instinctive tendency to speak, as we see in the babble of our young children; whilst no child has an instinctive tendency to brew, bake, or write. Moreover, no philogist now supposes that any language has been deliberately invented; it has been slowly and unconsciously developed by many steps. The sounds uttered by birds offer in several respects the nearest analogy to language, for all the members of the same species utter the same instinctive cries expressive of their emotions; and all the kinds which sing, exert their power instinctively; but the actual song, and even the call notes, are learnt from their parents or foster-parents.

87. . . . I cannot doubt that language owes its origin to the imitation and modification of various natural sounds, the voices of other animals, and man's own instinctive cries, aided by signs and gestures. When we treat of sexual selection we shall see that primeval man, or rather some early progenitor of man, probably first used his voice in producing true musical cadences, that is in singing, as do some of the gibbon-apes at the present day; and we may conclude from a widely-spread analogy, that this power would have been especially exerted during the courtship of the sexes— would have expressed various emotions, such as love, jealousy, triumph,—and would have served as a challenge to rivals. It is, therefore, probable that the imitation of musical cries by articulate sounds may have given rise to words expressive of various complex emotions. The strong tendency in our nearest allies, the monkeys, in microcephalous idiots, and in the barbarous races of mankind, to imitate whatever they hear deserves notice, as bearing on the subject of imitation.

88. Several writers, more especially Prof. Max Müller, have lately insisted that the use of language implies the power of forming general concepts; and that as no animals are supposed to possess this power, an impossible barrier is formed between them and man. With respect to animals, I have already endeavoured to show that they have this power, at least in a rude and incipient degree.

91. The perfectly regular and wonderfully complex construction of the languages of many barbarous nations has often been advanced as a proof, either of the divine origin of these languages, or of the high art and former civilization of their founders. . . . But it is assuredly an error to speak of any language as an art, in the sense of its having been elaborately and methodically formed. Philogists now admit that conjugations, declensions, etc., originally existed as distinct words since joined together; and as such words express the most obvious relations between objects and persons, it is not surprising that they should have been used by the men of most races during the earliest ages. With respect to perfection, the following illustration will best shew how easily we may err: a Crinoid sometimes consists of no less than 150,000 pieces of shell, all arranged with perfect symmetry in radiating lines; but a naturalist does not consider an animal of this kind as more perfect than a bilateral one with comparatively few parts, and with none of these parts alike, excepting on the opposite sides of the body. . . . So with languages; the most symmetrical and complex ought not to be ranked above irregular, abbreviated, and bastardised languages, which have borrowed expressive words and useful forms of construction from various conquering, conquered, or immigrant races.

92. *Sense of Beauty.*—This sense has been declared to be peculiar to man. I refer here only to the pleasure given by certain colours, forms, and sounds, and which may fairly be called a sense of the beautiful; with cultivated men such sensations are, however, intimately associated with complex ideas and trains of thought. When we behold a male bird elaborately displaying his graceful plumes or splendid colours before the female, whilst other birds, not thus decorated, make no such display, it is impossible to doubt that she admires the beauty of her male partner. As women everywhere deck themselves with these plumes, the beauty of such ornaments cannot be disputed. As we shall see later, the nests of humming-birds, and the playing passages of bower-birds are tastefully ornamented with gaily-coloured objects; and this shews that they must receive some kind of pleasure from the sight of such things. . . . Why certain bright colours should excite pleasure cannot, I presume, be explained, any more than why certain flavours and scents are agreeable; but habit has something to do with the result, for that which is at first unpleasant to our senses, ultimately becomes pleasant, and habits are inherited. With respect to sounds, Helmholtz has explained to a certain extent on physiological principles, why harmonies and certain cadences are agreeable. But besides this, sounds frequently recurring at irregular intervals are highly disagreeable, as every one will admit who has listened at night to the irregular flapping of a rope on board ship. The same principle seems to come into play with vision, as the eye prefers symmetry or figures with some regular recurrence. Patterns of this kind are employed by even the lowest savages as ornaments; and they have been developed through sexual selection for the adornment of some male animals. Whether we can or not give any reason for the pleasure thus derived from vision and hearing, yet man and many of the lower animals are alike pleased by the same colours, graceful shading and forms, and the same sounds.

The taste for the beautiful, at least as far as female beauty is concerned, is not of a special nature in the human mind; for it differs widely in the different races of man, and is not quite the same even in the different nations of the same race. Judging from the hideous ornaments and the equally hideous music admired by most savages, it might be urged that their aesthetic faculty was not so highly developed as in certain animals, for instance, as in birds. Obviously no animal would be capable of admiring such scenes as the heavens at night, a beautiful landscape, or refined music; but such high tastes are acquired through culture, and depend upon complex associations; they are not enjoyed by barbarians or by uneducated persons.

93. *Belief in God—Religion*—There is no evidence that man was aboriginally endowed with the ennobling belief in the existence of an Omnipotent God. On the contrary there is ample evidence,

derived not from hasty travelers, but from men who have long resided with savages, that numerous races have existed, and still exist, who have no idea of one or more gods, and who have no words
in their languages to express such an idea. The question is of course
wholly distinct from that higher one, whether there exists a Creator and Ruler of the Universe; and this has been answered in the
affirmative by some of the highest intellects that have ever existed.

If, however, we include under the term "religion" the belief in
unseen and spiritual agencies, the case is wholly different; for this
belief seems to be universal with the less civilized races. Nor is it
difficult to comprehend how it arose. As soon as the important
faculties of the imagination, wonder, and curiosity, together with
some power of reasoning, had become partially developed, man
would naturally crave to understand what was passing around him,
and would have vaguely speculated on his own existence.

95. The tendency in savages to imagine that natural objects and
agencies are animated by spiritual or living essences, is perhaps
illustrated by a little fact which I once noticed: my dog, a full-
grown and very sensible animal, was lying on the lawn during a
hot and still day; but at a little distance a slight breeze occasionally moved an open parasol, which would have been wholly disregarded by the dog, had any one stood near it. As it was, every
time that the parasol slightly moved, the dog growled fiercely and
barked. He must, I think have reasoned to himself in a rapid and
unconscious manner, that movement without any apparent cause
indicated the presence of some strange living agent, and that no
stranger had a right to be on his territory.

The belief in spiritual agencies would easily pass into the belief
in the existence of one or more gods. For savages would naturally
attribute to spirits the same passions, the same love of vengeance
or simplest form of justice, and the same affections which they
themselves feel. The Fuegians appear to be in this respect an intermediate condition, for when the surgeon on board the "Bea-

gle" shot some young ducklings as specimens, York Minster declared in the most solemn manner, "Oh, Mr. Bynoe, much rain,
much snow, blow much;" and this was evidently a retributive
punishment for wasting human food. So again he related how, when
his brother killed a "wild man" storms long raged, much rain and
snow fell. Yet we could never discover that the Fuegians believed
in what we should call a God, or practised any religious rites; and
Jemmy Button, with justifiable pride, stoutly maintained that there
was no devil in his land. This latter assertion is the more remarkable, as with savages the belief in bad spirits is far more common
than that in good ones.

The feeling of religious devotion is a highly complex one, consisting of love, complete submission to an exalted and mysterious
superior, and a strong sense of dependence, fear, reverence, gratitude, hope for the future, and perhaps other elements. No being
could experience so complex an emotion until advanced in his intellectual and moral faculties to at least a moderately high level.

100. *Sociability.*—Animals of many kinds are social; we find even
distinct species living together; for example some American monkeys; and united flocks of rooks, jackdaws, and starlings. Man shews
the same feeling in his strong love for the dog, which the dog returns with interest. . . .

Animals also render more important services to one another: thus
wolves and some other beasts of prey hunt in packs, and aid one
another in attacking their victims. . . .

106. The all-important emotion of sympathy is distinct from that
of love. A mother may passionately love her sleeping and passive
infant, but she can hardly at such times be said to feel sympathy
for it. The love of a man for his dog is distinct from sympathy, and
so is that of a dog for his master. Adam Smith formerly arugued,
as has Mr. Bain recently, that the basis of sympathy lies in our
strong retentiveness of former states of pain or pleasure. Hence

"the sight of another person enduring hunger, cold, fatigue, re-
vives in us some recollection of these states, which are painful even
in idea." We are thus impelled to relieve the sufferings of another, in order that our own painful feelings may be at the same
time relieved. In like manner we are led to participate in the
pleasures of others. But I cannot see how this view explains the
fact that sympathy is excited, in an immeasurably stronger degree, by a beloved, than by an indifferent person. The mere sight
of suffering, independently of love, would suffice to call up in us
vivid recollections and associations. The explanation may lie in the
fact that, with all animals, sympathy is directed solely towards the
members of the same community, and therefore towards known,
and more or less beloved members, but not to all the individuals
of the same species. This fact is not more surprising than that the
fears of many animals should be directed against special enemies.
Species which are not social, such as lions and tigers, no doubt
feel sympathy for the suffering of their own young, but not for
that of any other animal. With mankind, selfishness, experience
and imitation, probably add . . . to the power of sympathy; for
we are led by the hope of receiving good in return to perform acts
of sympathetic kindness to others; and sympathy is much
strengthened by habit. In however complex a manner this feeling
may have originated, as it is one of high importance to all those
animals which aid and defend one another, it will have been increased through natural selection; for those communities, which
included the greatest number of the most sympathetic members
would flourish best, and rear the greatest number of offspring.

108. *Man as a social animal.*—Every one will admit that man is
a social being. We see this in his dislike of solitude, and in his
wish for society beyond that of his own family. Solitary confinement is one of the severest punishments which can be inflicted.
Some authors suppose that man primevally lived in single families; but at the present day, though single families, or only two or
three together, roam the solitudes of some savage lands, they al-

ways, as far as I can discover, hold friendly relations with other families inhabiting the same district. Such families occasionally meet in council, and unite for their common defence. It is no argument against savage man being a social animal, that the tribes inhabiting adjacent districts are almost always at war with each other; for the social instincts never extend to all the individuals of the same species. . . . Although man, as he now exists, has few special instincts, having lost any which his early progenitors may have possessed, this is no reason why he should not have retained from an extremely remote period some degree of instinctive love and sympathy for his fellows. We are indeed all conscious that we do possess such sympathetic feelings; but our consciousness does not tell us whether they are instinctive, having originated long ago in the same manner as with the lower animals, or whether they have been acquired by each of us during our early years. As man is a social animal, it is almost certain that he would inherit a tendency to be faithful to his comrades, and obedient to the leader of his tribe for these qualities are common to most social animals. He would consequently possess some capacity for self-command. He would from an inherited tendency be willing to defend, in concert with others, his fellow-men; and would be ready to aid them in any way, which did not too greatly interfere with his own welfare or his own strong desires. . . .

Although man, as just remarked, has no special instincts to tell him how to aid his fellow-men, he still has the impulse, and with his improved intellectual faculties would naturally be much guided in this respect by reason and experience. Instinctive sympathy would also cause him to value highly the approbation of his fellows; for . . . the love of praise and the strong feeling of glory and the still stronger horror of scorn and infamy are due to the working of sympathy. Consequently man would be influenced in the highest degree by the wishes, approbation, and blame of his fellow-men, as expressed by their gestures and language. Thus the social instincts, which must have been acquired by man in a very rude state, and probably even by his early ape-like progenitors, still give the impulse to some of his best actions; but his actions are in a higher degree determined by the expressed wishes and judgment of his fellow men, and unfortunately very often by his own strong selfish desires. But as love, sympathy and self-command become strengthened by habit, and as the power of reasoning becomes clearer, so that man can value justly the judgments of his fellows, he will feel himself impelled apart from any transitory pleasure or pain, to certain lines of conduct. He might then declare—not that any barbarian or uncultivated man could thus think—I am the supreme judge of my own conduct, and in the words of Kant, I will not in my own person violate the dignity of humanity.

The more enduring Social Instincts conquer the less persistent Instincts.—We have not, however, as yet considered the main point on which, from our present point of view, the whole question of the moral sense turns. Why should a man feel that he ought to obey one instinctive desire rather than another? Why is he bitterly regretful, if he has yielded to a strong sense of self-preservation, and has not risked his life to save that of a fellow-creature? or why does he regret having stolen food from hunger?

It is evident in the first place, that with mankind the instinctive impulses have different degrees of strength; a savage will risk his own life to save that of a member of the same community, but will be wholly indifferent about a stranger: a young and timid mother urged by the maternal instinct will, without a moment's hesitation, run the greatest danger for her own infant, but not for a mere fellow-creature. Nevertheless many a civilized man, or even boy who never before risked his life for another, but full of courage and sympathy, has disregarded the instinct of self-preservation, and plunged at once into a torrent to save a drowning man, though a stranger. In this case man is impelled by the same instinctive motive, which made the heroic little American monkey, formerly described, save his keeper, by attacking the great and dreaded baboon. Such actions as the above appear to be the simple result of the greater strength of the social or maternal instincts than that of any other instinct or motive; for they are performed too instantaneously for reflection, or for pleasure or pain to be felt at the time; though, if prevented by any cause, distress or even misery might be felt. In a timid man, on the other hand, the instinct of self-preservation might be so strong, that he would be unable to force himself to run any such risk, perhaps not even for his own child.

I am aware that some persons maintain that actions performed impulsively, as in the above cases, do not come under the dominion of the moral sense, and cannot be called moral. They confine this term to actions done deliberately, after a victory over opposing desires, or when prompted by some exalted motive. But it appears scarcely possible to draw any clear line of distinction of this kind. As far as exalted motives are concerned, many instances have been recorded of savages, destitute of any feeling of general benevolence towards mankind, and not guided by any religious motive, who have deliberately sacrificed their lives as prisoners, rather than betray their comrades; and surely their conduct ought to be considered as moral. As far as deliberation, and the victory over opposing motives are concerned, animals may be seen doubting between opposed instincts, in rescuing their offspring or comrades from danger; yet their actions, though done for the good of others, are not called moral. Moreover, anything performed very often by us, will at last be done without deliberation or hesitation, and can then hardly be distinguished from an instinct; yet surely no one will pretend that such an action ceases to be moral. On the contrary, we feel that an act cannot be considered as perfect, or as performed in the most noble manner, unless it be done impulsively, without deliberation or effort, in the same manner as by a man in whom the requisite qualities are innate. He who is forced to overcome his fear or want of sympathy before he acts, deserves, however, in one way higher credit than the man whose innate disposition leads him to a good act without effort. As we cannot distinguish between motives, we rank all actions of a certain class as moral, if performed by a moral being. A moral being is one who is capable of comparing his past and future actions or motives, and of approving or disapproving of them. We have no reason to suppose that any of the lower animals have this capacity; therefore, when a Newfoundland dog drags a child out of the water, or a monkey faces danger to rescue its comrade, or takes charge of an orphan monkey, we do not call its conduct moral. But in the case of man, who alone can with certainty be ranked as a moral being, actions of a certain class are called moral, whether performed deliberately, after a struggle with opposing motives or impulsively through instinct, or from the effects of slowly-gained habit.

But to return to our more immediate subject. Although some instincts are more powerful than others, and thus lead to corresponding actions, yet it is untenable, that in man the social instincts (including the love of praise and fear of blame) possess greater strength, or have, through long habit, acquired greater strength than the instincts of self-preservation, hunger, lust, vengeance, etc,. Why then does man regret, even though trying to banish such regret, that he has followed the one natural impulse rather than the other; and why does he further feel that he ought to regret his conduct? Man in this respect differs profoundly from the lower animals. Nevertheless we can, I think, see with some degree of clearness the reason of this difference.

Man from the activity of his mental faculties, cannot avoid reflection: past impressions and images are incessantly and clearly passing through his mind. Now with those animals which live permanently in a body, the social instincts are ever present and persistent. Such animals are always ready to utter the danger-signal, to defend the community, and to give aid to their fellows in accordance with their habits; they feel at all times, without the stimulus of any special passion or desire, some degree of love and sympathy for them; they are unhappy if long separated from them, and always happy to be again in their company. So it is with ourselves. Even when we are quite alone, how often do we think with pleasure or pain of what others think of us,—of their imagined approbation or disapprobation; and this all follows from sympathy, a fundamental element of the social instincts. A man who possessed no trace of such instincts would be an unnatural monster. On the other hand, the desire to satisfy hunger, or any passion such as vengeance, is in its nature temporary, and can for a time be fully satisfied. Nor is it easy, perhaps hardly possible, to call up with complete vividness the feeling, for instance, of hunger; nor indeed, as has often been remarked, of any suffering. The instinct of self-preservation is not felt except in the presence of danger; and many a coward has thought himself brave until he has met his enemy face to face. The wish for another man's property is perhaps as persistent a desire as any that can be named; but even in this case the satisfaction of actual possession is generally a weaker feeling than the desire: many a thief, if not a habitual one, after success has wondered why he stole some article.

A man cannot prevent past impressions often repassing through his mind; he will thus be driven to make a comparison between the impressions of past hunger, vengeance satisfied, or danger shunned at other men's cost, with the almost ever-present instinct of sympathy, and with his early knowledge of what others consider as praiseworthy or blameable. This knowledge cannot be banished from his mind, and from instinctive sympathy is esteemed of great moment. He will then feel as if he had been baulked in following a present instinct or habit, and this with all animals causes dissatisfaction, or even misery. . . .

114. The nature and strength of the feelings which we call regret, shame, repentance or remorse, depend apparently not only on the strength of the violated instinct, but partly on the strength of the temptation, and often still more on the judgment of our fellows. How far each man values the appreciation of others, depends on the strength of his innate or acquired feelings of sympathy; and on his own capacity for reasoning out the remote consequences of his acts. Another element is most important, although not necessary, the reverence or fear of the Gods, or Spirits believed in by each man: and this applies especially in cases of remorse. . . .

115. Man prompted by his conscience, will through long habit acquire such perfect self-command, that his desires and passions will at last yield instantly and without a struggle to his social sym-

pathies and instincts, including his feeling for the judgment of his fellows. The still hungry, or the still revengeful man will not think of stealing food, or of wreaking his vengeance. It is possible, or as we shall hereafter see, even probable, that the habit of self-command may, like other habits, be inherited. Thus at last man comes to feel, through acquired and perhaps inherited habit, that it is best for him to obey his more persistent impulses. The imperious word *ought* seems merely to imply the conciousness of the existence of a rule of conduct, however it may have originated. Formerly it must have been often vehemently urged that an insulted gentleman *ought* to fight a duel. We even say that a pointer *ought* to point, and a retriever to retrieve game. If they fail to do so, they fail in their duty and act wrongly.

If any desire or instinct leading to an action opposed to the good of others still appears, when recalled to mind, as strong as, or stronger than, the social instinct, a man will feel no keen regret at having followed it; but he will be conscious that if his conduct were known to his fellows, it would meet with their disapprobation; and few are so destitute of sympathy as not to feel discomfort when this is realised. If he has no such sympathy, and if his desires leading to bad actions are at the time strong, and when recalled are not over-mastered by the persistent social instincts, and the judgment of others, then he is essentially a bad man; and the sole restraining motive left is the fear of punishment, and the conviction that in the long run it would be best for his own selfish interests to regard the good of others rather than his own.

It is obvious that every one may with an easy conscience gratify his own desires; if they do not interfere with his social instincts, that is with the good of others; but in order to be quite free from self-reproach, or at least of anxiety, it is almost necessary for him to avoid the disapprobation, whether reasonable or not, of his fellow-men. Nor must he break through the fixed habits of his life, especially if these are supported by reason; for if he does, he will assuredly feel dissatisfaction. He must likewise avoid the reprobation of the one God or gods in whom, according to his knowledge or superstition, he may believe; but in this case the additional fear of divine punishment often supervenes.

The strictly Social Virtues at first alone regarded.—The above view of the origin and nature of the moral sense, which tells us what we ought to do, and of the conscience which reproves us if we disobey it, accords well with what we see of the early and undeveloped condition of this faculty in mankind. The virtues which must be practiced, at least generally, by rude men, so that they may associate in a body, are those which are still recognized as the most important. But they are practised almost exclusively in relation to the men of the same tribe; and their opposites are not regarded as crimes in relation to the men of other tribes. No tribe could hold together if murder, robbery, treachery, etc., were common; consequently such crimes within the limits of the same tribe "are branded with everlasting infamy;" but excite no such sentiment beyond these limits. A North American Indian is well pleased with himself, and is honoured by others, when he scalps a man of another tribe; and a Dyak cuts off the head of an unoffending person, and dries it as a trophy. The murder of infants has prevailed on the largest scale throughout the world, and has met with no reproach; but infanticide, especially of females, has been taught to be good for the tribe, or at least not injurious. Suicide during former times was not generally considered as a crime, but rather, from the courage displayed, as an honourable act; and it is still practised by some semi-civilized and savage nations without reproach, for it does not obviously concern others of the tribe. It has been recorded that an Indian Thug conscientiously regretted that he had not robbed and strangled as many travellers as did his father before him. In a rude state of civilization the robbery of strangers is, indeed, generally considered as honourable.

Slavery, although in some ways beneficial during ancient times, is a great crime; yet it was not so regarded until quite recently, even by the most civilized nations. And this was especially the case, because the slaves belonged in general to a race different from that of their masters. As barbarians do not regard the opinion of their women, wives are commonly treated like slaves. Most savages are utterly indifferent to the sufferings of strangers, or even delight in witnessing them. It is well known that the women and children of the North-American Indians aided in torturing their enemies. Some savages take a horrid pleasure in cruelty to animals, and humanity is an unknown virtue. Nevertheless, besides the family affections, kindness is common, especially during sickness, between the members of the same tribe, and is sometimes extended beyond these limits. Mungo Park's touching account of the kindness of the negro women of the interior to him is well known. Many instances could be given of the noble fidelity of savages towards each other, but not to strangers; common experience justifies the maxim of the Spaniard, "Never, never trust an Indian." There cannot be fidelity without truth; and this fundamental virtue is not rare between the members of the same tribe: thus Mungo Park heard the negro women teaching their young children to love the truth. This, again, is one of the virtues which becomes so deeply rooted in the mind, that it is sometimes practised by savages, even at a high cost, towards strangers; but to lie to your enemy has rarely been thought a sin, as the history of modern diplomacy too plainly shews. As soon as a tribe has a recognised leader, disobedience becomes a crime, and even abject submission is looked at as a sacred virtue. . . .

118. The other so called self-regarding virtues, which do not obviously, though they may really, affect the welfare of the tribe, have never been esteemed by savages, though now highly appreciated by civilized nations. The greatest intemperance is no reproach with savages. Utter licentiousness, and unnatural crimes, prevail to an astounding extent. As soon, however, as marriage, whether polygamous, or monogamous, becomes common, jealously will lead to the inculcation of female virtue; and this, being honoured, will tend to spread to the unmarried females. How slowly it spreads to the male sex, we see at the present day. Chastity eminently requires self-command; therefore it has been honoured from a very early period in the moral history of civilised man. As

a consequence of this, the senseless practice of celibacy has been ranked from a remote period as a virtue. The hatred of indecency, which appears to us so natural as to be thought innate, and which is so valuable an aid to chastity, is a modern virtue, appertaining exclusively . . . to civilized life. This is shewn by the ancient religious rites of various nations, by drawings on the walls of Pompeii, and by the practices of many savages.

We have now seen that actions are regarded by savages, and were probably so regarded by primeval man, as good or bad, solely as they obviously affect the welfare of the tribe,—not that of the species, nor that of an individual member of the tribe. This conclusion agrees well with the belief that the so-called moral sense is aboriginally derived from the social instincts, for both relate at first exclusively to the community. The chief causes of the low morality of savages, as judged by our standard, are, firstly, the confinement of sympathy to the same tribe. Secondly, powers of reasoning insufficient to recognize the bearing of many virtues, especially of the self-rewarding virtues, on the general welfare of the tribe. Savages, for instance, fail to trace the multiplied evils consequent on a want of temperance, chastity, etc. And, thirdly, weak power of self-command; for this power has not been strengthened through long-continued, perhaps inherited, habit, instruction and religion.

I have entered into the above details on the immorality of savages, because some authors have recently taken a high view of their moral nature, or have attributed most of their crimes to mistaken benevolence. These authors appear to rest their conclusion on savages possessing those virtues which are serviceable, or even necessary, for the existence of the family and of the tribe—qualities which they undoubtedly do possess, and often in a high degree.

127. The subjects to be discussed in this chapter are of the highest interest, but are treated by me in an imperfect and fragmentary manner. Mr. Wallace, in an admirable paper before referred to, argues that man, after he had partially acquired those intellec-

tual and moral faculties which distinguish him from the lower animals, would have been but little liable to bodily modifications
through natural selection or any other means. For man is enabled
through his mental faculties "to keep with an unchanged body in
harmony with the changing universe." He has great power of
adapting his habits to new conditions of life. He invents weapons,
tools, and various stratagems to procure food and to defend himself. When he migrates into a colder climate he uses clothes, builds
sheds, and makes fire; and by the aid of fire cooks food otherwise
indigestible. He aids his fellow-men in many ways, and antici-
pates future events. Even at a remote period he practised some
division of labour.

The lower animals, on the other hand, must have their bodily
structure modified in order to survive under greatly changed conditions. They must be rendered stronger, or acquire more effec-
tive teeth or claws, for defence against new enemies; or they must
be reduced in size, so as to escape detection and danger. When
they migrate into a colder climate, they must become clothed with
thicker fur, or have their constitutions altered. If they fail to be
thus modified, they will cease to exist.

The case, however, is widely different, as Mr. Wallace has with
justice insisted, in relation to the intellectual and moral faculties
of man. These faculties are variable; and we have every reason to
believe that the variations tend to be inherited. Therefore, if they
were formerly of high importance to primeval man and to his ape-
like progenitors, they would have been perfected or advanced
through natural selection. Of the high importance of the intellectual faculties there can be no doubt, for man mainly owes to them
his predominant position in the world. We can see, that in the
rudest state of society, the individuals who were the most sagacious, who invented and used the best weapons or traps, and who
were best able to defend themselves, would rear the greatest
number of offspring. The tribes, which included the largest number of men thus endowed, would increase in number and supplant other tribes. Numbers depend primarily on the means of
subsistence, and this depends partly on the physical nature of the

country, but in a much higher degree on the arts which are there practiced. As a tribe increases and is victorious, it is often still further increased by the absorption of other tribes. The stature and strength of the men of a tribe are likewise of some importance for its success, and these depend in part on the nature and amount of the food which can be obtained. In Europe the men of the Bronze period were supplanted by a race more powerful, and judging from their sword-handles, with larger hands, but their success was probably still more due to their superiority in the arts.

All that we know about savages, or may infer from their traditions and from old monuments, the history of which is quite forgotten by the present inhabitants, shew that from the remotest times successful tribes have supplanted other tribes. Relics of extinct or forgotten tribes have been discovered throughout the civilised regions of the earth, on the wild plains of America, and on the isolated islands in the Pacific Ocean. At the present day civilised nations are everywhere supplanting barbarous nations, excepting where the climate opposes a deadly barrier; and they succeed mainly, though not exclusively, through their arts, which are the products of the intellect. It is, therefore, highly probable that with mankind the intellectual faculties have been mainly and gradually perfected through natural selection; and this conclusion is sufficient for our purpose. Undoubtedly it would be interesting to trace the development of each separate faculty from the state in which it exists in the lower animals to that in which it exists in man; but neither my ability nor knowledge permits this attempt.

It deserves notice that, as soon as the progenitors of man became social (and this probably occurred at a very early period), the principle of imitation, and reason, and experience would have increased, and much modified the intellectual powers in a way, of which we see only traces in the lower animals. . . . Now, if some one man in a tribe, more sagacious than the others, invented a new snare or weapon, or other means of attack or defence, the plainest self-interest, without the assistance of much reasoning power, would prompt the other members to imitate him; and all would thus profit. The habitual practice of each new art must likewise in some slight degree strengthen the intellect. If the new invention were an important one, the tribe would increase in number, spread, and supplant other tribes. In a tribe thus rendered more numerous there would always be a rather greater chance of the birth of other superior and inventive members. If such men left children to inherit their mental superiority, the chance of the birth of still more ingenious members would be somewhat better, and in a very small tribe decidedly better. Even if they left no children, the tribe would still include their blood-relations; and it has been ascertained by agriculturists that by preserving and breeding from the family of an animal, which when slaughtered was found to be valuable, the desired character has been obtained.

Turning now to the social and moral faculties. In order that primeval men, or the ape-like pregenitors of man, should become social, they must have acquired the same instinctive feelings, which impel other animals to live in a body; and they no doubt exhibited the same general disposition. They would have felt uneasy when separated from their comrades, for whom they would have felt some degree of love; they would have warned each other of danger, and have given mutual aid in attack or defence. All this implies some degree of sympathy, fidelity, and courage. Such social qualities, the paramount importance of which to the lower animals is disputed by no one, were no doubt acquired by the progenitors of man in a similar manner, namely, through natural selection aided by inherited habit. . . .

130. But it may be asked, how within the limits of the same tribe did a large number of members first become endowed with these social and moral qualities, and how was the standard of excellence raised? It is extremely doubtful whether the offspring of the more sympathetic and benevolent parents, of those who were the most faithful to their comrades, would be reared in greater numbers than the children of selfish and treacherous parents belonging to the same tribe. He who was ready to sacrifice his life, as many a savage has been, rather than betray his comrades, would often leave

no offspring to inherit his noble nature. The bravest men, who were always willing to come to the front in war, and who freely risked their lives for others, would on an average perish in larger numbers than other men. Therefore it hardly seems probable, that the number of men gifted with such virtues, or that of the standard of their excellence, could be increased through natural selection, that is, by the survival of the fittest; for we are not here speaking of one tribe being victorious over another.

Although the circumstances, leading to an increase in the number of those thus endowed within the same tribe, are too complex to be clearly followed out, we can trace some of the probable steps. In the first place, as the reasoning powers and foresight of the members became improved, each man would soon learn that if he aided his fellow-men, he would commonly receive aid in return. From this low motive he might acquire the habit of aiding his fellows; and the habit of performing benevolent actions certainly strengthens the feeling of sympathy which gives the first impulse to benevolent actions. Habits, moreover, followed during many generations probably tend to be inherited.

But another and much more powerful stimulus to the development of the social virtues, is afforded by the praise and the blame of our fellow-men. To the instinct of sympathy, as we have already seen, it is primarily due, that we habitually bestow both praise and blame on others, whilst we love the former and dread the latter when applied to ourselves; and this instinct no doubt was originally acquired, like all the other social instincts, through natural selection. At how early a period the progenitors of man in the course of their development, became capable of feeling and being impelled by, the praise or blame of their fellow-creatures, we cannot of course say. But it appears that even dogs appreciate encouragement, praise and blame. The rudest savages feel the sentiment of glory, as they clearly show by preserving the trophies of their prowess, by their habit of excessive boasting, and even by the extreme care which they take of their personal appearance and decorations; for unless they regarded the opinion of their comrades, such habits would be senseless.

They certainly feel shame at the breach of some of their lesser rules, and apparently remorse, as shewn by the case of the Australian who grew thin and could not rest from having delayed to murder some other woman, so as to propitiate his dead wife's spirit. Though I have not met with any other recorded case, it is scarcely credible that a savage, who will sacrifice his life rather than betray his tribe, or one who will deliver himself up as a prisoner rather than break his parole, would not feel remorse in his inmost soul, if he had failed in a duty, which he held sacred.

We may therefore conclude that primeval man, at a very remote period, was influenced by the praise and blame of his fellows. It is obvious, that the members of the same tribe would approve of conduct which appeared to them to be for the general good, and would reprobate that which appeared evil. To do good unto others—to do unto others as ye would they should do unto you—is the foundation of morality. It is, therefore, hardly possible to exaggerate the importance during rude times of the love of praise and the dread of blame. A man who was not impelled by any deep, instinctive feeling, to sacrifice his life for the good of others, yet was roused to such actions by a sense of glory, would by his example excite the same wish for glory in other men, and would strengthen by exercise the noble feeling of admiration. He might thus do far more good to his tribe than by begetting offspring with a tendency to inherit his own high character.

With increased experience and reason, man perceives the more remote consequences of his actions, and the self-regarding virtues, such as temperance, chastity, etc., which during early times are, as we have before seen, utterly disregarded, come to be highly esteemed or even held sacred. I need not, however, repeat what I have said on this head in the fourth chapter. Ultimately our moral sense or conscience becomes a highly complex sentiment—originating in the social instincts, largely guided by the approbation of our fellow-men, ruled by reason, self-interest, and in later times by deep religious feelings, and confirmed by instruction and habit.

It must not be forgotten that although a high standard of morality gives but a slight or no advantage to each individual man and his children over the other men of the same tribe, yet that an increase in the number of well-endowed men and an advancement in the standard of morality will certainly give an immense advantage to one tribe over another. A tribe including many members who, from possessing in a high degree the spirit of patriotism, fidelity, obedience, courage, and sympathy, were always ready to aid one another, and to sacrifice themselves for the common good, would be victorious over most other tribes; and this would be natural selection. At all times throughout the world tribes have supplanted other tribes; and as morality is one important element in their success, the standard of morality and the number of well-endowed men will thus everywhere tend to rise and increase.

It is, however, very difficult to form any judgment why one particular tribe and not another has been successful and has risen in the scale of civilization. Many savages are in the same condition as when first discovered several centuries ago. . . . [W]e are apt to look at progress as normal in human society; but history refutes this. The ancients did not even entertain the idea, nor do the Oriental nations at the present day. According to another high authority, Sir Henry Maine, "the greatest part of mankind has never shewn a particle of desire that its civil institutions should be improved." Progress seems to depend on many concurrent favourable conditions, far too complex to be followed out. But it has often been remarked, that a cool climate, from leading to industry and to the various arts, has been highly favourable thereto. The Esquimaux, pressed by hard necessity, have succeeded in many ingenious inventions, but their climate has been too severe for continued progress. Nomadic habits, whether over wide plains, or through the dense forests of the tropics, or along the shores of the sea have in every case been highly detrimental. Whilst observing the barbarous inhabitants of Tierra del Fuego, it struck me that the possession of some property, a fixed abode, and the union of many families under a chief, were the indispensable requisites for civilization. Such habits almost necessitate the cultivation of the ground; and the first steps in cultivation would probably result, as

I have elsewhere shewn, from some some such accident as the seeds of a fruit-tree falling on a heap of refuse, and producing an unusually fine variety. The problem, however, of the first advance of savages towards civilisation is at present much too difficult be solved.

Natural Selection as affecting Civilized Nations.—I have hitherto only considered the advancement of man from a semi-human condition to that of the modern savage. But some remarks on the action of natural selection on civilised nations may be worth adding. This subject has been ably discussed by Mr. W. R. Greg, and previously by Mr. Wallace and Mr. Galton. Most of my remarks are taken from these three authors. With savages, the weak in body or mind are soon eliminated; and those that survive commonly exhibit a vigorous state of health. We civilised men, on the other hand, do our utmost to check the process of elimination; we build asylums for the imbecile, the maimed, and the sick; we institute poor-laws; and our medical men exert their utmost skill to save the life of every one to the last moment. There is reason to believe that vaccination has preserved thousands, who from a weak constitution would formerly have succumbed to small-pox. Thus the weak members of civilised society propagate their kind. No one who has attended to the breeding of domestic animals will doubt that this must be highly injurious to the race of man. It is surprising how soon a want of care, or care wrongly directed, leads to the degeneration of a domestic race; but excepting in the case of man himself, hardly any one is so ignorant as to allow his worst animals to breed.

The aid which we feel impelled to give to the helpless is mainly an incidental result of the instinct of sympathy, which was originally acquired as part of the social instincts, but subsequently rendered, in the manner previously indicated, more tender and more widely diffused. Nor could we check our sympathy, even at the urging of hard reason, without deterioration in the noblest part of our nature. The surgeon may harden himself whilst performing an operation, for he knows that he is acting for the good of his patient; but if we were intentionally to neglect the weak and helpless, it could only be for a contingent benefit, with an overwhelming present evil. We must therefore bear the undoubtedly bad effects of the weak surviving and propagating their kind; but there appears to be at least one check in steady action, namely that the weaker and inferior members of society do not marry so freely as the sound; and this check might be indefinitely increased by the weak in body or mind refraining from marriage, though this is more to be hoped for than expected.

In every country in which a large standing army is kept up, the finest young men are taken by the conscription or are enlisted. They are thus exposed to early death during war, are often tempted into vice, and are prevented from marrying during the prime of life. On the other hand the shorter and feebler men, with poor constitutions, are left at home, and consequently have a much better chance of marrying and propagating their kind.

Man accumulates property and bequeaths it to his children, so that the children of the rich have an advantage over the poor in the race for success, independently of bodily or mental superiority. On the other hand, the children of parents who are short-lived, and are therefore on an average deficient in health and vigour, come into the their property sooner than other children, and will be likely to marry earlier and leave a larger number of offspring to inherit their inferior constitutions. But the inheritance of property by itself is very far from an evil; for without the accumulation of capital the arts could not progress; and it is chiefly through their power that the civilised races have extended, and are now everywhere extending their range, so as to take the place of the lower races. Nor does the moderate accumulation of wealth interfere with the process of selection. When a poor man becomes moderately rich, his children enter trades or professions in which there is struggle enough, so that the able in body and mind succeed best. The presence of a body of well-instructed men, who have not to labour for their daily bread, is important to a degree which cannot be over-estimated; as all high intellectual work is carried on by them, and on such work, material progress of all kinds mainly depends, not to mention other and higher advantages. No doubt wealth when very great tends to convert men into useless drones, but their number is never large; and some degree of elimination here occurs, for we daily see rich men, who happen to be fools or profligate, squandering away their wealth.

Primogeniture with entailed estates is a more direct evil, though it may formerly have been a great advantage by the creation of a dominant class, and any government is better than none. Most eldest sons, though they may be weak in body or mind, marry, whilst the younger sons, however superior in these respects, do not so generally marry. Nor can worthless eldest sons with entailed estates squander their wealth. But here, as elsewhere, the relations of civilised life are so complex that some compensatory checks intervene. The men who are rich through primogeniture are able to select generation after generation the more beautiful and charming women; and these must generally be healthy in body and active in mind. The evil consequences, such as they may be, of the continued preservation of the same line of descent, without any selection, are checked by men of rank always wishing to increase their wealth and power; and this they effect by marrying heiresses. But the daughters of parents who have produced single children, are themselves, as Mr. Galton has shewn, apt to be sterile; and thus noble families are continually cut off in the direct line, and their wealth flows into some side channel; but unfortunately this channel is not determined by superiority of any kind.

Although civilization thus checks in many ways the action of natural selection, it apparently favours the better development of the body, by means of good food and the freedom from occasional hardships. This may be inferred from civilised men having been found, wherever compared, to be physically stronger than savages. They appear also to have equal powers of endurance, as has been proved in many adventurous expeditions. Even the great luxury of the rich can be but little detrimental for the expectation of life of our aristocracy, at all ages and of both sexes, is very little inferior to that of healthy English lives in the lower classes.

We will now look to the intellectual faculties. If in each grade of society the members were divided into two equal bodies, the one including the intellectually superior and the other the inferior, there can be little doubt that the former would succeed best in all occupations, and rear a greater number of children. Even in the lowest walks of life, skill and ability must be of some advantage; though in many occupations, owing to the great division of labour, a very small one. Hence in civilised nations there will be some tendency to an increase both in the number and in the standard of the intellectually able. But I do not wish to assert that this tendency may not be more than counterbalanced in other ways, as by the multiplication of the reckless and improvident; but even to such as these, ability must be some advantage.

It has often been objected to views like the foregoing, that the most eminent men who have ever lived have left no offspring to inherit their great intellect. Mr. Galton says, "I regret I am unable to solve the simple question whether, and how far, men and women who are prodigies of genius are infertile. I have, however, shewn that men of eminence are by no means so." Great lawgivers, the founders of beneficent religions, great philosophers and discovers in science, aid the progress of mankind in a far higher degree by their works than by leaving a numerous progeny. In the case of corporeal structures, it is the selection of the slightly better-endowed and the elimination of the slightly less well-endowed individuals, and not the preservation of strongly-marked and rare anomalies, that leads to the advancement of a species. So it will be with the intellectual faculties, since the somewhat abler men in each grade of society succeed rather better than the less able, and consequently increase in number, if not otherwise prevented. When in any nation the standard of intellect and the number of intellectual men have increased, we may expect from the law of the deviation from an average, that prodigies of genius will, as shewn by Mr. Galton, appear somewhat more frequently than before.

In regard to the moral qualities, some elimination of the worst dispositions is always in progress even in the most civilised nations. Malefactors are executed, or imprisoned for long periods, so that they cannot freely transmit their bad qualities. Melancholic and insane persons are confined, or commit suicide. Violent and quarrelsome men often come to a bloody end. The restless who will not follow any steady occupation—and this relic of barbarism is a great check to civilization—emigrate to newly-settled countries, where they prove useful pioneers. . . .

With civilized nations, as far as an advanced standard of morality, and an increased number of fairly good men are concerned, natural selection apparently effects but little; though the fundamental social instincts were originally thus gained. But I have already said enough, whilst treating of the lower races, on the causes which lead to the advance of morality, namely, the approbation of our fellow-men—the strengthening of our sympathies by habit—example and imitation—reason—experience, and even self-interest—instruction during youth, and religious feelings.

A most important obstacle in civilised countries to an increase in the number of men of a superior class has been strongly insisted on by Mr. Greg and Mr. Galton, namely, the fact that the very poor and reckless, who are often degraded by vice, almost invariably marry early, whilst the careful and frugal, who are generally otherwise virtuous, marry late in life, so that they may be able to support themselves and their children in comfort. Those who marry early produce within a given period not only a greater number of generations, but, as shewn by Dr. Duncan, they produce many more children. The children, moreover, that are born by mothers during the prime of life are heavier and larger, and therefore probably more vigorous, than those born at other periods. Thus the reckless, degraded, and often vicious members of society, tend to increase at a quicker rate than the provident and generally virtuous members. . . .

There are, however, some checks to this downward tendency. We have seen that the intemperate suffer from a high rate of mortality, and the extremely profligate leave few offspring. The poorest classes crowd into towns, and it has been proved by Dr. Stark from the statistics of ten years in Scotland, that at all ages the death-rate is higher in towns than in rural districts, "and during the first five years of life the town death-rate is almost exactly double that of the rural districts." As these returns include both the rich and the poor, no doubt more than twice the number of births would be requisite to keep up the number of the very poor inhabitants in the towns, relatively to those in the country. With women, marriage at too early an age is highly injurious; for it has been found in France that, "twice as many wives under twenty die in the year, as died out of the same number of the unmarried." The mortality, also, of husbands under twenty is "excessively high," but what the cause of this may be, seems doubtful. Lastly, if the men who prudently delay marrying until they can bring up their families in comfort, were to select, as they often do women in the prime of life, the rate of increase in the better class would be only slightly lessened. . . .

140. If the various checks specified in the two last paragraphs, and perhaps others as yet unknown, do not prevent the reckless, the vicious and otherwise inferior members of society from increasing at a quicker rate than the better class of men, the nation will retrograde, as has too often occurred in the history of the world. We must remember that progress is no invariable rule. It is very difficult to say why one civilised nation rises, becomes more powerful, and spreads more widely, than another; or why the same nation progresses more quickly at one time than at another. We can only say that it depends on an increase in the actual number of the population, on the number of the men endowed with high intellectual and moral faculties, as well as on their standard of excellence. Corporeal structure appears to have little influence, except so far as vigour of body leads to vigour of mind.

It has been argued by several writers that as high intellectual powers are advantageous to a nation, the old Greeks, who stood some grades higher in intellect than any race that has ever existed, ought, if the power of natural selection were real, to have risen still higher in the scale, increased in number, and stocked the whole of Europe. Here we have the tacit assumption, so often made with respect to corporeal structures, that there is some innate tendency towards continued development in mind and body.

But development of all kinds depends on many concurrent favourable circumstances. Natural selection acts only tentatively. Individuals and races may have acquired certain indisputable advantages, and yet have perished from failing in other characters. The Greeks may have retrograded from a want of coherence between the many small states, from the small size of their whole country, from the practice of slavery, or from extreme sensuality; for they did not succumb until "they were enervated and corrupt to the very core." The western nations of Europe, who now so immeasurably surpass their former savage progenitors, and stand at the summit of civilisation, owe little or none of their superiority to direct inheritance from the old Greeks, though they owe much to the written works of that wonderful people. . . .

142. The remarkable success of the English as colonists, compared to other European nations has been ascribed to their "daring and persistent energy;" a result which is well illustrated by comparing the progress of the Canadians of English and French extraction; but who can say how the English gained their energy? There is apparently much truth in the belief that the wonderful progress of the United States, as well as the character of the people, are the results of natural selection; for the more energetic, restless, and courageous men from all parts of Europe have emigrated during the last ten or twelve generations to that great country, and have there succeeded best. . . .

Natural selection follows from the struggle for existence; and this from a rapid rate of increase. It is impossible not to regret bitterly, but whether wisely is another question, the rate at which man tends to increase; for this leads in barbarous tribes to infanticide and many other evils, and in civilised nations to abject poverty, celibacy, and to the late marriages of the prudent. But as man suffers from the same physical evils as the lower animals, he has no right to expect an immunity from the evils consequent on the struggle for existence. Had he not been subjected during primeval times to natural selection, assuredly he would never have attained to his present rank. Since we see in many parts of the world enormous areas of the most fertile land capable of support-ing numerous happy homes, but peopled only by a few wandering savages, it might be argued that the struggle for existence had not been sufficiently severe to force man upwards to his highest stan-dard. Judging from all that we know of man and the lower ani-mals, there has always been sufficient variability in their intellec-tual and moral faculties, for a steady advance through natural selection. No doubt such advance demands many favourable con-current circumstances; but it may well be doubted whether the most favourable would have sufficed, had not the rate of increase been rapid, and the consequent struggle for existence extremely severe. It even appears from what we see, for instance, in parts of S. America, that a people which may be called civilised, such as the Spanish settlers, is liable to become indolent and to retro-grade, when the conditions of life are very easy. With highly civ-ilised nations continued progress depends in a subordinate degree on natural selection; for such nations do not supplant and exter-minate one another as do savage tribes. Nevertheless the more intelligent members within the same community will succeed better in the long run than the inferior, and leave a more numerous progeny, and this is a form of natural selection. The more efficient causes of progress seem to consist of a good education during youth whilst the brain is impressible, and of a high standard of excel-lence, inculcated by the ablest and best men, embodied in the laws, customs and traditions of the nation, and enforced by public opinion. It should, however, be borne in mind, that the enforce-ment of public opinion depends on our appreciation of the appro-bation and disapprobation of others; and this appreciation is founded on our sympathy, which it can hardly be doubted was originally developed through natural selection as one of the most important elements of the social instincts.

144. The evidence that all civilised nations are the descendants of barbarians, consists, on the one side, of clear traces of their for-mer low condition in still-existing customs, beliefs, language, etc.; and on the other side, of proofs that savages are independently able to raise themselves a few steps in the scale of civilisation, and have actually thus risen.

156. The great break in the organic chain between man and his nearest allies, which cannot be bridged over by any extinct or living species, has often been advanced as a grave objection to the belief that man is descended from some lower form; but this objection will not appear of much weight to those who, from general reasons, believe in the general principle of evolution. Breaks often occur in all parts of the series, some being wide, sharp and defined, others less so in various degrees; as between the orang and its nearest allies—between the Tarsius and the other Lemuridae—between the elephant, and in a more striking manner between the Ornithorhynchus or Echindna, and all other mammals. But these breaks depend merely on the number of related forms which have become extinct. At some future period, not very distant as measured by centuries, the civilised races of man will almost certainly exterminate, and replace, the savage races throughout the world. At the same time the anthropomorphous apes, as Professor Schaaffhausen has remarked, will no doubt be exterminated. The break between man and his nearest allies will then be wider, for it will intervene between man in a more civilised state, as we may hope, even than the Caucasian, and some ape as low as a baboon, instead of as now between the negro or Australian and the gorilla.

167... Even the most distinct races of man are much more like each other in form than would at first be supposed; certain negro tribes must be excepted, whilst others, as Dr. Rohlfs writes to me, and as I have myself seen, have Caucasian features. This general similarity is well shewn by the French photographs in the Collection Anthropologique du Museum de Paris of the men belonging to various races, the greater number of which might pass for Europeans, as many persons to whom I have shewn them have remarked. Nevertheless, these men, if seen alive, would undoubtedly appear very distinct, so that we are clearly much influenced in our judgment by the mere colour of the skin and hair, by slight differences in the features, and by expression.

There is, however, no doubt that the various races, when carefully compared and measured, differ much from each other,—as in the texture of the hair, the relative proportions of all parts of the body, the capacity of the lungs, the form and capacity of the skull, and even the convolutions of the brain. . . . The races differ also in constitution, in acclimatisation, and in liability to certain diseases. Their mental characteristics are likewise very distinct; chiefly as it would appear in their emotional, but partly in their intellectual faculties. Every one who has had the opportunity of comparision, must have been struck with the contrast between the taciturn, even morose, aborigines of S. America and the light-hearted, talkative negroes. There is a nearly similar contrast between the Malays and the Papuans, who live under the same physical conditions, and are separated from each other only by a narrow space of sea.

We will first consider the arguments which may be advanced in favour of classing the races of man as distinct species, and then the arguments on the other side. If a naturalist, who had never before seen a Negro, Hottentot, Australian, or Mongolian, were to compare them, he would at once perceive that they differed in a multitude of characters, some of slight and some of considerable importance. On enquiry he would find that they were adapted to live under widely different climates, and that they differed somewhat in bodily constitution and mental disposition. If he were then told that hundreds of similar specimens could be brought from the same countries, he would assuredly declare that they were as good species as many to which he had been in the habit of affixing specific names. . . .

170. Our supposed naturalist having proceeded thus far in his investigation, would next enquire whether the races of men, when crossed, were in any degree sterile. . . .

Even if it should hereafter be proved that all the races of men were perfectly fertile together, he who was inclined from other reasons to rank them as distinct species, might with justice argue that fertility and sterility are not safe criterions of specific distinctness. . . .

Independently of fertility, the characters presented by the offspring from a cross have been thought to indicate whether or not the parent-forms ought to be ranked as species or varieties; but after carefully studying the evidence, I have come to the conclusion that no general rules of this kind can be trusted. . . .

We have now seen that a naturalist might feel himself fully justified in ranking the races of man as distinct species; for he has found that they are distinguished by many differences in structure and constitution, some being of importance. These differences have, also, remained nearly constant for very long periods of time. Our naturalist will have been in some degree influenced by the enormous range of man, which is a great anomaly in the class of mammals, if mankind be viewed as a single species. He will have been struck with the distribution of the several so-called races, which accords with that of other undoubtedly distinct species of mammals. Finally he might urge that the mutual fertility of all the races has not as yet been fully proved, and even if proved would not be an absolute proof of their specific identity.

173. On the other side of the question, if our supposed naturalist were to enquire whether the forms of man keep distinct like ordinary species, when mingled together in large numbers in the same country, he would immediately discover that this was by no means the case. In Brazil he would behold an immense mongrel population of Negroes and Portuguese; in Chiloe, and other parts of South America, he would behold the whole population consisting of Indians and Spaniards blended in various degrees. In many parts of the same continent he would meet with the most complex crosses between Negroes, Indians, and Europeans; and judging from the vegetable kingdom, such triple crosses afford the severest test of the mutual fertility of the parent forms. In one island of the Pacific he would find a small population of mingled Polynesian and English blood; and in the Fiji Archipelago a population of Polynesian and Negritos crossed in all degrees. Many analogous cases could be added; for instance, in Africa. Hence the races of man are not sufficiently distinct to inhabit the same country without fusion; and the absence of fusion affords the usual and best test of specific distinctness.

Our naturalist would likewise be much disturbed as soon as he perceived that the distinctive characters of all the races were highly variable. This fact strikes every one on first beholding the negro slaves in Brazil, who have been imported from all parts of Africa. The same remark holds good with the Polynesians, and with many other races. It may be doubted whether any character can be named which is distinctive of a race and is constant. Savages, even within the limits of the same tribe, are not nearly so uniform in character, as has been often asserted. . . .

But the most weighty of all the arguments against treating the races of man as distinct species, is that they graduate into each other, independently in many cases, as far as we can judge, of their having intercrossed. Man has been studied more carefully than any other animal, and yet there is the greatest possible diversity amongst capable judges whether he should be classed as a single species or race, or as two (Virey), as three (Jacquinot), as four (Kant), five (Blumenbach), six (Buffon), seven (Hunter), eight (Agassiz), eleven (Pickering), fifteen (Bory St. Vincent), sixteen (Desmoulins), twenty-two (Merton), sixty (Crawford), or as sixty-three, according to Burke. This diversity of judgment does not prove that the races ought not to be ranked as species, but it shews that they graduate into each other, and that it is hardly possible to discover clear distinctive characters between them. . . .

178. Although the existing races of man differ in many respects, as in colour, hair, shape of skull, proportions of the body, etc., yet if their whole structure be taken into consideration they are found to resemble each other closely in a multitude of points. Many of these are of so unimportant or of so singular a nature, that it is extremely improbable that they should have been independently acquired by aboriginally distinct species or races. The same re-

mark holds good with equal or greater force with respect to the numerous points of mental similarity between the most distinct races of man. The American aborigines, Negroes, and Europeans are as different from each other in mind as any three races that can be named; yet I was incessantly struck, whilst living with the Fuegians on board the "Beagle," with the many little traits of character, shewing how similar their minds were to ours; and so it was with a full-blooded negro with whom I happened once to be intimate.

He who will read Mr. Tylor's and Sir John Lubbock's interesting works can hardly fail to be deeply impressed with the close similarity between the men of all races in tastes, dispositions and habits. This is shewn by the pleasure which they all take in dancing, rude music, acting, painting, tattooing and otherwise decorating themselves; in their mutual conprehension of gesture-language, by the same expression in their features, and by the same inarticulate cries, when excited by the same emotions. This similarity, or rather identity, is striking, when contrasted with the different expressions and cries made by distinct species of monkeys. There is good evidence that the art of shooting with bows and arrows has not been handed down from any common progenitor of mankind, yet . . . the stone arrow-heads, brought from the most distant parts of the world, and manufactured at the most remote periods, are almost identical; and this fact can only be accounted for by the various races having similar inventive or mental powers. The same observation has been made by archaeologists with respect to certain widely-prevalent ornaments, such as zig-zags, etc.; and with respect to various simple beliefs and customs, such as the burying of the dead under megalithic structures. . . .

Now when naturalists observe a close agreement in numerous small details of habits, tastes, and dispositions between two or more domestic races, or between nearly-allied natural forms, they use this fact as an argument that they are descended from a common progenitor who was thus endowed; and consequently that all should be classed under the same species. The same argument may be applied with much more force to the races of man.

As it is improbable that the numerous and unimportant points of resemblance between the several races of man in bodily structure and mental faculties (I do not here refer to similar customs) should all have been independently acquired, they must have been inherited from progenitors who had these same characters. We thus gain some insight into the early state of man, before he had spread step by step over the face of the earth.

198. We have now seen that the external characteristic differences between the races of man cannot be accounted for in a satisfactory manner by the direct action of the conditions of life, nor by the effects of the continued use of parts, nor through the principle of correlation. We are therefore led to inquire whether slight individual differences, to which man is eminently liable, may not have been preserved and augmented during a long series of generations through natural selection. But here we are at once met by the objection that beneficial variations alone can be thus preserved; and as far as we enabled to judge, although always liable to err on this head, none of the differences between the races of man are of any direct or special service to him. The intellectual, and moral or social faculties must of course be excepted from this remark. The great variability of all the external differences between the races of man, likewise indicates that they cannot be of much importance; for if important, they would long ago have been either fixed and preserved, or eliminated. In this respect man resembles those forms, called by naturalists protean or polymorphic, which have remained extremely variable, owing, as it seems, to such variations being of an indifferent nature, and to their having thus escaped the action of natural selection.

Sexual Selection in Relation to Man

557. Man is more courageous, pugnacious, and energetic than woman, and has a more inventive genius. His brain is absolutely larger, but whether or not proportionately to his larger body has not, I believe, been fully ascertained. In woman the face is rounder; the jaws and the base of the skull smaller; the outlines of the body rounder, in parts more prominent; and her pelvis is broader than in man; but this latter character may perhaps be considered rather as a primary than a secondary sexual character. She comes to maturity at an earlier age than man.

561. *Law of Battle.*—With savages, for instance the Australians, the women are the constant cause of war both between members of the same tribe and between distinct tribes. So no doubt it was in ancient times; . . .

563. There can be little doubt that the greater size and strength of man, in comparison with woman, together with his broader shoulders, more developed muscles, rugged outline of body, his greater courage and pugnacity, are all due in chief part to inheritance from his half-human male ancestors. These characters would, however, have been preserved or even augmented during the long ages of man's savagery, by the success of the strongest and boldest men, both in the general struggle for life and in their contests for wives; a success which would have ensured their leaving a more numerous progeny than their less favoured brethren. It is not probable that the greater strength of man was primarily acquired through the inherited effects of his having worked harder than woman for his own subsistence and that of his family; for the women in all barbarous nations are compelled to work at least as hard as the men. With civilized people the arbitrament of battle for the possession of the women has long ceased; on the other hand, the men, as a general rule, have to work harder than the women for their joint subsistence, and thus their greater strength will have been kept up.

563. *Differences in the Mental Powers of the two Sexes.*—With respect to differences of this nature between man and woman, it isprobable that sexual selection has played a highly important part. I am aware that some writers doubt whether there is any such inherent difference; but this is at least probable from the analogy of the lower animals which present other secondary sexual characters. . . . Woman seems to differ from man in mental disposition, chiefly in her greater tenderness and less selfishness; and this holds good even with savages, as shewn by a well-known passage in Mungo Park's Travels, and by statements made by many other travellers. Woman, owing to her maternal instincts, displays these qualities towards her infants in an eminent degree; therefore it is likely that she would often extend them towards her fellow-creatures. Man is the rival of other men; he delights in competition, and this leads to ambition which passes too easily into selfishness. These latter qualities seem to be his natural and unfortunate birthright. It is generally admitted that with woman the powers of intuition, of rapid perception, and perhaps of imitation, are more strongly marked than in man; but some, at least, of these faculties are characteristic of the lower races, and therefore of a past and lower state of civilization.

The chief distinction in the intellectual powers of the two sexes is shewn by man's attaining to a higher eminence, in whatever he takes up, than can woman—whether requiring deep thought, reason, or imagination, or merely the use of the senses and hands. If two lists were made of the most eminent men and women in poetry, painting, sculpture, music (inclusive of both composition and performance), history, science, and philosophy, with a half-a-dozen names under each subject, the two lists would not bear comparision. . . .

Amongst the half-human progenitors of man, and amongst savages, there have been struggles between the males during many generations for the possession of the females. But mere bodily strength and size would do little for victory, unless associated with courage, perseverance, and determined energy. . . .

Now, when two men are put into competition, or a man with a woman, both possessed of every mental quality in equal perfection, save that one has higher energy, perserverance, and courage, the latter will generally become more eminent in every pursuit, and will gain the ascendancy. He may be said to possess genius—for genius has been declared by a great authority to be patience; and patience, in this sense, means unflinching, undaunted perseverance. But this view of genius is perhaps deficient; for without the higher powers of the imagination and reason, no eminent success can be gained in many subjects. These latter faculties, as well as the former, will have been developed in man, partly through sexual selection—that is, through the contest of rival males, and partly through natural selection,—that is from success in the general struggle for life; and as in both cases the struggle will have been during maturity, the characters gained will have been transmitted more fully to the male than to the female offspring.

570. We see that the musical faculties, which are not wholly deficient in any race, are capable of prompt and high development, for Hottentots and Negroes have become excellent musicians, although in their native countries they rarely practice anything that we should consider music.

573. *The Influence of Beauty in determining the Marriages of Mankind.*—In civilized life man is largely, but by no means exclusively, influenced in the choice of his wife by external appearance; but we are chiefly concerned with primeval times, and our only means of forming a judgment on this subject is to study the habits of existing semi-civilized and savage nations. If it can be shewn that the men of different races prefer women having various characteristics, or conversely with the women, we have then to enquire whether such choice, continued during many generations, would produce any sensible effect on the race, either on one sex or both according to the form of inheritance which has prevailed.

It will first be shewn in some detail that savages pay the greatest attention to their personal appearance. That they have a passion for ornament is notorious; and an English philosopher goes so far as to maintain, that clothes were first made for ornament not for warmth. . . .

577. Having made these preliminary remarks on the admiration felt by savages for various ornaments, and for deformities most unsightly to our eyes, let us see how far the men are attracted by the appearance of their women, and what are their ideas of beauty. I have heard it maintained that savages are quite indifferent about the beauty of their women, valuing them solely as slaves; it may therefore be well to observe that this conclusion does not at all agree with the care which the women take in ornamenting themselves, or with their vanity.

581. We thus see how widely the different races of man differ in their taste for the beautiful. In every nation sufficiently advanced to have made effigies of their gods or of their deified rulers, the sculptors no doubt have endeavoured to express their highest ideal of beauty and grandeur. Under this point of view it is well to compare in our mind the Jupiter or Apollo of the Greeks with the Egyptian or Assyrian statues; and these with the hideous bas-reliefs of the ruined buildings of Central America.

590. Although the manner of development of the marriage-tie is an obscure subject, as we may infer from the divergent opinions on several points between the three authors who have studied it most closely, namely, Mr. Morgan, Mr. Mc'lennan, and Sir J. Lubbock, yet from the foregoing and several other lines of evidence it seems probable that the habit of marriage in any strict sense of the word, has been gradually developed; and that almost promiscuous or very loose intercourse was once extremely common throughout the world. Nevertheless from the strength of the feeling of jealousy all through the animal kingdom, as well as from the analogy of the lower animals, more particularly of those which come nearest to man, I cannot believe that absolutely promiscuous intercourse prevailed in times past, shortly before man attained to his present rank in the zoological scale. Man, as I have attempted to shew, is certainly descended from some ape-like creature. With the existing Quadrumana, as far as their habits are known, the males of some species are monogamous, but live dur-

ing only a part of the year with the females; of this the orang seems
to afford an instance. Several kinds, for example some of the Indian and American monkeys, are strictly monogamous, and associate all the year round with their wives. Others are polygamous,
for example the gorilla and several American species, and each
family lives separate. Even when this occurs, the families inhabi-
tating the same district are probably somewhat social: the chimpanzee, for instance, is occasionally met with in large bands. Again,
other species are polygamous, but several males, each with his own
females, live associated in a body, as with several species of baboons. We may indeed conclude from what we know of the jealousy of all male quadrupeds, armed, as many of them are, with
special weapons for battling with their rivals, that promiscuous intercourse in a state of nature is extremely improbable. The pair-
ing may not last for life, but only for each birth; yet if the males
which are the strongest and best able to defend or otherwise assist their females and young, were to select the more attractive
females, this would suffice for sexual selection.

Therefore, looking far enough back in the stream of time, and
judging from the social habits of man as he now exists, the most
probable view is that he aboriginally lived in small communities,
each with a single wife, or if powerful with several, whom he jealously guarded against all other men. Or he may not have been a
social animal, and yet have lived with several wives, like the gorilla; for all the natives "agree that but one adult male is seen in
a band; when the young male grows up, a contest takes place for
mastery, and the strongest, by killing or driving out of the others,
establishes himself as the head of the community." The younger
males, being thus expelled and wandering about, would, when at
last successful in finding a partner, prevent too close interbreed-
ing within the limits of the same family.

Although savages are now extremely licentious, and although
communal marriages may formerly have largely prevailed, yet many
tribes practise some form of marriage, but of a far more lax nature
than that of civilised nations. Polygamy, as just stated, is almost
universally followed by the leading men in every tribe. Neverthe-

less there are tribes, standing almost at the bottom of the scale, which are strictly monogamous. This is the case with the Veddahs of Ceylon: they have a saying, according to Sir J. Lubbock, "that death alone can separate husband and wife." . . . Whether savages who now enter into some form of marriage, either polygamous or monogamous, have retained this habit from primeval times, or whether they have returned to some form of marriage, after passing through a stage of promiscuous intercourse, I will not pretend to conjecture.

Infanticide.—This practice is now very common throughout the world, and there is reason to believe that it prevailed much more extensively during former times. Barbarians find it difficult to support themselves and their children, and it is a simple plan to kill their infants. In South America some tribes, according to Azara, formerly destroyed so many infants of both sexes, that they were on the point of extinction. . . .

When, owing to female infanticide, the women of a tribe were few, the habit of capturing wives from neighbouring tribes would naturally arise. Sir J. Lubbock, however, as we have seen, attributes the practice in chief part, to the former existence of communal marriage, and to the men having consequently captured women from other tribes to hold as their sole property. Additional causes might be assigned, such as the communities being very small, in which case, marriageable women would often be deficient. That the habit was most extensively practised during former times, even by the ancestors of civilised nations, is clearly shewn by the preservation of many curious customs and ceremonies, of which Mr. Mc'lennan has given an interesting account.

593. The scarcity of women, consequent on female infanticide, leads, also, to another practice, that of polyandry, still common in several parts of the world, and which formerly, as Mr. Mc'lennan believes, prevailed almost universally; but this latter conclusion is doubted by Mr. Morgan and Sir. J. Lubbock. Whenever two or more men are compelled to marry one woman, it is certain that all the women of the tribe will get married, and there will be no

selection by the men of the more attractive women. But under these circumstances the women no doubt will have the power of choice, and will prefer the more attractive men. . . .

Early Betrothals and Slavery of Women.—With many savages it is the custom to betroth the females whilst mere infants; and this would effectually prevent preference being exerted on either side according to personal appearance. But it would not prevent the more attractive women from being afterwards stolen or taken by force from their husbands by the more powerful men; and this often happens in Australia, America and elsewhere. The same consequences with reference to sexual selection would to a certain extent follow, when women are valued almost solely as slaves or beasts of burden, as is the case with many savages. The men, however, at all times would prefer the handsomest slaves according to their standard of beauty.

We thus see that several customs prevail with the savages which must greatly interfere with, or completely stop, the action of sexual selection. On the other hand, the conditions of life to which savages are exposed, and some of their habits, are favourable to natural selection; and this comes into play at the same time with sexual selection. Savages are known to suffer severely from recurrent famines; they do not increase their food by artificial means; they rarely refrain from marriage, and generally marry whilst young. Consequently they must be subjected to occasional hard struggles for existence, and the favoured individuals will alone survive.

At a very early period, before man attained to his present rank in the scale, many of his conditions would be different from what obtains amongst savages. Judging from the analogy of the lower animals he would then either live with a single female, or be a polygamist. The most powerful and able males would succeed best in obtaining attractive females. They would also succeed best in the general struggle for life, and in defending their females, as well as their offspring, from enemies of all kinds. At this early period the ancestors of man would not be sufficiently advanced in intellect to look forward to distant contingencies; they would not foresee that the rearing of all their children, especially the female children, would make the struggle for life severer for the tribe. They would be governed more by their instincts and less by their reason, than are savages at the present day. They would not at that period have partially lost one of the strongest of all instincts, common to all the lower animals, namely the love of their young offspring; and consequently they would not have practiced female infanticide. Women would not have been thus rendered scarce, and polyandry would not have been practised; for hardly any other cause, except the scarcity of women seems sufficient to break down the natural and widely prevalent feeling of jealousy, and the desire of each male to possess a female for himself. Polyandry would be a natural stepping-stone to communal marriages or almost promiscuous intercourse; though the best authorities believe that the latter habit preceded polyandry. During primordial times there would be no early betrothals, for this implies foresight. Nor would women be valued merely as useful slaves or beasts of burthen. Both sexes, if the females as well as the males were permitted to exert any choice, would choose their partners not for mental charms, or property, or social position, but almost solely from external appearance. All the adults would marry or pair, and all the offspring, as far as that was possible, would be reared; so that the struggle for existence would be periodically excessively severe. Thus during these times all the conditions for sexual selection would have been more favourable than at a later period, when man had advanced in his intellectual powers but had retrograded in his instincts. Therefore, whatever influence sexual selection may have had in reducing the differences between the races of man, and between man and the higher Quadrumana, this influence would have been more powerful at a remote period than at the present day, though probably not yet wholly lost.

595. *The Manner of Action of Sexual Selection with Mankind.*— With primeval men under the favourable conditions just stated, and with those savages who at the present time enter into any marriage tie, sexual selection has probably acted in the following manner, subject to greater or less interference from female infanticide, early betrothals, etc. The strongest and most vigorous men,—those who could best defend and hunt for their families, who were provided with the best weapons and possessed the most property, such as a large number of dogs or other animals,—would succeed in rearing a greater average number of offspring than the weaker and poorer members of the same tribes. There can, also, be no doubt that such men would generally be able to select the more attractive women. At present the chiefs of nearly every tribe throughout the world succeed in obtaining more than one wife. . . .

596. Let us suppose the members of a tribe, practising some form of marriage, to spread over an unoccupied continent; they would soon split up into distinct hordes, separated from each other by various barriers, and still more effectually by the incessant wars between all barbarous nations. The hordes would thus be exposed to slightly different conditions and habits of life, and would sooner or later come to differ in some small degree. As soon as this occurred, each isolated tribe would form for itself a slightly different standard of beauty; and then unconscious selection would come into action through the more powerful and leading men preferring certain women to others. Thus the differences between tribes, at first very slight, would gradually and inevitably be more or less increased.

597. Man is more powerful in body and mind than woman, and in the savage state he keeps her in a far more abject state of bondage than does the male of any other animal; therefore it is not surprising that he should have gained the power of selection. Women are everywhere conscious of the value of their own beauty; and when they have the means, they take more delight in decorating themselves with all sorts of ornaments than do men. They borrow the plumes of male birds, with which nature has decked this sex in order to charm the females. As women have long been selected for beauty, it is not surprising that some of their successive variations should have been transmitted exclusively to the same sex; consquently that they should have transmitted beauty in a somewhat higher degree to their female than to their male off-spring, and thus have become more beautiful, according to general opinion, than men. Women however, certainly transmit most of their characters, including some beauty, to their offspring of both sexes; so that the continued preference by the men of each race for the more attractive women, according to their standard of taste, will have tended to modify in the same manner all the individuals of both sexes belonging to the race.

With respect to the other form of sexual selection (which with the lower animals is much the more common), namely, when the females are the selectors, and accept only those males which excite or charm them most, we have reason to believe that it formerly acted on our progenitors. Man in all probability owes his beard, and perhaps some other characters, to inheritance from an ancient progenitor who thus gained his ornaments. But this form of selection may have occasionally acted during later times; for in utterly barbarous tribes the women have more power in choosing, rejecting, and tempting their lovers, or of afterwards changing their husbands, than might have been expected. . . .

599. We thus see that with savages the women are not in quite so abject a state in relation to marriage, as has often been supposed. They can tempt the men whom they prefer, and can sometimes reject those whom they dislike either before or after marriage. Preference on the part of the women, steadily acting in any one direction, would ultimately affect the character of the tribe; for the women would generally choose not merely the handsomest men, according to the standard of taste, but those who were at the same time best able to defend and support them. Such well-endowed pairs would commonly rear a large number of offspring than the less favoured. The same result would obviously follow in a still more marked manner, if there was selection on both sides; that is if the more attractive, and at the same time more powerful men were to prefer, and were preferred by, the more attractive women. And this double form of selection seems actually to have occurred, especially during the earlier periods of our long history.

601. Some races are much more hairy than others, especially the males; but it must not be assumed that the more hairy races, such as the European, have retained their primordial condition more completely than the naked races, such as the Kalmucks or Americans. It is more probable that the hairiness of the former is due to partial reversion; for characters which have been at some former period long inherited, are always apt to return. We have seen that idiots are often very hairy, and they are apt to revert in other characters to a lower animal type. It does not appear that a cold climate has been influential in leading to this kind of reversion; excepting perhaps with the negroes who have been reared during several generations in the United States, and possibly with the Ainos, who inhabit the northern islands of the Japan archipelago.

604. *Colour of the Skin.*—The best kind of evidence that in man the colour of the skin has been modified through sexual selection is scanty; for in most races the sexes do not differ in this respect, and only slightly, as we have seen in others. We know, however, from the many facts already given that the colour of the skin is regarded by the men of all races as a highly important element in their beauty; so that it is a character which would be likely to have been modified through selection, as has occurred in innumerable instances with the lower animals. It seems at first sight a monstrous supposition that the jet-blackness of the negro should have been gained through sexual selection; but this view is supported by various analogies, and we know that negroes admire their own colour.

618. The main conclusion arrived at in this work, namely that man is descended from some lowly organised form, will, I regret to think, be highly distasteful to many. But there can hardly be a doubt that we are descended from barbarians. The astonishment which I felt on first seeing a party of Fuegians on a wild and broken shore will never be forgotten by me, for the reflection at once rushed into my mind—such were our ancestors. These men were absolutely naked and bedaubed with paint, their long hair was tangled, their mouths frothed with excitement, and their expression was wild, startled, and distrustful. They possessed hardly any arts, and like wild animals lived on what they could catch; they had no government, and were merciless to every one not of their own small tribe. He who has seen a savage in his native land will not feel much shame, if forced to acknowledge that the blood of some more humble creature flows in his veins. For my own part I would as soon be descended from that heroic little monkey, who braved his dreaded enemy in order to save the life of his keeper, or from that old baboon, who descending from the mountains, carried away in triumph his young comrade from a crowd of astonished dogs—as from a savage who delights to torture his enemies, offers up bloody sacrifices, practises infanticide without remorse, treats his wives like slaves, knows no decency, and is haunted by the grossest superstitions.

Man may be excused for feeling some pride at having risen, though not through his own exertions, to the very summit of the organic scale; and the fact of his having thus risen, instead of having been aboriginally placed there, may give him hope for a still higher destiny in the distant future. But we are not here concerned with hopes or fears, only with the truth as far as our reason permits us to discover it; and I have given the evidence to the best of my ability. We must, however, acknowledge, as it seems to me, that man with all his noble qualities, with sympathy which feels for the most debased, with benevolence which extends not only to other men but to the humblest living creature, with his god-like intellect which has penetrated into the movements and constitution of the solar system—with all these exhalted powers—Man still bears in his bodily frame the indelible stamp of his lowly origin.

THE EXPRESSION OF
THE EMOTIONS IN MAN
AND ANIMALS

12. No doubt as long as man and all other animals are viewed as independent creations, an effectual stop is put to our natural desire to investigate as far as possible the causes of Expression. By this doctrine, anything and everything can be equally well explained; and it has proved as pernicious with respect to Expression as to every other branch of natural history. With mankind some expressions, such as the bristling of the hair under the influence of extreme terror, or the uncovering of the teeth under that of furious rage, can hardly be understood, except on the belief that man once existed in a much lower and animal-like condition. The community of certain expressions in distinct though allied species, as in the movements of the same facial muscles during laughter by man and by various monkeys, is rendered somewhat more intelligible, if we believe in their descent from a common progenitor. He who admits on general grounds that the structure and habits of all animals have been gradually evolved, will look at the whole subject of Expression in a new and interesting light.

The study of Expression is difficult, owing to the movements being often extremely slight, and of a fleeting nature. A difference may be clearly perceived, and yet it may be impossible, at least I have found it so, to state in what the difference consists. When we witness any deep emotion, our sympathy is so strongly excited, that close observation is forgotten or rendered almost impossible; of which fact I have had many curious proofs. Our imagination is another and still more serious source of error; for if from the nature of the circumstances we expect to see any expression, we readily imagine its presence. Notwithstanding Dr. Duchenne's great experience, he for a long time fancied, as he states, that several muscles contracted under certain emotions, whereas he ultimately convinced himself that the movement was confined to a single muscle.

In order to acquire as good a foundation as possible, and to ascertain, independently of common opinion, how far particular movements of the features and gestures are really expressive of certain states of the mind, I have found the following means the most serviceable. In the first place, to observe infants; for they exhibit many emotions, as Sir C. Bell remarks, "with extraordinary force;" whereas, in after life, some of our expressions "cease to have the pure and simple source from which they spring in infancy."

In the second place, it occurred to me that the insane ought to be studied, as they are liable to the strongest passions, and give uncontrolled vent to them. I had, myself, no opportunity of doing this, so I applied to Dr. Maudsley and received from him an introduction to Dr. J. Crichton Browne, who had charge of an immense asylum near Wakefield, and who, as I found, had already attended to the subject. This excellent observer has with unwearied kindness sent me copious notes and descriptions, with valuable suggestions on many points; and I can hardly over-estimate the value of his assistance. I owe also, to the kindness of Mr. Patrick Nicol, of the Sussex Lunatic Asylum, interesting statements on two or three points.

Thirdly Dr. Duchenne galvanized, as we have already seen, certain muscles in the face of an old man, whose skin was little sensitive, and thus produced various expressions which were photographed on a large scale. It fortunately occurred to me to show several of the best plates, without a word of explanation, to above twenty educated persons of various ages and both sexes, asking them, in each case, by what emotion or feeling the old man was supposed to be agitated; and I recorded their answers in the words which they used. Several of the expressions were instantly recognised by almost everyone, though described in not exactly the same terms; and these may, I think, be relied on as truthful, and will hereafter be specified. On the other hand, the most widely different judgments were pronounced in regard to some of them. This exhibition was of use in another way, by convincing me how easily we may be misguided by our imagination; for when I first looked through Dr. Duchenne's photographs, reading at the same time the text, and thus learning what was intended, I was struck with admiration at the truthfulness of all, with only a few exceptions. Nevertheless, if I had examined them without any explanation, no doubt I should have been as much perplexed, in some cases, as other persons have been.

Fourthly, I had hoped to derive much aid from the great masters in painting and sculpture, who are such close observers. Accordingly, I have looked at photographs and engravings of many well-known works; but, with a few exceptions, have not thus profited. The reason no doubt is, that in works of art, beauty is the chief object; and strongly contracted facial muscles destroy beauty. The story of the composition is generally told with wonderful force and truth by skillfully given accessories.

Fifthly, it seemed to me highly important to ascertain whether the same expressions and gestures prevail, as has often been asserted without much evidence, with all the races of mankind, expecially with those who have associated but little with Europeans. Whenever the same movements of the features or body express the same emotions in several distinct races of man, we may infer with much probability, that such expressions are true ones,— that is, are innate or instinctive. Conventional expressions or gestures, acquired by the individual during early life, would probably have differed in the different races, in the same manner as do their languages. Accordingly I circulated, early in the year 1867, the following printed queries with a request, which has been fully responded to, that actual observations, and not memory, might be trusted. These queries were written after a considerable interval of time, during which my attention had been otherwise directed, and I can now see that they might have been greatly improved. To some of the later copies, I appended, in manuscript, a few additional remarks:—

1. Is astonishment expressed by the eyes and mouth being opened wide, and by the eyebrows being raised?
2. Does shame excite a blush when the colour of the skin allows

it to be visible? and especially how low down the body does the blush extend?

3. When a man is indignant or defiant does he frown, hold his body and head erect, square his shoulders and clench his fists?

4. When considering deeply on any subject, or trying to understand any puzzle, does he frown, or wrinkle the skin beneath the lower eyelids?

5. When in low spirits, are the corners of the mouth depressed, and the inner corner of the eyebrows raised by that muscle which the French call the "Grief muscle"? The eyebrow in this state becomes slightly oblique, with a little swelling at the inner end; and the forehead is transversely wrinkled in the middle part, but not across the whole breadth, as when the eyebrows are raised in surprise.

6. When in good spirits do the eyes sparkle, with the skin a little wrinkled round and under them, and with the mouth a little drawn back at the corners?

7. When a man sneers or snarls at another, is the corner of the upper lip over the canine or eye tooth raised on the side facing the man whom he addresses?

8. Can a dogged or obstinate expression be recognized, which is chiefly shown by the mouth being firmly closed, a lowering brow and a slight frown?

9. Is contempt expressed by a slight protrusion of the lips and by turning up the nose, and with a slight expiration?

10. Is disgust shown by the lower lip being turned down, the upper lip slightly raised, with a sudden expiration, something like incipient vomiting, or like something spit out of the mouth?

11. Is extreme fear expressed in the same general manner as with Europeans?

12. Is laughter ever carried to such an extreme as to bring tears into the eyes?

13. When a man wishes to show that he cannot prevent something being done, or cannot himself do something, does he shrug his shoulders, turn inwards his elbows, extend outwards his hands and open the palms; with the eyebrows raised?

14. Do the children when sulky, pout or greatly protrude the lips?

15. Can guilty, or sly, or jealous expressions be recognized? though I know not how these can be defined.

16. Is the head nodded vertically in affirmation, and shaken laterally in negation?

Observations on natives who have had little communication with Europeans would be of course the most valuable, though those made on any natives would be of much interest to me. General remarks on expression are of comparatively little value; and memory is so deceptive that I earnestly beg it may not be trusted. A definite description of the countenance under any emotion or frame of mind, with a statement of the circumstances under which it occurred, would possess much value.

To these queries I have received thirty-six answers from different observers, several of them missionaries or protectors of the aborigines, to all of whom I am deeply indebted for the great trouble which they have taken, and for the valuable aid thus received. I will specify their names, &c., towards the close of this chapter, so as not to interrupt my present remarks. The answers relate to several of the most distinct and savage races of man. In many instances, the circumstances have been recorded under which each expression was observed, and the expression itself described. In such cases, much confidence may be placed in the answers. When the answers have been simply yes or no, I have always received them with caution. It follows, from the information thus acquired, that the same state of mind is expressed throughout the world with remarkable uniformity; and this fact is in itself interesting as evidence of the close similarity in bodily structure and mental disposition of all the races of mankind.

Sixthly, and lastly, I have attended, as closely as I could, to the expression of the several passions in some of the commoner animals; and this I believe to be of paramount importance, not of course for deciding how far in man certain expressions are characteristic of certain states of mind, but as affording the safest basis for generalisation on the causes, or origin, of the various movements of Expression. In observing animals, we are not so likely to be biassed by our imagination; and we may feel safe that their expressions are not conventional.

From the reasons above assigned, namely, the fleeting nature of some expressions (the changes in the features being often extremely slight); our sympathy being easily aroused when we behold any strong emotion, and our attention thus distracted; our imagination deceiving us, from knowing in a vague manner what to expect, though certainly few of us know what the exact changes in the countenance are; and lastly, even our long familiarity with the subject,—from all these causes combined, the observation of Expression is by no means easy, as many persons, whom I have asked to observe certain points, have so discovered. Hence it is difficult to determine, with certainty, what are the movements of the features and of the body, which commonly characterize certain states of the mind. Nevertheless, some of the doubts and difficulties have, as I hope, been cleared away by the observation of infants,—of the insane,—of the different races of man,—of works of art,—and lastly, of the facial muscles under the action of galvanism, as effected by Dr. Duchenne.

But there remains the much greater difficulty of understanding the cause or origin of the several expressions, and of judging whether any theoretical explanation is trustworthy. Besides, judging as well as we can by our reason, without the aid of any rules, which of two or more explanations is the most satisfactory, or are quite unsatisfactory, I see only one way of testing our conclusions. This is to observe whether the same principle by which one expression can, as it appears, be explained, is applicable in other allied cases; and especially, whether the same general principles can be applied with satisfactory results, both to man and the lower animals. This latter method, I am inclined to think, is the most serviceable of all. The difficulty of judging of the truth of any theoretical explanation, and of testing it by some distinct line of investigation, is the great drawback to that interest which the study seems well fitted to excite.

Finally, with respect to my own observations, I may state that they were commenced in the year 1838; and, from that time to the present day, I have occasionally attended to the subject. At the above date, I was already inclined to believe in the principle of evolution, or of the derivation of species from other and lower forms. Consequently, when I read Sir C. Bell's great work, his view, that man had been created with certain muscles specially adapted for the expression of his feelings, struck me as unsatisfactory. It seemed probable that the habit of expressing our feelings by certain movements, though now rendered innate, had been in some manner gradually acquired. But to discover how such habits had been acquired was perplexing in no small degree. The whole subject had to be viewed under a new aspect, and each expression demanded a rational explanation. This belief led me to attempt the present work, however imperfectly it may have been executed.

I will now give the names of the gentlemen to whom, as I have said, I am deeply indebted for information in regard to the expressions exhibited by various races of man, and I will specify some of the circumstances under which the observations were in each case made. Owing to the great kindness and powerful influence of Mr. Wilson, of Hayes Place, Kent, I have received from Australia no less than thirteen sets of answers to my queries. This has been particularly fortunate, as the Australian aborigines rank amongst the most distinct of all the races of man. It will be seen that the observations have been chiefly made in the south, in the outlying parts of the colony of Victoria; but some excellent answers have been received from the north.

Mr. Dyson Lacy has given me in detail some valuable observations, made several hundred miles in the interior of Queensland. To Mr. R. Brough Smyth, of Melbourne, I am much indebted for observations made by himself, and for sending me several of the following letters, namely:—From the Rev. Mr. Hagenauer, of Lake Wellington, a missionary in Gippsland, Victoria, who has had much experience with the natives. From Mr. Samuel Wilson, a landowner, residing at Langerenong, Wimmera, Victoria. From the Rev. George Taplin, superintendent of the native Industrial Settlement at Port Macleay. From Mr. Archibald G. Lang, of Coranderik, Victoria, a teacher at a school where aborigines, old and young, are collected from all parts of the colony. From Mr. H. B. Lane, of Belfast, Victoria, a police magistrate and warden, whose observations, as I am assured, are highly trustworthy. From Mr. Templeton Bunnett, of Echuca, whose station is on the borders of the colony of Victoria, and who has thus been able to observe many aborigines who have had little intercourse with white men. He compared his observations with those made by two other gentlemen long resident in the neighbourhood. Also from Mr. J. Bulmer, a missionary in a remote part of Gippsland, Victoria.

I am also indebted to the distinguished botanist, Dr. Ferdinand Müller, of Victoria, for some observations made by himself, and for sending me others made by Mrs. Green, as well as for some of the foregoing letters.

In regard to the Maoris of New Zealand, the Rev. J. W. Stack has answered only a few of my queries; but the answers have been remarkably full, clear, and distinct, with the circumstances recorded under which the observations were made.

The Rajah Brooke has given me some information with respect to the Dyaks of Borneo.

Respecting the Malays, I have been highly successful; for Mr. F. Geach (to whom I was introduced by Mr. Wallace), during his residence as a mining engineer in the interior of Malacca, observed many natives, who had never before associated with white men. He wrote me two long letters with admirable and detailed observations on their expressions. He likewise observed the Chinese immigrants in the Malay archipelago.

The well-known naturalist, H. M. Consul, Mr. Swinhoe, also observed for me the Chinese in their native country; and he made inquiries from others whom he could trust.

In India Mr. H. Erskine, whilst residing in his official capacity in the Admednugur District in the Bombay Presidency, attended to the expression of the inhabitants, but found much difficulty in arriving at any safe conclusions, owing to their habitual concealment of all emotions in the presence of Europeans. He also obtained information for me from Mr. West, the Judge in Canara, and he consulted some intelligent native gentlemen on certain points. In Calcutta Mr. J. Scott, curator of the Botanic Gardens, carefully observed the various tribes of men therein employed during a considerable period, and no one has sent me such full and valuable details. The habit of accurate observation, gained by his botanical studies, has been brought to bear on our present subject. For Ceylon I am much indebted to the Rev. S. O. Glenie for answers to some of my queries.

Turning to Africa, I have been unfortunate with respect to the negroes, though Mr. Winwood Reade aided me as far as lay in his power. It would have been comparatively easy to have obtained information in regard to the negro slaves in America; but as they have long associated with white men, such observations would have possessed little value. In the southern parts of the continent Mrs. Barber observed the Kafirs and Fingoes, and sent me many distinct answers. Mr. J. P. Mansel Weale also made some observations on the natives, and procured for me a curious document, namely, the opinion, written in English, of Christian Gaika, brother of the Chief Sandilli, on the expressions of his fellow-countrymen. In the northern regions of Africa Captain Speedy, who long resided with the Abyssinians, answered my queries partly from memory and partly from observations made on the son of King Theodore, who was then under his charge. Professor and Mrs. Asa Gray attended to some points in the expressions of the natives, as observed by them whilst ascending the Nile.

On the great American continent Mr. Bridges, a catechist residing with the Fuegians, answered some few questions about their expression, addressed to him many years ago. In the northern half of the continent Dr. Rothrock attended to the expressions of the wild Atnah and Espyox tribes on the Nasse River, in North-Western America. Mr. Washington Matthews, Assistant-Surgeon in the United States Army, also observed with special care (after having seen my queries, as printed in the 'Smithsonian Report') some of the wildest tribes in the Western parts of the United States, namely, the Tetons, Grosventres, Mandans, and Assinaboines; and his answers have proved of the highest value.

Lastly, besides these special sources of information, I have collected some few facts incidentally given in books of travels.

27. I will begin by giving the three Principles, which appear to me to account for most of the expressions and gestures involuntarily used by man and the lower animals, under the influence of various emotions and sensations. I arrived, however, at these three Principles only at the close of my observations. They will be discussed in the present and two following chapters in a general manner. Facts observed both with man and the lower animals will here be made use of; but the latter facts are preferable, as less likely to deceive us. In the fourth and fifth chapters, I will describe the special expressions of some of the lower animals; and in the succeeding chapters those of man. Everyone will thus be able to judge for himself, how far my three principles throw light on the theory of the subject. It appears to me that so many expressions are thus explained in a fairly satisfactory manner, that probably all will hereafter be found to come under the same or closely analogous heads. I need hardly premise that movements or changes in any part of the body,—as the wagging of a dog's tail, the drawing back of a horse's ears, the shrugging of a man's shoulders, or the dilatation of the capillary vessels of the skin,—may all equally well serve for expression. The three Principles are as follows.

I. *The principle of serviceable associated Habits.*—Certain complex actions are of direct or indirect service under certain states of the mind, in order to relieve or gratify certain sensations, desires, &c.; and whenever the same state of mind is induced, however feebly, there is a tendency through the force of habit and association for the same movements to be performed, though they may not them be of the least use. Some actions ordinarily associated through habit with certain states of the mind may be partially repressed through the will, and in such cases the muscles which are least under the separate control of the will are the most liable still to act, causing movements which we recognize as expressive. In certain other cases the checking of one habitual movement requires other slight movements; and these are likewise expressive.

II. *The principle of Antithesis.*—Certain states of the mind lead to certain habitual actions, which are of service, as under our first principle. Now when a directly opposite state of mind is induced, there is a strong and involuntary tendency to the performance of movements of a directly opposite nature, though these are of no use; and such movements are in some cases highly expressive.

III. *The principle of actions due to the constitution of the Nervous System, independently from the first of the Will, and independently to a certain extent of Habit.*—When the sensorium is strongly excited, nerve-force is generated in excess, and is transmitted in certain definite directions, depending on the connection of the nerve-cells, and partly on habit: or the supply of nerve-force may, as it appears, be interrupted. Effects are thus produced which we recognize as expressive. This third principle may, for the sake of brevity, be called that of the direct action of the nervous system.

With respect to our *first Principle*, it is notorious how powerful is the force of habit. The most complex and difficult movements can in time be performed without the least effort or consciousness. It is not positively known how it comes that habit is so efficient in facilitating complex movements; but physiologists admit "that the conducting power of the nervous fibres increases with the frequency of their excitement." This applies to the nerves of motion and sensation, as well as to those connected with the act of thinking. That some physical change is produced in the nerve-cells or nerves which are habitually used can hardly be doubted, for otherwise it is impossible to understand how the tendency to certain acquired movements is inherited. That they are inherited we see with horses in certain transmitted paces, such as cantering and ambling, which are not natural to them,—in the pointing of young pointers and the setting of young setters—in the peculiar manner of flight of certain breeds of the pigeon, &c. We have analogous cases with mankind in the inheritance of tricks or unusual gestures, to which we shall presently recur. To those who admit the gradual evolution of species, a most striking instance of the perfection with which the most difficult consensual movements can be transmitted, is afforded by the humming-bird Sphinx-moth (Macroglossa); for this moth, shortly after its emergence from the cocoon, as shown by the bloom on its unruffled scales, may be seen poised stationary in the air, with its long hair-like proboscis uncurled and inserted into the minuter orifices of flowers; and no one, I believe, has ever seen this moth learning to perform its difficult task, which requires such unerring aim.

When there exists an inherited or instinctive tendency to the performance of an action, or an inherited taste for certain kinds of food, some degree of habit in the individual is often or generally requisite. We find this in the paces of the horse, and to a certain extent in the pointing of dogs; although some young dogs point excellently the first time they are taken out, yet they often associate the proper inherited attitude with a wrong odor, and even with eyesight. I have heard it asserted that if a calf be allowed to suck its mother only once, it is much more difficult afterwards to rear it by hand. Caterpillars which have been fed on the leaves of one kind of tree, have been known to perish from hunger rather than to eat the leaves of another tree, although this afforded them their proper food, under a state of nature; and so it is in many other cases.

The power of Association is admitted by everyone. Mr. Bain remarks, that "actions, sensations and states of feeling, occurring together or in close succession, tend to grow together, or cohere, in such a way that when any one of them is afterwards presented to the mind, the others are apt to be brought up in idea." It is so important for our purpose fully to recognize that actions readily become associated with other actions and with various states of the mind, that I will give a good many instances, in the first place relating to man, and afterwards to the lower animals. Some of the instances are of a very trifling nature, but they are good as for our purpose as more important habits. It is known to everyone how difficult, or even impossible it is, without repeated trials, to move the limbs in certain opposed directions which have never been practised. Analogous cases occur with sensations, as in the common experiment of rolling a marble beneath the tips of two crossed fingers, when it feels exactly like two marbles. Everyone protects himself when falling to the ground by extending his arms, and as Professor Alison has remarked, few can resist acting thus, when voluntarily falling on a soft bed. A man when going out of doors puts on his gloves quite unconsciously; and this may seem an extremely simple operation, but he who has taught a child to put on gloves, knows that this is by no means the case.

When our minds are much affected, so are the movements of our bodies; but here another principle besides habit, namely the undirected overflow of nerve-force, partially comes into play. Norfolk, in speaking of Cardinal Wolsey, says—

"Some strange commotion
Is in his brain; he bites his lip and starts;
Stops on a sudden, looks upon the ground,
Then, lays his finger on his temple: straight,
Springs out into fast gait; then, stops again,
Strikes his breast hard; and anon, he casts
His eye against the moon: in most strange postures
We have seen him set himself."—*Hen. VIII.*, act3, sc.2.

A vulgar man often scratches his head when perplexed in mind; and I believe that he acts thus from habit, as if he experienced a slightly uncomfortable bodily sensation, namely, the itching of his head, to which he is particularly liable, and which he thus relieves. Another man rubs his eyes when perplexed, or gives a little cough when embarrassed, acting in either case as if he felt a slightly uncomfortable sensation in his eyes or windpipe.

From the continued use of the eyes, these organs are especially liable to be acted on through association under various states of the mind, although there is manifestly nothing to be seen. A man, as Gratiolet remarks, who vehemently rejects a proposition, will almost certainly shut his eyes or turn away his face; but if he accepts the proposition, he will nod his head in affirmation and open his eyes widely. The man acts in his latter case as if he clearly saw the thing, and in the former case as if he did not or would not see it. I have noticed that persons in describing a horrid sight often shut their eyes momentarily and firmly, or shake their heads, as if not to see or to drive away something disagreeable; and I have caught myself, when thinking in the dark of a horrid spectacle, closing my eyes firmly. In looking suddenly at any object, or in looking all around, everyone raises his eyebrows, so that the eyes may be quickly and widely opened; and Duchenne remarks that a person in trying to remember something often raises his eyebrows, as if to see it. A Hindoo gentleman made exactly the same remark to Mr. Erskine in regard to his countrymen. I noticed a young lady earnestly trying to recollect a painter's name, and she first looked to one corner of the ceiling and then to the opposite corner, arching the one eyebrow on that side; although, of course, there was nothing to be seen there.

In most of the foregoing cases, we can understand how the associated movements were acquired through habit; but with some individuals, certain strange gestures or tricks have arisen in association with certain states of the mind, owing to wholly inexplicable causes, and are undoubtedly inherited. I have elsewhere given one instance from my own observation of an extraordinary and complex gesture, associated with pleasurable feelings, which was transmitted from a father to his daughter, as well as some other analogous facts. Another curious instance of an odd inherited movement, associated with the wish to obtain an object, will be given in the course of this volume.

There are other actions which are commonly performed under certain circumstances, independently of habit, and which seem to be due to imitation or some sort of sympathy. Thus persons cutting anything with a pair of scissors may be seen to move their jaws simultaneously with the blades of the scissors. Children learning to write often twist about their tongues as their fingers move, in a ridiculous fashion. When a public singer suddenly becomes a little hoarse, many of those present may be heard, as I have been assured by a gentleman on whom I can rely, to clear their throats; but here habit probably comes into play, as we clear our own throats under similar circumstances. I have also been told that at leaping matches, as the performer makes his spring, many

[handwritten marginalia]: human can use tools and perform work more properly and effect than animals. became human can create ideas, etc.

of the spectators, generally men and boys, move their feet; but here again habit probably comes into play, for it is very doubtful whether women would thus act.

Reflex actions.—Reflex actions, in the strict sense of the term, are due to the excitement of a peripheral nerve, which transmits its influence to certain nerve-cells, and these in their turn excite certain muscles or glands into action; and all this may take place without any sensation or consciousness on our part, though often thus accompanied. As many reflex actions are highly expressive, the subject must here be noticed at some little length. We shall also see that some of them graduate into, and can hardly be distinguished from actions which have arisen through habit. Coughing and sneezing are familiar instances of reflex actions. With infants the first act of respiration is often a sneeze, although this requires the co-ordinated movement of numerous muscles. Respiration is partly voluntary, but mainly reflex, and is performed in the most natural and best manner without the interference of the will. A vast number of complex movements are reflex. As good an instance as can be given is the often-quoted one of a decapitated frog, which cannot of course feel, and cannot consciously perform, any movement. Yet if a drop of acid be placed on the lower surface of the thigh of a frog in this state, it will rub off the drop with the upper surface of the foot of the same leg. If this foot be cut off, it cannot thus act. "After some fruitless efforts, therefore, it gives up trying in that way, seems restless, as though, says Pfluger, it was seeking some other way, and at last it makes use of the foot of the other leg and succeeds in rubbing off the acid. Notably we have here not merely contractions of muscles, but combined and harmonized contractions in due sequence for a special purpose. These are actions that have all the appearance of being guided by intelligence and instigated by will in an animal, the recognized organ of whose intelligence and will has been removed."

176. To sum up this chapter, weeping is probably the result of some such chain of events as follows. Children, when wanting food

or suffering in any way, cry out loudly, like the young of most
other animals, partly as a call to their parents for aid, and partly
from any great exertion serving as a relief. Prolonged screaming
inevitably leads to the gorging of the blood-vessels of the eye; and
this will have led, at first consciously and at last habitually, to the
contraction of the muscles round the eyes in order to protect them.
At the same time the spasmodic pressure on the surface of the
eye, and the distension of the vessels within the eye, without necessarily entailing any conscious sensation, will have affected,
through reflex action, the lacrymal glands. Finally, through the
three principles of nerve-force readily passing along accustomed
channels—of association, which is so widely extended in its power—
and of certain actions, being more under the control of the will
than others—it has come to pass that suffering readily causes the
secretion of tears, without being necessarily accompanied by any
other action.

Although in accordance with this view we must look at weeping
as an incidental result, as purposeless as the secretion of tears from
a blow outside the eye, or as a sneeze from the retina being affected by a bright light, yet this does not present any difficulty in
our understanding how the secretion of tears serves as a relief to
suffering. And by as much as the weeping is more violent or hys-
terical, by so much will the relief be greater,—on the same principle that the writhing of the whole body, the grinding of the teeth,
and the uttering of piercing shrieks, all give relief under an agony
of pain.

187. The expression of grief, due to the contraction of the grief-
muscles, is by no means confined to Europeans, but appears to
be common to all the races of mankind. I have, at least, received
trustworthy accounts in regard to Hindoos, Dhangars (one of the
aboriginal hill-tribes of India, and therefore belonging to a quite
distinct race from the Hindoos), Malays, Negroes and Australians.
With respect to the latter, two observers answer my query in the
affirmative, but enter into no details. Mr. Taplin, however, ap-
pends to my descriptive remarks the words "this is exact." With
respect to negroes, the lady who told me of Fra Angelico's pic-

ture, saw a negro towing a boat on the Nile, and as he encountered an obstruction, she observed his grief-muscles in strong action, with the middle of the forehead well wrinkled. Mr. Geach watched a Malay man in Malacca, with the corners of his mouth much depressed, the eyebrows oblique, with deep short grooves on the forehead. This expression lasted for a very short time; and Mr. Geach remarks it "was a strange one, very much like a person about to cry at some great loss."

In India Mr. H. Erskine found that the natives were familiar with this expression; and Mr. J. Scott, of the Botanic Gardens, Calcutta, has obligingly sent me a full description of two cases. He observed during some time, himself unseen, a very young Dhangar woman from Nagpore, the wife of one of the gardeners, nursing her baby who was at the point of death; and he distinctly saw the eyebrows raised at the inner corners, the eyelids drooping, the forehead wrinkled in the middle, the mouth slightly open, with the corners much depressed. He then came from behind a screen of plants and spoke to the poor woman, who started, burst into a bitter flood of tears, and besought him to cure her baby. The second case was that of a Hindustani man, who from illness and poverty was compelled to sell his favourite goat. After receiving the money, he repeatedly looked at the money in his hand and then at the goat, as if doubting whether he would not return it. He went to the goat, which was tied up ready to be led away, and the animal reared up and licked his hands. His eyes then wavered from side to side; his "mouth was partially closed, with the corners very decidedly depressed." At last the poor man seemed to make up his mind that he must part with his goat, and then, as Mr. Scott saw, the eyebrows became slightly oblique, with the characteristic puckering or swelling at the inner ends, but the wrinkles on the forehead were not present. The man stood thus for a minute, then heaving a deep sigh, burst into tears, raised up his two hands, blessed the goat, turned round, and without looking again, went away.

208. I was anxious to know whether tears are freely shed during excessive laughter by most of the races of men, and I hear from

my correspondents that this is the case. One instance was observed with the Hindoos, and they themselves said that it often
occurred. So it is with the Chinese. The women of a wild tribe of
Malays in the Malacca peninsula, sometimes shed tears when they
laugh heartily, though this seldom occurs. With the Dyaks of Borneo it must frequently be the case, at least with the women, for I
hear from the Rajah C. Brooke that it is common expression with
them to say "we nearly made tears from laughter." The aborigines
of Australia express their emotions freely, and they are described
by my correspondents as jumping about and clapping their hands
for joy, and as often roaring with laughter. No less than four observers have seen their eyes freely watering on such occasions; and
in one instance the tears rolled down their cheeks. Mr. Bulmer,
a missionary in a remote part of Victoria, remarks, "that they have
a keen sense of the ridiculous; they are excellent mimics, and when
one of them is able to imitate the peculiarities of some absent
member of the tribe, it is very common to hear all in the camp
convulsed with laughter." With Europeans hardly anything excites laughter so easily as mimicry; and it is rather curious to find
the same fact with the savages of Australia, who constitute one of
the most distinct races in the world.

In Southern Africa with two tribes of Kafirs, especially with the
women, their eyes often fill with tears during laughter. Gaika, the
brother of the chief Sandilli, answers my query on this head, with
the words, "Yes, this is their common practice." Sir Andrew Smith
has seen the painted face of a Hottentot woman all furrowed with
tears after a fit of laughter. In Northern Africa, with the Abyssinians, tears are secreted under the same circumstances. Lastly, in
North America, the same fact has been observed in a remarkably
savage and isolated tribe, but chiefly with the women; in another
tribe it was observed only on a single occasion.

213. With all the races of man the expression of good spirits appears to be the same, and is easily recognized. My informants,
from various parts of the Old and New Worlds, answer in the affirmative to my queries on this head, and they give some partic-

ulars with respect to Hindos, Malays, and New Zealanders. the brightness of the eyes of the Australians has struck four observers, and the same fact has been noticed with Hindoos, New Zealanders, and the Dyaks of Borneo.

Savages sometimes express their satisfaction not only by smiling, but by gestures derived from the pleasure of eating. Thus Mr. Wedgwood quotes Pethrick that the negroes on the Upper Nile began a general rubbing of their bellies when he displayed his beads; and Leichhardt says that the Australians smacked and clacked their mouths at the sight of his horses and bullocks, and more especially of his kangaroo dogs. The Greenlanders, "when they affirm anything with pleasure, such down air with a certain sound;" and this may be an imitation of the act of swallowing savoury food.

233. From inquiries which I have made in several large families, pouting does not seem very common with European children; but it prevails throughout the world, and must be both common and strongly marked with most savage races, as it has caught the attention of many observers. It has been noticed in eight different districts of Australia; and one of my informants remarks how greatly the lips of the children are then protruded. Two observers have seen pouting with the children of Hindoos; three, with those of the Kafirs and Fingoes of South Africa, and with the Hottentots; and two, with the children of the wild Indians of North America. Pouting has also been observed with the Chinese, Abyssinians, Malays of Malacca, Dyaks of Borneo, and often with the New Zealanders. Mr. Mansel Weale informs me that he has seen the lips much protruded, not only with the children of the Kafirs, but with the adults of both sexes when sulky; and Mr. Stack has sometimes observed the same thing with the men, and very frequently with the women of New Zealand. A trace of the same expression may occasionally be detected even with adult Europeans.

247. Rage, anger, and indignation are exhibited in nearly the same manner throughout the world; and the following descriptions may be worth giving as evidence of this, and as illustrations of some of the foregoing remarks. There is, however, an exception with respect to clenching the fists, which seems confined chiefly to the men who fight with their fists. With the Australians only one of my informants has seen the fists clenched. All agree about the body being held erect; and all, with two exceptions, state that the brows are heavily contracted. Some of them allude to the firmly-compressed mouth, the distended nostrils, and flashing eyes. According to the Rev. Mr. Taplin, rage, with the Australians, is expressed by the lips being protruded, the eyes being widely open; and in the case of the women by their dancing about and casting dust into the air. Another observer speaks of the native men, when enraged, throwing their arms wildly about.

I have received similar accounts, except as to the clenching of the fists in regard to the Malays of the Malacca peninsula, the Abyssinians, and the natives of South Africa. So it is with the Dakota Indians of North America; and, according to Mr. Matthews, they then hold their heads erect, frown, and often stalk away with long strides. Mr. Bridges states that the Fuegians, when enraged, frequently stamp on the ground, walk distractedly about, sometimes cry and grow pale. The Rev. Mr. Stack watched a New Zealand man and woman quarreling, and made the following entry in his note-book: "Eyes dilated, body swayed violently backwards and forwards, head inclined forwards, fists clenched, now thrown behind the body, now directed towards each other's faces." Mr. Swinhoe says that my description agrees with what he has seen of the Chinese, excepting that an angry man generally inclines his body towards his antagonist, and pointing at him, pours forth a volley of abuse.

Lastly, with respect to the natives of India, Mr. J. Scott has sent me a full description of their gestures and expression when enraged. Two low-caste Bengalees disputed about a loan. At first they were calm, but soon grew furious and poured forth the grossest abuse on each other's relations and progenitors for many generations past. Their gestures were very different from those of Europeans; for though their chests were expanded and shoulders squared, their arms remained rigidly suspended, with the elbows turned inwards and the hands alternately clenched and opened. Their shoulders were often raised high, and then again lowered. They looked fiercely at each other from under their lowered and strongly wrinkled brows, and their protruded lips were firmly closed. They approached each other, with heads and necks stretched forwards, and pushed, scratched, and grasped at each other. This protrusion of the head and body seems a common gesture with the enraged; and I have noticed it with degraded English women whilst quarrelling violently in the streets. In such cases it may be presumed that neither party expects to receive a blow from the other.

260. From the answers received from my correspondents it appears that the various movements, which have now been described as expressing contempt and disgust, prevail throughout a large part of the world. Dr. Rothrock, for instance, answers with a decided affirmative with respect to certain wild Indian tribes of North America. Crantz says that when a Greenlander denies anything with contempt or horror he turns up his nose, and gives a slight sound through it. Mr. Scott has sent me a graphic description of the face of a young Hindoo at the sight of castor-oil, which he was compelled occasionally to take. Mr. Scott has also seen the same expression on the faces of high-caste natives who have approached close to some defiling object. Mr. Bridges says that the Fuegians "express contempt by shooting out the lips and hissing through them, and by turning up the nose." The tendency either to snort through the nose, or to make a noise expressed by *ugh* or *ach*, is noticed by several of my correspondents.

Spitting seems an almost universal sign of contempt or disgust; and spitting obviously represents the rejection of anything offensive from the mouth. Shakespeare makes the Duke of Norfolk say, "I spit at him—call him a slanderous coward and a villain." So, again, Falstaff says, "Tell thee what, Hal,—if I tell thee a lie, spit in my face." Leichhardt remarks that the Australians "interrupted their speeches by spitting, and uttering a noise like pooh! pooh!

apparently expressive of their disgust." And Captain Burton speaks of certain negroes "spitting with disgust upon the ground." Captain Speedy informs me that this is likewise the case with the Abyssinians. Mr. Geach says that with the Malays of Malacca the expression of disgust "answers to spitting from the mouth;" and with the Fuegians, according to Mr. Bridges "to spit at one is the highest mark of contempt."

267. As it appeared to me at one time improbable in a high degree that so complex a gesture as shrugging the shoulders, together with the accompanying movements, should be innate, I was anxious to ascertain whether the blind and deaf Laura Bridgman, who could not have learnt the habit by imitation, practised it. And I have heard, through Dr. Innes, from a lady who has lately had charge of her, that she does shrug her shoulders, turn in her elbows, and raise her eyebrows in the same manner as other people, and under the same circumstances. I was also anxious to learn whether this gesture was practised by the various races of man, especially by those who never have had much intercourse with Europeans. We shall see that they act in this manner; but it appears that the gesture is sometimes confined to merely raising or shrugging the shoulders, without the other movements.

Mr. Scott has frequently seen this gesture in the Bengalees and Dhangars (the latter constituting a distinct race) who are employed in the Botanic Garden at Calcutta; when, for instance, they have declared that they could not do some work, such as lifting a heavy weight. He ordered a Bengalee to climb a lofty tree; but the man, with a shrug of his shoulders and a lateral shake of his head, said he could not. Mr. Scott knowing that the man was lazy, thought he could, and insisted on his trying. His face now became pale, his arms dropped to his sides, his mouth and eyes were widely opened, and again surveying the tree, he looked askant at Mr. Scott, shrugged his shoulders, inverted his elbows, extended his open hands, and with a few quick lateral shakes of the head declared his inability. Mr. H. Erskine has likewise seen the natives of India shrugging their shoulders; but he has never seen the elbows turned so much inwards as with us; and whilst shrugging their shoulders they sometimes lay their uncrossed hands on their breasts.

With the wild Malays of the interior of Malacca, and with the Bugis (true Malays, though speaking a different language), Mr. Geach has often seen this gesture. I presume that it is complete, as, in answer to my query descriptive of the movements of the shoulders, arms, hands, and face, Mr. Geach remarks, "it is performed in a beautiful style." I have lost an extract from a scientific voyage, in which shrugging the shoulders by some natives (Micronesians) of the Caroline Archipelago in the Pacific Ocean, was well described. Capt. Speedy informs me that the Abyssinians shrug their shoulders, but enters into no details. Mrs. Asa Gray saw an Arab dragoman in Alexandria acting exactly as described in my query, when an old gentleman, on whom he attended, would not go in the proper direction which had been pointed out to him.

Mr. Washington Matthews says, in reference to the wild Indian tribes of the western parts of the United States, "I have on a few occasions detected men using a slight apologetic shrug, but the rest of the demonstration which you describe I have not witnessed." Fritz Müller informs me that he has seen the negroes in Brazil shrugging their shoulders; but it is of course possible that they may have learnt to do so by imitating the Portuguese. Mrs. Barber has never seen this gesture with the Kafirs of South Africa; and Gaika, judging from his answer, did not even understand what was meant by my description. Mr. Swinhoe is also doubtful about the Chinese; but he has seen them, under the circumstances which would make us shrug our shoulders, press their right elbow against their side, raise their eyebrows, lift up their hand with the palm directed towards the person addressed, and shake it from right to left. Lastly, with respect to the Australians, four of my informants answer by a simple negative, and one by a simple affirmative. Mr. Bunnett, who has had excellent opportunities for observation on the borders of the Colony of Victoria, also answers by a "yes," adding that the gesture is performed "in a more subdued and less demonstrative manner than is the case with civilized nations." This circumstance may account for its not having been noticed by four of my informants.

These statements, relating to Europeans, Hindoos, the hill-tribes of India, Malays, Micronesians, Abyssinians, Arabs, Negroes, Indians of North America, and apparently to the Australians—many of these natives having had scarcely any intercourse with Europeans—are sufficient to show that shrugging the shoulders, accompanied in some cases by the other proper movements, is a gesture natural to mankind.

274. That these signs are innate or instinctive, at least with Anglo-Saxons, is rendered highly probable by the blind and deaf Laura Bridgman "constantly accompanying her *yes* with the common affirmative nod, and her *no* with our negative shake of the head." Had not Mr. Lieber stated to the contrary, I should have imagined that these gestures might have been acquired or learnt by her, considering her wonderful sense of touch and appreciation of the movements of others. With microcephalous idiots, who are so degraded that they never learn to speak, one of them is described by Vogt, as answering, when asked whether he wished for more food or drink, by inclining or shaking his head. Schmalz, in his remarkable dissertation on the education of the deaf and dumb, as well as of children raised only one degree above idiocy, assumes that they can always both make and understand the common signs of affirmation and negation.

Nevertheless if we look to the various races of man, these signs are not so universally employed as I should have expected; yet they seem too general to be ranked as altogether conventional or artificial. My informants assert that both signs are used by the Malays, by the natives of Ceylon, the Chinese, the negroes of the Guinea coast, and, according to Gaika, by the Kafirs of South Africa, though with these latter people Mrs. Barber has never seen a lateral shake used as a negative. With respect to the Australians, seven observers agree that a nod is given in affirmation; five agree about a lateral shake in negation, accompanied or not by some word; but Mr. Dyson Lacy has never seen this latter sign in Queensland, and Mr. Bulmer says that in Gipps' Land a negative is expressed by throwing the head a little backwards and putting out the tongue. At the northern extremity of the continent, near Torres Straits, the natives when uttering a negative "don't shake the head with it, but holding up the right hand, shake it by turning it half round and back again two or three times." The throwing back of the head with a click of the tongue is said to be used as a negative by the modern Greeks and Turks, the latter people expressing *yes* by a movement like that made by us when we shake our heads. The Abyssinians, as I am informed by Captain Speedy, express a negative by jerking the head to the right shoulder, together with a slight cluck, the mouth being closed; an affirmation is expressed by the head being thrown backwards and the eyebrows raised for an instant. The Tagals of Luzon, in the Philippine Archipelago, as I hear from Dr. Adolf Meyer, when they say "yes," also throw the head backwards. According to the Rajah Brooke, the Dyaks of Borneo express an affirmation by raising the eyebrows, and a negation by slightly contracting them, together with a peculiar look from the eyes. With the Arabs on the Nile, Professor and Mrs. Asa Gray concluded that nodding in affirmation was rare, whilst shaking the head in negation was never used, and was not even understood by them. With the Esquimaux a nod means *yes* and a wink *no*. The New Zealanders "elevate the head and chin in place of nodding acquiescence."

With the Hindoos Mr. H. Erskine concludes from inquiries made from experienced Europeans, and from native gentlemen, that the signs of affirmation and negation vary—a nod and a lateral shake being sometimes used as we do; but a negative is more commonly expressed by the head being thrown suddenly backwards and a little to one side, with a cluck of the tongue. What the meaning may be of this cluck of the tongue, which has been observed with various people, I cannot imagine. A native gentleman stated that affirmation is frequently shown by the head being thrown to the left. I asked Mr. Scott to attend particularly to this point, and, after repeated observations, he believes that a vertical nod is not commonly used by the natives in affirmation, but that the head is first thrown backwards either to the left or right, and then jerked obliquely forwards only once. This movement would perhaps have been described by a less careful observer as a lateral shake. He also states that in negation the head is usually held nearly upright, and shaken several times.

Mr. Bridges informs me that the Fuegians nod their heads vertically in affirmation, and shake them laterally in denial. With the wild Indians of North America, according to Mr. Washington Matthews, nodding and shaking the head have been learnt from Europeans, and are not naturally employed. They express affirmation "by describing with the hand (all the fingers except the index being flexed) a curve downwards and outwards from the body, whilst negation is expressed by moving the open hand outwards, with the palm facing inwards." Other observers state that the sign of affirmation with these Indians is the forefinger being raised, and then lowered and pointed to the ground, or the hand is waved straight forward from the face; and that the sign of negation is the finger or whole hand shaken from side to side. This latter movement probably represents in all cases the lateral shaking of the head. The Italians are said in like manner to move the lifted finger from right to left in negation, as indeed we English sometimes do.

On the whole we find considerable diversity in the signs of affirmation and negation in the different races of man. With respect to negation, if we admit that the shaking of the finger or hand from side to side is symbolic of the lateral movement of the head; and if we admit that the sudden backward movement of the head represents one of the actions often practised by young children in refusing food, then there is much uniformity throughout the world in the signs of negation, and we can see how they originated. The most marked exceptions are presented by the Arabs, Esquimaux, some Australian tribes, and Dyaks. With the latter a frown is the sign of negation, and with us frowning often accompanies a lateral shake of the head.

With respect to nodding in affirmation, the exceptions are rather more numerous, namely with some of the Hindoos, with the Turks,

Abyssinians, Dyaks, Tagals, and New Zealanders. The eyebrows are sometimes raised in affirmation, and as a person in bending his head forwards and downwards naturally looks up to the person whom he addresses, he will be apt to raise his eyebrows, and this sign may thus have arisen as an abbreviation. So again with the New Zealanders, the lifting up the chin and head in affirmation may perhaps represent in an abbreviated form the upward movement of the head after it has been nodded forwards and downwards.

280. The well-known Australian explorer, Mr. Stuart, has given a striking account of stupefied amazement together with terror in a native who had never before seen a man on horseback. Mr. Stuart approached unseen and called to him from a little distance. "He turned round and saw me. What he imagined I was I do not know; but a finer picture of fear and astonishment I never saw. He stood incapable of moving a limb, riveted to the spot, mouth open and eyes staring. . . . He remained motionless until our black got within a few yards of him, when suddenly throwing down his waddies, he jumped into a mulga bush as high as he could get." He could not speak, and answered not a word to the inquiries made by the black, but, trembling from head to foot, "waved with his hand for us to be off."

294. With respect to fear, as exhibited by the various races of man, my informants agree that the signs are the same as with Europeans. They are displayed in an exaggerated degree with the Hindoos and natives of Ceylon. Mr. Geach has seen Malays when terrified turn pale and shake; and Mr. Brough Smyth states that a native Australian "being on one occasion much frightened, showed a complexion as nearly approaching to what we call paleness, as can well be conceived in the case of a very black man." Mr. Dyson Lacy has seen extreme fear shown in an Australian, by a nervous twitching of the hands, feet, and lips; and by the perspiration standing on the skin. Many savages do not repress the signs of fear so much as Europeans; and they often tremble greatly. With the Kafir, Gaika says, in his rather quaint English, the shaking "of the body is much experienced, and the eyes are widely open." With savages, the sphincter muscles are often relaxed, just as may be observed in much frightened dogs, and as I have seen with monkeys when terrified by being caught.

316. *Blushing in the various races of man.*—The small vessels of the face become filled with blood, from the emotion of shame, in almost all the races of man, though in the very dark races no distinct change of colour can be perceived. Blushing is evident in all the Aryan nations of Europe, and to a certain extent with those of India. But Mr. Erskine has never noticed that the necks of the Hindoos are decidedly affected. With the Lepchas of Sikhim, Mr. Scott has often observed a faint blush on the cheeks, base of the ears, and sides of the neck, accompanied by sunken eyes and lowered head. This has occurred when he has detected them in a falsehood, or has accused them of ingratitude. The pale, sallow complexions of these men render a blush much more conspicuous than in most of the other natives of India. With the latter, shame, or it may be in part fear, is expressed, according to Mr. Scott, much more plainly by the head being averted or bent down, with the eyes wavering or turned askant, than by any change of colour in the skin.

The Semitic races blush freely, as might have been expected, from their general similitude to the Aryans. Thus with the Jews, it is said in the Book of Jeremiah (chap. vi. 15), "Nay, they are not at all ashamed, neither could they blush." Mrs. Asa Gray saw an Arab managing his boat clumsily on the Nile, and when laughed at by his companions, "he blushed quite to the back of his neck." Lady Duff Gordon remarks that a young Arab blushed coming into her presence.

Mr. Swinhoe has seen the Chinese blushing, but he thinks it is rare; yet they have the expression "to redden with shame." Mr. Geach informs me that the Chinese settled in Malacca and the native Malays of the interior both blush. Some of these people go nearly naked, and he particularly attended to the downward extension of the blush. Omitting the cases in which the face alone was seen to blush, Mr. Geach observed that the face, arms, and breast of a Chinaman, aged 24 years, reddened from shame; and with another Chinese, when asked why he had not done his work in better style, the whole body was similarly affected. In two Malays he saw the face, neck, breast, and arms blushing; and in a third Malay (a Bugis) the blush extended down to the waist.

The Polynesians blush freely. The Rev. Mr. Stack has seen hundreds of instances with the New Zealanders. The following case is worth giving, as it related to an old man who was unusually dark-coloured and partly tattooed. After having lent his land to an Englishman for a small yearly rental, a strong passion seized him to buy a gig, which had lately become the fashion with the Maoris. He consequently wished to draw all the rent for four years from his tenant, and consulted Mr. Stack whether he could do so. The man was old, clumsy, poor, and ragged, and the idea of his driving himself about in his carriage for display amused Mr. Stack so much that he could not help bursting out into a laugh; and then "the old man blushed up to the roots of his hair." Forster says that "you may easily distinguish a spreading blush" on the cheeks of the fairest women in Tahiti. The natives also of several of the other archipelagoes in the Pacific have been seen to blush.

Mr. Washington Matthews has often seen a blush on the faces of the young squaws belonging to various wild Indian tribes of North America. At the opposite extremity of the continent in Tierra del Fuego, the natives, according to Mr. Bridges, "blush much, but chiefly in regard to women; but they certainly blush also at their own personal appearance." This latter statement agrees with what I remember of the Fuegian, Jemmy Button, who blushed when he was quizzed about the care which he took in polishing his shoes, and in otherwise adorning himself. With respect to the Aymara Indians on the lofty plateaus of Bolivia, Mr. Forbes says, that from the colour of their skins it is impossible that their blushes should be as clearly visible as in the white races; still under such circumstances as would raise a blush in us, "there can always be seen the same expression of modesty or confusion; and even in the dark, a rise of temperature of the skin of the face can be felt, exactly as occurs in the European."

319. Several trustworthy observers have assured me that they have seen on the faces of negroes an appearance resembling a blush, under circumstances which would have excited one in us, though their skins were of an ebony-black tint. Some describe it as blushing brown, but most say that the blackness becomes more intense. An increased supply of blood in the skin seems in some manner to increase its blackness; thus certain exanthematous diseases cause the affected places in the negro to appear blacker, instead of, as with us, redder. The skin, perhaps, from being rendered more tense by the filling of the capillaries, would reflect a somewhat different tint to what it did before. That the capillaries of the face in the negro become filled with blood, under the emotion of shame, we may feel confident; because a perfectly characterized albino negress, described by Buffon, showed a faint tinge of crimson on her cheeks when she exhibited herself naked. Cicatrices of the skin remain for a long time white in the negro, and Dr. Burgess, who had frequent opportunities of observing a scar of this kind on the face of a negress, distinctly saw that it "invariably became red whenever she was abruptly spoken to, or charged with any trivial offence. The blush could be seen proceeding from the circumference of the scar towards the middle, but it did not reach the center. Mulattoes are often great blushers, blush succeeding blush over their faces. From these facts there can be no doubt that negroes blush, although no redness is visible on the skin.

I am assured by Gaika and by Mrs. Barber that the Kafirs of South Africa never blush; but this may only mean that no change of colour is distinguishable. Gaika adds that under the circumstances which would make a European blush his countrymen "look ashamed to keep their heads up."

It is asserted by four of my informants that the Australians, who are almost as black as negroes, never blush. A fifth answers doubtfully, remarking that only a very strong blush could be seen, on account of the dirty state of their skins. Three observers state that they do blush; Mr. S. Wilson adding that this is noticeable only under a strong emotion, and when the skin is not too dark from long exposure and want of cleanliness. Mr. Lang answers, "I have noticed that shame almost always excites a blush, which frequently extends as low as the neck." Shame is also shown, as he adds, "by the eyes being turned from side to side." As Mr. Lang was a teacher in a native school, it is probable that he chiefly observed children; and we know that they blush more than adults.

338. The belief that blushing was *specially* designed by the Creator is opposed to the general theory of evolution, which is now so largely accepted; but it forms no part of my duty here to argue on the general question. Those who believe in design, will find it difficult to account for shyness being the most frequent and efficient of all the causes of blushing, as it makes the blusher to suffer and the beholder uncomfortable, without being of the least service to either of them. They will also find it difficult to account for negroes and other dark-coloured races blushing, in whom a change of colour in the skin is scarcely or not at all visible.

No doubt a slight blush adds to the beauty of a maiden's face; and the Circassian women who are capable of blushing, invariably fetch a higher price in the seraglio of the Sultan than less susceptible women. But the firmest believer in the efficacy of sexual selection will hardly suppose that blushing was acquired as a sexual ornament. This view would also be opposed to what has just been said about the dark-coloured races blushing in an invisible manner.

351. That the chief expressive actions, exhibited by man and by the lower animals, are now innate or inherited,—that is, have not been learnt by the individual,—is admitted by every one. So little has learning or imitation to do with several of them that they are from the earliest days and throughout life quite beyond our control; for instance, the relaxation of the arteries of the skin in blushing, and the increased action of the heart in anger.

352. When, however, we turn to less common gestures in ourselves, which we are accustomed to look at as artificial or conventional,—such as shrugging the shoulders, as a sign of impotence, or the raising of the arms with open hands and extended fingers, as a sign of wonder,—we feel perhaps too much surprise at finding that they are innate. That these and some other gestures are inherited, we may infer from their being performed by very young children, by those born blind, and by the most widely distinct races of man. We should also bear in mind that new and highly peculiar tricks, in association with certain states of the mind, are known to have arisen in certain individuals, and to have been afterwards transmitted to their offspring, in some cases, for more than one generation.

Certain other gestures, which seem to us so natural that we might easily imagine that they were innate, apparently have been learnt like the words of a language. This seems to be the case with the joining of the uplifted hands, and the turning up of the eyes, in prayer. So it is with kissing as a mark of affection; but this is innate, in so far as it depends on the pleasure derived from contact with a beloved person. The evidence with respect to the inheritance of nodding and shaking the head, as signs of affirmation and negation, is doubtful; for they are not universal, yet seem too general to have been independently acquired by all the individuals of so many races.

355. The power of communication between the members of the same tribe by means of language has been of paramount importance in the development of man; and the force of language is much aided by the expressive movements of the face and body. We perceive this at once when we converse on an important subject with any person whose face is concealed. Nevertheless there are no grounds, as far as I can discover, for believing that any muscle has been developed or even modified exclusively for the sake of expression. The vocal and other sound-producing organs, by which various expressive noises are produced, seem to form a partial exception; but I have elsewhere attempted to show that these organs were first developed for sexual purposes, in order that one sex might call or charm the other. Nor can I discover grounds for believing that any inherited movement, which now serves as a means of expression, was at first voluntarily and consciously performed for this special purpose,—like some of the gestures and the finger-language used by the deaf and dumb. On the contrary, every true or inherited movement of expression seems to have had some natural and independent origin. But when once acquired, such movements may be voluntarily and consciously employed as a means of communication.

357. In the course of the foregoing remarks and throughout this volume, I have often felt much difficulty about the proper application of the terms, will, consciousness, and intention. Actions, which were at first voluntary, soon became habitual, and at last hereditary, and may then be performed even in opposition to the will. Although they often reveal the state of the mind, this result was not at first either intended or expected. Even such words as that "certain movements serve as a means of expression" are apt to mislead, as they imply that this was their primary purpose or object. This, however, seems rarely or never to have been the case; the movements having been at first either of some direct use, or the indirect effect of the excited state of the sensorium. An infant may scream either intentionally or instinctively to show that it wants food; but it has no wish or intention to draw its features into the peculiar form which so plainly indicates misery; yet some of the most characteristic expressions exhibited by man are derived from the act of screaming, as has been explained.

361. I have endeavoured to show in considerable detail that all the chief expressions exhibited by man are the same throughout the world. This fact is interesting, as it affords a new argument in favour of the several races being descended from a single parent-stock, which must have been almost completely human in structure, and to a large extent in mind, before the period at which the races diverged from each other. No doubt similar structures,

adapted for the same purpose, have often been independently acquired through variation and natural selection by distinct species;
but this view will not explain close similarity between distinct
species in a multitude of unimportant details. Now if we bear in
mind the numerous points of structure having no relation to
expression, in which all the faces of man closely agree, and then
add to them the numerous points, some of the highest importance
and many of the most trifling value, on which the movements of
expression directly or indirectly depend, it seems to me improbable in the highest degree that so much similarity, or rather identity of structure, could have been acquired by independent means.
Yet this must have been the case if the races of man are descended from several aboriginally distinct species. It is far more
probable that the many points of close similarity in the various
races are due to inheritance from a single parent-form, which had
already assumed a human character.

367. We have seen that the study of the theory of expression con-
firms to a certain limited extent the conclusion that man is derived from some lower animal form, and supports the belief of the
specific or subspecific unity of the several races; but as far as my
judgment serves, such confirmation was hardly needed. We have
also seen that expression in itself, or the language of the emotions, as it has sometimes been called, is certainly of importance
for the welfare of mankind. To understand, as far as possible, the
source or origin of the various expressions which may be hourly
seen on the faces of the men around us, not to mention our domesticated animals, ought to possess much interest for us. From
these several causes, we may conclude that the philosophy of our
subject has well deserved the attention which it has already received from several excellent observers, and that it deserves still
further attention, especially from any able physiologist.

INDEX